Corporate Integrity

D0181107

What do corporations look like when they have integrity, and how can we move more companies in that direction? *Corporate Integrity* offers a timely, comprehensive framework – and practical business lessons – bringing together questions of organizational design, communication practices, working relationships, and leadership styles to answer this question. Dr. Marvin T. Brown explores the five key challenges facing modern businesses as they try to respond ethically to cultural, inter-personal, organizational, civic, and environmental requirements. He demonstrates that if corporations are to meet the needs of civil society, they must facilitate inclusive communication patterns based on mutual recognition and civic cooperation. *Corporate Integrity* is essential reading for professionals in organizational ethics, business leaders, and graduate students looking for practical and reflective insights into doing business with integrity and purpose.

MARVIN T. BROWN teaches at the University of San Francisco and at Saybrook Graduate School, and has been working in the field of organizational ethics and communication for more than twenty years as an educator, writer, and consultant. He is the author of *The Ethical Process: An Approach to Disagreement and Controversial Issues* (2002) and *Working Ethics: Strategies for Decision Making and Organizational Responsibility* (1990).

Corporate Integrity

Rethinking Organizational Ethics and Leadership

MARVIN T. BROWN

CAMBRIDGE UNIVERSITY PRESS
Cambridge, New York, Melbourne, Madrid, Cape Town, Singapore, São Paulo
Cambridge University Press
The Edinburgh Building, Cambridge, CB2 2RU, UK
Published in the United States of America by Cambridge University Press, New York

www.cambridge.org
Information on this title:www.cambridge.org/9780521844819

First published 2005

Printed in the United Kingdom at the University Press, Cambridge

Typeset in Sabon 10/13pt system Advent 3B2 8.07f   [TB]

A catalogue record for this book is available from the British Library

Library of Congress Cataloguing in Publication data

Brown, Marvin T., 1943–
    Corporate Integrity: Rethinking Organizational Ethics and Leadership /
    Marvin T. Brown.
        p.   cm.
    Includes bibliographical references and index.
    ISBN 0 521 84481 9 – ISBN 0 521 60657 8 (pbk.)
    1. Social responsibility of business.   2. Business ethics.
    3. Business communication. 4. Leadership.   I. Title.

    HD60.B766 2005
    174'.4 – dc22   2004057062

ISBN-13 978-0-521-84481-9 hardback
ISBN-10 0-521-84481-9 hardback
ISBN-13 978-0-521-60657-8 paperback
ISBN-10 0-521-60657-8 paperback

Contents

Preface

What would corporations look like if they were to have integrity and how can we move them in that direction? In an effort to answer this question, *Corporate Integrity* takes a different path than most books that have distinguished themselves either in business ethics or corporate social responsibility. For one thing, this book overrides that distinction and provides a model of organizational ethics that is truly integrative. With a strong sense of integrity as wholeness, the book explores five dimensions of corporate life: the cultural, interpersonal, organizational, civic, and environmental. This exploration moves from an analysis of the integrity challenge on each of the five dimensions to a leadership strategy for meeting them.

The book is unusual in some other ways as well. It offers a particular perspective, a somewhat singular focus, and a special method. It explores the challenges of corporate integrity from a civic perspective. This perspective views corporations as members of civil society and corporate members as citizens. Instead of relying on the persuasiveness of the "business case," which needs to show that doing well will result from doing good, the civic case relies on shared civic values of meeting human needs and respecting human rights. This allows an examination of how these values are realized not only in interpersonal relationships, but also in corporate relationships with other groups in civic society as they struggle to work together to design a sustainable world.

To bring these and other values into the analysis, the book focuses on relationships. It follows the implications of understanding integrity as wholeness, which requires us to see individuals as part of the relational whole to which they belong and corporations as part of the larger whole to which they belong. In each of the five dimension of corporate life, the integrity challenge is to develop appropriate relationships for individuals, for corporations, and for corporations and other civic organizations. Improving the quality of these relationships will improve integrity.

Of course you cannot directly observe relationships, but you can observe the patterns of communication in which they are embedded. So the method for improving the integrity of relationships is to analyze, evaluate, and redesign communication patterns. These patterns include much more than verbal pronouncements. They also include nonverbal behaviors and actions. Actions sometimes do speak louder than words. In organizations, however, communication patterns often speak the loudest. The daily routines, schedules, structures, everyday conversations, reward systems, shared images, and interpretive schemes largely determine the quality of relationships on all five dimensions of corporate life.

So the book takes up a civic perspective to explore corporate relations by examining communication patterns so that we will understand the challenges of integrity and learn what is necessary to meet them. Behind this approach lie some basic assumptions. These will be explored in chapter 1, and others will be examined throughout the book. The book's overall purpose is quite simple: to show what corporations would look like if they were to have integrity, and to explore how to move them in that direction. Once we know what corporate integrity entails, we will know what to expect of them, and corporate and civic leaders will know how to design them.

To assist readers in evaluating and applying the book's various themes, each chapter is followed by a series of questions for reflection and dialogue. In addition, the appendix contains worksheets for each chapter to facilitate the exploration of existing patterns of communication and for developing strategies to improve them.

This book has evolved from the fusion of multiple disciplines and experiences. Business ethics has provided most of the material for the conversations in which this book participates. The focus on communication has its roots in the study of theological and philosophical hermeneutics (theories of interpretation) and conversations years ago with Edward Hobbs. My interest in designing communication patterns has evolved from my earlier work on ethical decision making to a concern about how to create the conditions in which people could make ethical decisions. The civic perspective is an answer to a question that I probably should have asked much sooner than I did: "Who am I when I am engaged in ethical analysis?" I realized I had always done this work, at least implicitly, as a citizen, rather than as an economist, or even a philosopher. Once I became clear about this, my interest focused on making that stance explicit. Conversations with Mark

Brown have also increased my knowledge of research in political theory and democratic practices. The relational focus has several sources, including feminist ethics and the professional perspectives of Erdmut Brown and Kirsten Brown on relational distress and wholeness in couples therapy and social work.

The experiences behind the book include years of teaching graduate and undergraduate students, who have always challenged me to make ideas relevant and practical. There is also my early experience as an intern, and later as a researcher, in the lay academies in Germany, which then provided a variety of conferences for workers and managers to explore controversial issues. More recently, I have had the opportunity to help design corporate training programs as well as ethics and compliance programs at such companies as Levi Strauss and Company and the California State Automobile Association. Colleagues in Germany, Poland, Venezuela, and Argentina have invited me to give lectures and workshops, which have increased my understanding of what a contemporary corporate ethic requires. The chapter on corporations and cities was originally a paper I presented at an ethics conference in Buenos Aires sponsored by the Asociación Argentina de Investigaciones Éticas. Ideas from the other chapters were also previously presented in papers at conferences of the Society of Business Ethics, the International Society of Business, Economics and Ethics, and the Association of Professional and Practical Ethics. Collegial responses to these papers, as well as dinner conversations, have usually been enlightening.

The book has benefited from conversations with many colleagues, including W. Barnett Pearce, Nancy Southern, David Gill, Barbara McGraw, Toni Wilson, Eugene Muscat, John Moyer, and Horacio Bolaños. I am grateful to Georges Enderle, Joseph DesJardins, Heidi von Weitzien Hoivik, and Joseph Rost for reading the whole manuscript or parts of it and providing valuable comments. Mark Brown's reading of the completed draft was especially helpful. The reviewers at Cambridge University Press were also helpful in clarifying the book's overall direction. The Press's editor, Katy Plowright, has been nothing but generous throughout this project. I am deeply grateful for her guidance. I am also grateful to Linda Lancione Moyer, a friend and poet, who gave the various chapters her attention as they were written. I dedicate this book to Erdmut Brown, who has held our relationship as a life-giving source of support, renewal, and joy.

1 | *The context for corporate integrity*

T he scandals of Enron, World-Com, Arthur Andersen, and others in the past few years have once again destroyed the naiveté of those who trusted corporations and confirmed the suspicions of those who did not. This is not the first time that corporate behavior has confirmed the opinions of its critics and shattered the opinions of its supporters. The difference today is that corporate conduct, whether good or bad, makes a much greater footprint than ever before, not only on human communities, but also on the natural environment. Furthermore, as corporations have become more powerful, the civic institutions that have saved them in the past have become weaker. The overall direction of global corporations today gives us some notion of what it must have been like traveling on the *Titanic*: to be slowly moving in the wrong direction, but too big and powerful to change course.

There is another side of the story, of course. It is the story of the increased involvement of corporations in ethics, social responsibility, and corporate citizenship. It will be told in the chapters ahead. Both stories are important. Taken together they create the context for rethinking organizational ethics and leadership. In contrast to the narratives that make prime-time viewing and TV entertainment/ news, these stories are not focused primarily on individuals. They are mostly about designing and redesigning the ongoing conversational patterns that constitute corporations as human organizations. These stories are also multidimensional. For the stories to be told well, and for the telling to show what can and needs to be done, these different dimensions must become available for analysis, evaluation, and change. The five dimensions of corporate stories include the cultural, the interpersonal, the organizational, the civic, and environmental. All five dimensions much be taken into account, because any one can hold back the other four, and any one can also improve the whole. At the same time, not one of the five can become an adequate substitute for any of the other four. Exploring these five dimensions represents the core of this book.

On each of these dimensions of corporate life there is always more than one way of getting things done. The cultural dimension, for example, can prevent or promote the introduction of new ideas. The environmental dimension can hide or reveal knowledge about the sustainability of consumer products. The same is true for the other three dimensions as well. Not every accomplishment, however, can be justified. How can we tell which ones are justified? Not how can *I* tell, but how can *we* tell? I can tell because I know what is right and wrong. The problem is you also know, and you and I may disagree. What can we do then? *We* need a shared standard that we can use to make good judgments. I think that integrity can serve as such a standard.

Integrity could become *our* standard for corporate conduct because it is closely tied to the implicit issue raised by both the critic's disdain for corporations and the supporter's disappointment in corporate scandals: the issue of trust. If people have integrity, then we can usually trust them. If we could design corporations with integrity, people could trust them too. They could work in them and with them to develop a viable future for us and for our children.

So what would that design look like? It could involve the arrangement of physical things, of course, such as the design of interior office space. Interior design certainly reveals a corporation's view of how people should relate to each other at work, but that is only a small portion of the life of a corporation. We need to examine how the whole corporation is designed, and we can if we look at the design of the ongoing verbal and nonverbal communication patterns that constitute a corporation as a social system. It is the quality of the communication patterns, in other words, that will give us the data to evaluate a corporation's integrity.

Much of the information about communicative patterns is very accessible. We just need to listen and reflect on what is being said (and not said), who is speaking (and not speaking), what is talked about (and not talked about), and so on. After listening, we can learn how the conversations create the conditions and the expectations for how people should act towards each other, toward the organization, and toward nature.

This exploration of corporate integrity rests on a series of assumptions about corporations and about integrity. Perhaps the most important assumptions are definitions. Corporations can be defined in several ways, but a definition that is especially relevant for corporate integrity is to see them as human systems designed to achieve some purpose. Systems are sets of interactive parts that constitute a whole. Integrity is also about parts and whole. To integrate is to make whole. So the initial connection between systems and integrity is that while a systems approach examines how parts and wholes are related to each other, an integrity approach investigates how they *should* be related. Some human systems, such as individual persons, are both biological and linguistic systems. Corporations, of course, are not biological. They are, however, constituted by language, or, we could say, by ongoing communication patterns. These patterns include both verbal and non-verbal communications. The verbal communication includes mission and policy statements as well as daily conversations. The nonverbal includes work design, daily schedules, and practical skills. If we look at corporate systems as ongoing communications, then corporate integrity will depend on the character of these communications.

Corporations are not only systems themselves; they also belong to larger social and natural systems. To investigate their integrity in these larger systems, it is necessary to find the best angle from which to examine how corporations should relate to the other parts of these systems. I think the best angle is from a civic perspective. Instead of putting corporations in a separate sphere of economics, for example, the civic perspective places them in the context of civic life, and in relationship with other civic agents, such as nonprofits and government agencies. Exploring and evaluating the types of conversations in which these different agencies participate will give us a picture of the requirements of corporate integrity in terms of society and the environment.

Chapters 2–6 examine and evaluate internal and external corporate relationships. The final chapter explores the leader's role in designing corporate integrity. This chapter clarifies three key ideas: the meanings of integrity, the rationale for a civic perspective, and the idea of corporations as ongoing communication patterns.

The meanings of integrity

Sometimes integrity is simply used as a substitute for the good or the right. Richard DeGeorge uses the term in this way: "Acting with integrity is the same as acting ethically or morally."[1] There is certainly something right about this definition; integrity does have a normative meaning. In fact it has several meanings, and each one can help us understand its significance, not as a substitute for ethics, but as a significant addition to other ethical standards. To understand these various meanings, we need to begin with its original meaning, which comes from the notion of "integral." An integral represents a whole.[2] Wholeness, of course, always implies the presence of parts, so integrity requires not only wholeness, but also the right relationships among the parts of a whole. To create integrity, therefore, is to integrate the parts into a whole. The relationships between the parts and the whole offer various meanings of integrity, including integrity as consistency, as relational awareness, as inclusion, and as pursuing a worthwhile purpose.

Integrity as consistency

Perhaps the most common meaning of integrity is consistency. Integrity here refers to the alignment between what one does and what one says. Doing and saying should belong to the same whole. This is the way Charles Watson uses integrity in his book *Managing with Integrity*:

There is wholeness in what the person with integrity says and does. There is consistency between his actions and what he purports to honor. He pursues his aims along the high road and is uninterrupted and undiminished by temptations for quick or easy personal gain. He seems undisturbed by the opinions others hold or express about him and what he honors. His upright conduct is made possible through steadfast adherence to unbending principles and standards, and his character is marked by an undaunted quest for important ends far larger than his own needs, comfort, and interests.[3]

This understanding of personal integrity is certainly praiseworthy in some cases. Taken as the complete definition of integrity, however, it leaves us with a potentially dangerous use of the term. Imagine for a

---

[1] Richard T. DeGeorge, *Competing with Integrity in International Business* (New York and Oxford: Oxford University Press, 1993), p. 5.
[2] *The American Heritage Dictionary of The English Language*, third edition (Boston: Houghton Mifflin, 1992), p. 937.
[3] Charles E. Watson, *Managing with Integrity: Insights from America's CEOs* (New York: Praeger, 1991), p. 171.

moment that this person with integrity is a totally unconscious individual, who is unaware of his privileges, but believes that everyone has had similar opportunities as he has had. Does his integrity here – being undisturbed by the opinions of others and practicing steadfast adherence to unbending principles and standards – help or prevent him from becoming conscious of his relationships with others in larger social and economic systems? If integrity means wholeness, and if a particular consistency prevents one from an awareness of one's whole situation, then consistency would actually prevent the creation of integrity. To be fair to Watson, his book argues elsewhere that managers have a "duty to think" and to consider different points of view.[4] Still, his description of managerial integrity expresses a common attitude about the self: at its best the self is isolated from others, true to its own principles, and is a complete "whole."

As most of us know from our own experience, this notion of the isolated self is less than a half-truth. We are born to live in relationships with others. The relational self exists prior to, and serves as the foundation for, expressions of the individual self. So integrity as wholeness must be defined not only by consistency but also by relational awareness.

Integrity as relational awareness

In a book on executive integrity, Suresh Srivastva and Frank Barrett write that: "The 'wholeness' that the word integrity refers to is the wholeness of the relationship, the wholeness of the interaction."[5] Robert Solomon also defines integrity as relational: " 'Wholeness' means that one's identity is not that of an isolated atom but rather the product of a larger social molecule, and that wholeness includes – rather than excludes – other people and one's social role."[6] For individuals to have real integrity, they must be conscious of the relationships in

---

[4] Ibid., p. 57.
[5] Suresh Srivastva and Frank J. Barrett, "Foundations for Executive Integrity: Dialogue, Diversity, Development," in *Executive Integrity: The Search for High Human Values in Organizational Life*, ed. Suresh Srivastva and Associates (San Francisco, CA: Jossey-Bass, 1989), p. 291.
[6] Robert C. Solomon, *A Better Way to Think About Business: How Personal Integrity Leads to Corporate Success* (New York: Oxford University Press, 1999), p. 40.

which they live. Does that mean that we should throw out the notion of consistency? Not completely, because the self has two quite different ways of beings.

In my business ethics classes, I ask students to write out a description of who they are. They usually write down specific characteristics, such as honest, caring, hard working, and so on. I take these to refer to how they think they will respond or act in specific circumstances. They can be understood as virtues or dispositions to act in certain ways rather than others.[7] Sometimes the students write out a very different set of terms. They use such terms as sons, daughters, students, parents, and so on. These are all relational terms. Instead of identifying dispositions toward action, like the first set of terms, this set identifies persons in terms of their involvements and memberships, as related persons. Integrity applies to both aspects of the self. As a relational self, integrity requires a relational awareness, a consciousness of the relations in which one participates.[8] In terms of human action, integrity requires consistency in action; a consistency between what one says and what one does. So both aspects of integrity are necessary because the self is both relational and an agent. This is also true of corporations. Corporate designers also have to answer questions of identity (the who-are-we? question) and questions of action (the what-should-we-do? question). Chapter 3, on interpersonal relationships, focuses more on the corporation as a relational entity, and chapter 4, on organizational purpose, focuses more on the corporation as an agent. Relational awareness, of course, does not necessarily determine the type of relationship one should strive for. One can be aware of relationships of inclusion or exclusion. To affirm wholeness, however, requires inclusion, which is the third meaning of integrity.

---

[7] I take this to be Aristotle's understanding of the virtues. They were dispositions or habitual ways of responding to situations. The virtues, in other words, are related to actions.

[8] A similar notion of the individual-in-relationships or in-community can be found in several business ethics books, such as Michael Rion, *The Responsible Manager: Practical Strategies for Ethical Decision Making* (Amherst, MA: Human Resource Development Press, 1996), as well as the writings of Robert Solomon, *Ethics and Excellence: Cooperation and Integrity in Business* (New York and Oxford: Oxford University Press, 1993), and Edwin Hartman, *Organizational Ethics and the Good Life* (Oxford: Oxford University Press, 1996).

Integrity as inclusion

In groups and teams, inclusion requires an openness to differences and disagreements, which is the topic of chapter 2. On the organizational level, it can also refer to listening to different voices, even disagreeable ones. The idea of integrity as inclusion has also been used to talk about including ethics and compliance programs in everyday business practices. Lynn Sharp Paine, for example, has suggested that instead of imposing compliance programs to constrain corporate behavior, managers should integrate compliance programs into their daily operations. In this way, ethics becomes included in the business.[9]

Kaptein and Wempe have developed a theory of corporate integrity that relies on all three meanings of integrity reviewed so far: integrity as consistency, as relational, and as inclusion.[10] The consistency aspect of integrity refers to the union of words and deeds. The relational aspect refers to the multiple relationships with various stakeholders. The inclusion meaning refers to the integration of the ethical theories of virtue ethics, deontology and utilitarianism in guiding corporate decisions. When they put these three meanings of integrity together, they see corporate integrity as balancing the different claims and obligations that arise from both inside and outside the corporation.

The balancing metaphor certainly expresses the process of trying to include different interests and ethical standards, but it does not indicate the reason for the balancing act. In other words, what is the corporation pursuing that gives its whole process integrity? Kaptein and Wempe's answer is that people create businesses to be more efficient than they could be alone.[11] Efficiency, however, is not the kind of

---

[9] Lynn Sharp Paine, "Managing for Organizational Integrity," *Harvard Business Review* (March/April, 1994), pp. 106–17. Other authors also have used corporate integrity as an integration of ethical theory or as an integration of ethics and corporate practices. See Debbie Thorne LeClair, O. C. Ferrell, and John P. Fraedrich, *Integrity Management: A Guide to Managing Legal and Ethical Issues in the Workplace* (Tampa, FL: University of Tampa Press, 1998), and Joseph A. Petrick and John F. Quinn's *Management Ethics: Integrity at Work* (Thousand Oaks, CA: Sage, 1997).

[10] Muel Kaptein and Johan Wempe, *The Balanced Company: A Theory of Corporate Integrity* (Oxford: Oxford University Press, 2002).

[11] Ibid., p. 165.

purpose that elicits integrity. Drug dealers may be efficient, but that does not mean they should be praised for having integrity. What is missing in Kaptein and Wempe's theory is the notion of a good corporate purpose. A complete understanding of integrity must include this fourth meaning – integrity as pursuing a worthwhile purpose.

Integrity as pursuing a worthwhile purpose

When we say that someone or something has integrity, it is a way of praising them. Integrity, in other words, is a virtue, not a vice. To use integrity only as a means of integrating ethical principles into business practices, or even as a balancing of different claims, largely overlooks the fact that integrity itself is an ethical principle. Integrity, in other words, has a normative connotation that provides a guideline for right action.

The goodness implicit in the notion of integrity comes from its place in the larger language system to which it belongs. In this system, it has a positive meaning. We do not blame people for having integrity. We praise them. And we praise them not only because they are consistent, aware of relationships, and able to include different theories and claims, but also because they are pursuing something that is worthwhile.

These various meanings of integrity are not really opposed to each other, but rather together give us a strong notion of what integrity means. Since the corporation consists of multiple relationships, the relational meaning dominates. The other meanings – consistency, inclusion, and pursuing a worthwhile purpose – are not far behind. The most significant relationships occur in five dimensions of corporate life: the cultural, interpersonal, organizational, civic, and natural. Each of these dimensions can either block or enable corporate integrity.

The five dimensions of corporate integrity

Of the five dimensions, the cultural dimension is perhaps the most fundamental, because culture is what holds things together. Its language, rituals, and patterns of communication provide a rich context in which we discover how to relate to persons, experiences, and things. The second dimension, the interpersonal, focuses on the relationships that define the self. The third dimension, the organizational, refers to

Figure 1.1. Five dimensions of corporate integrity

corporations as agents. Agents have integrity when their actions are in alignment with their purposes, assuming these purposes are worthwhile. At this level, integrity as consistency is important, but so is the inclusive meaning of integrity, in the sense that corporations are included in their social and natural environments. Corporate relationships to society and to nature constitute the fourth and fifth dimensions of corporate integrity.

In light of the growing environmental crisis, designing relationships of integrity between corporations and nature may seem to deserve first place among the five dimensions. However, only by creating integrity in the cultural dimension, which requires the openness necessary to explore the environmental question, can we critically examine the relationship between corporations and nature. Actually, all five dimensions need to be integrated to achieve a high degree of corporate integrity. Figure 1.1 illustrates the contextual relationships among the five dimensions. As the figure illustrates, the cultural and the natural provide the context or contain the other three: the interpersonal, organizational, and social. Furthermore, the social contains the organizational, and the organizational contains the interpersonal. All five dimensions are interrelated and interdependent, but each one presents its own challenge.

Five challenges of corporate integrity

Each of the five dimensions presents its own particular challenge to corporate integrity. The challenge on the cultural level is to be open to differences and disagreements. In a sense, every culture is already holistic. That is one of the meanings of culture. In a pluralistic society, however, we continually encounter other cultures, which means that our culture is now a part of a larger whole – a multicultural society. Integrity as wholeness requires the recognition of cultural otherness, and an openness to the value of differences and disagreements. Chapter 2 provides a framework for exploring different cultural types and offers strategies for designing cultural openness.

On the interpersonal level, the challenge is to acknowledge the relationships that constitute one's relational self. The more extreme forms of individualism make such an acknowledgment particularly difficult. They tend to see the individual as separated from others rather than dependent on them. They also tend to ignore the meaning of the context in which an individual person exists. The paradox is that this individualism, which denies cultural bias, is a cultural bias. We all are particular persons, in particular relationships, living in a particular time and in particular social patterns. Integrity as wholeness requires that persons become aware of each other's relational identity, and of themselves as members of different types of relationships. In the workplace, for example, people are not only members of the workforce, but also are family and civic members. Since each person belongs to family and civic relationships, recognizing the whole person means that these key relationships should partly determine relationships at work. Holding all three types of relationships together – family, civic, and work – allows us to acknowledge the challenge of respecting the need for security from family relationships, the right to participate from civic relationships, as well as the virtue of reciprocity from work relationships. These relational concepts will be more completely developed in chapter 3.

On the organizational level, the challenge is to insure consistency between organizational purpose and conduct. The corporate mission, in other words, must express such a worthwhile purpose that when a decision is in alignment with that mission, one can say that the decision was right. These decisions are a part of a whole, which is identified by the corporate mission. For corporations to have integrity, they must have a worthwhile purpose that can be a reliable guide for their decisions. Since the meaning of corporate purpose is quite complicated, chapter 4 develops a framework that clearly distinguishes a corporation's organizational purpose from the individual and the social purposes of corporations.

The challenge of the fourth dimension, a corporation's social context, is for corporations to develop cooperative relationships with other private and government agencies. Businesses require a space for freedom and innovation and a legal structure to protect themselves from tyranny and anarchy. Civil society provides the space. The rule of law provides the protection. Given the "less government" ideology of many in the business community, the essential role of government is not always recognized, even in business ethics. In any case, corporations, both nonprofit and for-profit, exist in this larger civic whole, with public or government agencies, and integrity requires that corporations find their appropriate relationships with them. Chapter 5 explores six different models of corporate/city relationships and evaluates them in terms of how corporations should be included in society.

Finally, the fifth challenge calls for the inclusion of corporations in the natural environment so that they acknowledge the links between their fate and the fate of the earth. Although many corporations have made significant progress in decreasing the environmental destruction of our modern economy and working toward sustainability, the natural environment remains at risk. Over the long term, economic prosperity cannot continue to be at the expense of nature. For the modern economy to have integrity, it must be designed to fit with nature. Corporate integrity at this level requires that all of nature, both human and nonhuman communities, prosper together. Chapter 6 examines current conversations about sustainability, world trade, and the integrity of nature, and explores how to integrate them for the sake of natural prosperity. Drawing all five challenges together results in figure 1.2. The full significance of these five challenges will only become clear in the following chapters, which present a new way of analyzing, evaluating, and changing corporate conduct by working with existing communication patterns and imagining new ones that meet the challenges of integrity. The final chapter will draw these different dimensions of corporate integrity together and explore what they might tell us about the integrity of corporate leadership and what corporate leaders can do as designers of corporate integrity.

The book's civic perspective looks at corporations as members of civil society and corporate members as citizens. This way of interpreting corporations and employees and employers has three advantages: it represents the next step in the development of the idea of corporate citizenship; it provides a framework for mediating the conflict between

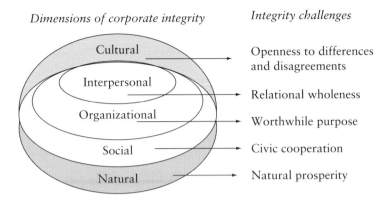

Dimensions of corporate integrity   *Integrity challenges*

Figure 1.2. Five integrity challenges

those who emphasize corporate responsibility and those who emphasize corporate corruption and domination; and it returns us to a new reading of Aristotle's ethic as a public, civic ethic. Once we have grounded corporate ethics in civic or public ethics, even more positive results will occur, as the following chapters will demonstrate. The following section demonstrates the significance of these three advantages, beginning with a brief review of different theories of corporate responsibility.

Theories of corporate responsibility

Corporate social responsibility has become a popular notion in business circles, with a variety of meanings. As Richard DeGeorge has pointed out, the notion can refer to either moral or nonmoral obligations.[12] It can also refer to obligations or to voluntary actions. In spite of these different interpretations, the following statement by Julio Moura, the CEO of GrupoNueva, in Costa Rica, illustrates much about its current usage:

As a company, we are part of this society; we have a certain privilege; we are educated; we have access to resources, and we have been entrusted with those

[12] Richard T. DeGeorge, *Business Ethics*, fifth edition (Upper Saddle River, NJ: Prentice Hall, 1999), p. 207.

responses, so we have also responsibilities to do something good, to make the community around us prosper.[13]

The understanding of responsibility here is that a company should respond *to* society because it has the ability to respond and because it is a part *of* society. Is this a moral obligation? Would it be a moral failure if a company did not do something good to make a community prosper? The answer depends on your assumptions about business corporations.

In the following review of different assumptions about corporations, I will use the term "corporate responsibility" rather than "corporate social responsibility," since corporate responsibilities certainly include moral responsibilities for individuals and the natural environment as well as for society.[14] The analysis will employ a three-level approach to business ethics suggested by Georges Enderle that examines the micro, meso, and macro levels of conduct.[15] The micro corresponds to our interpersonal dimension, the meso to the organizational dimension, and the macro to our social dimension. The five theories are the classic, contractual, stakeholder, corporate agent, and corporate citizen theories of corporate responsibility.

The classic theory of corporate responsibility

Although the first business corporations in the United States were chartered for specific public purposes, many today call the "classic" view of corporations the view represented by such economists as Milton Friedman.[16] In his famous essay on corporate responsibility,

---

[13] Quoted in Charles O. Holliday, Jr., Stephan Schmidheiny, and Philip Watts, *Walking the Talk: The Business Case for Sustainable Development* (San Francisco, CA: Berrett-Koehler, 2002), p. 103.

[14] For an extensive analysis of the uses of terms such as corporate responsibility and corporate social responsibility, see Sandra Waddock, "Parallel Universes: Companies, Academics, and the Progress of Corporate Citizenship," *Business and Society Review*, vol. 109, no. 1 (Spring, 2004), pp. 2–42.

[15] Georges Enderle, "Towards Business Ethics as an Academic Discipline," *Business Ethics Quarterly*, vol. 6, no. 1 (January, 1996), p. 47.

[16] Examples of this classification can be found in John Boatright, *Ethics and the Conduct of Business*, fourth edition (Upper Saddle River, NJ: Prentice Hall, 2003), and Joseph DesJardins, *An Introduction to Business Ethics* (Boston: McGraw Hill, 2003).

Friedman argued that the only social responsibility of business is to make a profit.[17] In terms of the individual, organizational, and social levels, Friedman's essay focuses only on individual behaviors. For him, corporate managers are the agents of the principals or owners, and their obligation is to do what the principals (owners) want. From this perspective, the notion of responsibility applies only to the managers or executives of a business, not the business organization itself. The corporation's responsibility to society might be understood from this perspective as a duty to obey the laws, but upon closer examination, it really does not have any responsibility, because corporations are not seen as actors, only individuals are. In fact, in the classical view of corporations, corporations are seen as instruments or as property of the owners, so they could not themselves have responsibilities, since corporations, as entities, do not really exist. At the social level, the classical theory sees individual managers responsive to market conditions and responsible for obeying laws and social norms.

In the past couple of decades, this classical approach has been given a new twist by the socially responsible investment movement. The 2003 report on socially responsible investing states that over $2.16 trillion in assets are now used in one of three investment strategies: screening, shareholder advocacy, or community investing. Furthermore, more than one out of every nine dollars under professional management in the United States is involved in socially responsible funding.[18] Without a doubt, socially responsible investors, and the mutual funds and other financial institutions that carry out their wishes, have become a significant force in today's market. Their key assumption, however, is that businesses are essentially financial or economic organizations.

Another movement, sometimes in alignment with, and sometimes opposed to, the social investment movement, is the growing activism of large financial institutions in corporate governance. James Hawley and Andrew Williams see this movement as bringing about a shift from an older managerial capitalism to a new "fiduciary capitalism." Moreover, as the subtitle of their book on fiduciary capitalism proclaims, they

---

[17] Milton Friedman, "The Social Responsibility of Business Is to Increase its Profits," in *Ethical Theory and Business*, sixth edition, ed. Tom Beauchamp and Norm Bowie (Upper Saddle River, NJ: Prentice Hall, 2000) pp. 51–5.

[18] See www.socialinvest.org/.

believe that "institutional investors can make corporate America more democratic."[19]

Their argument goes like this. Financial institutions, which manage the investments of various types of pension funds, as well as other types of funds, now control over half of the total equity in the US market. Because of their size and duty to exercise care, these financial institutions invest in many different corporations, which give them the status of what Hawley and Williams call "universal owners."[20] As universal owners, they are concerned not just about the performance of one company, but rather the economy as a whole, since they are invested in many aspects of the economy. Therefore, they should pressure corporations to conduct themselves for long-term economic prosperity, and support those activities, such as charitable giving, which may not be in the narrow interest of one firm, but would be in the interest of all firms. The corporate community needs a healthy environment in which to conduct business. Corporations will practice social responsibility, in other words, because their investors are interested in a sustainable economy.

Even though fiduciary capitalism may give investors a stronger voice in corporate decisions, it also reinforces the view that corporations are merely instruments for making money. Something like Kaptein and Wempe, Hawley and Williams seem to be trying to control the impact of corporations on society, rather than focusing on what corporations are good for. Fiduciary capitalism may promote democracy in "corporate America," as Hawley and William's book's subtitle suggests, but I would call this a "private democracy," rather than a "public democracy." It is a democracy for private investors, or those whose retirement is in the hands of private investors. A public democracy, on the other hand, is open to all citizens and for all citizens. Also, their form of capitalism, like classical capitalism, relies solely on the relationship between the owners (investors) and managers. It does not recognize the existence of corporations as organizational agents.

---

[19] James P. Hawley and Andrew T. Williams, *The Rise of Fiduciary Capitalism: How Institutional Investors Can Make Corporate America More Democratic* (Philadelphia: University of Pennsylvania Press, 2003).

[20] Ibid., p. xv.

The contractual theory of corporate responsibility

Our second theory of corporate responsibility more or less continues the previous view's emphasis on relationships among individuals, but does offer a different view of business organizations. The contractual theory sees a business organization as comprised of various contracts among individuals and groups, arranged for the purpose of satisfying their interests. Even though all of these contracts would appear to have equal value, this theory gives priority to the contract with shareholders and their interest in profit maximization. As Boatright points out, shareholders have first place because of the assumption that an emphasis on profit will increase wealth for all more than any other alternative.[21] Instead of limiting corporate responsibility to increasing the owner's profits, however, this view sees the responsibility of corporations as one of increasing prosperity for the whole society. At the social level, the contractual approach replaces the "invisible hand" as the coordinator of market transactions with a set of social institutions. Some of these institutions are encoded in laws, such as laws protecting private property, and some are not, such as the institution of putting in a day's work for a day's pay. Such institutions provide the cooperative basis for competitive markets.

Thomas Donaldson and Thomas Dunfee have developed a more recent contractual approach that also looks at corporations as sets of agreements or contracts among different parties.[22]

At the heart of the social contract effort is a simple assumption, namely, that we can understand better the obligations of key social institutions, such as business or government, by attempting to understand what is entailed in a fair agreement or "contract" between those institutions and society, and also in the implicit contracts that exist among the different communities and institutions within society.[23]

Central to Donaldson and Dunfee's contract theory is a distinction between local and general norms that express local and universal

---

[21] Boatright, *Ethics and the Conduct of Business*, p. 387.
[22] Thomas Donaldson and Thomas Dunfee, *Ties That Bind: A Social Contracts Approach to Business Ethics* (Boston, MA: Harvard Business School Press, 1999).
[23] Ibid., pp. 16–17.

agreements. They call the general or overriding agreements "hyper-norms."[24] These hypernorms serve as standards for the evaluation of local or specific community norms. Although the status of hypernorms has been controversial, their significance here resides in the view of corporate responsibility they express. Responsibility means clarifying the validity of both explicit and implicit local contracts by appealing to relevant hypernorms, and following those that are valid.

It does seem that a process of examining the actual agreements of a local community and then evaluating them by hypernorms or more general agreements could promote corporate responsibility. All three levels (the individual, organizational, and social) could be described in terms of contractual relations. The question is whether the language of contract can express the richness of human relations. Edwin Hartman, for example, believes that social contacts cannot cover all that needs to be said about corporations. For him, the basic issue is the development of a "good community that encourages the good life," and the good life is not just about following contracts, but also about developing appropriate dispositions or virtues.[25] In other words, if a good community facilitates the development of a good life, then the interaction among communal members will be much richer than con-tractual language expresses. The distinction that makes a difference is the distinction between a language based on contracts and a language based on membership as a way of revealing the dynamics of human relationships at work. This distinction between membership and con-tract could also apply to the next theory: the stakeholder theory of corporations.

The stakeholder view of corporate responsibility

A third theory of corporations, the stakeholder view, sees corporations as constituted by the various groups that have a stake in their conduct. R. Edward Freeman developed figure 1.3 to show what groups would

---

[24] Ibid., p. 50.
[25] Hartman, *Organizational Ethics and the Good Life*. Timothy L. Fort makes a similar critique of contractual thinking in his *Ethics and Governance: Business as Mediating Institution* (New York: Oxford University Press, 2001).

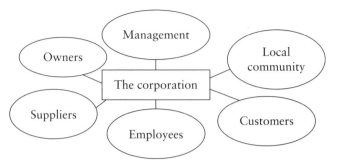

Figure 1.3. Stakeholders

be among a corporation's stakeholders.[26] If you delete one group from this picture, such as customers, the corporation no longer exists. All the parts, in other words, are necessary for the whole. The stakeholder view could be interpreted from a contractual or a membership perspective. I could imagine different types of contracts or different types of memberships among the various stakeholders. Either way, the stakeholder view has more in common with the previous views than the next view, which sees the corporation itself as a decision maker.

The corporate agent theory of corporate responsibility

How can you hold corporations responsible for the impact of their conduct or the design of their workplace if they are not seen as decision makers? And yet, the notion of corporate agency has been very controversial in the business ethics literature. Some of the arguments on both sides are explored in chapter 4 in the context of defining a corporation's purpose. The conclusion from that chapter is that the qualifications for agency are really quite simple. A corporation qualifies as an agent if it meets three conditions: the capacity to make decisions, the presence of real options or choices, and the ability to give reasons for a choice. Corporations are designed to make decisions in the sense they provide structures for persons to decide together what

[26] R. E. Freeman, "A Stakeholder Theory of the Modern Corporation," in *Ethical Theory and Business*, sixth edition, ed. T. Beauchamp and N. Bowie (Upper Saddle River, NJ: Prentice Hall, 1997).

the corporation should do. Corporations also have options. Finally, they also have corporate reasons expressed in their mission statement and other documents that can justify their decision. So corporations do make decisions, and they can be held responsible for them.

In contrast to the previous views, the corporate agent theory focuses more on the organizational level than the individual. This theory sees individuals as both persons and personnel. They are individual persons, responsible for their decisions, and they are personnel – members of the corporation that act as officers or managers of the corporation. As personnel, they use corporate reasons for making corporate decisions rather than individual reasons, so the corporation can be held responsible for the decision.

Although the corporate agent view of corporations goes beyond the other views, it does not replace them. The stakeholder/membership theory highlights the corporation as a community. The corporate agent view highlights that corporations are also agents. Both of these aspects are present in the theory of corporations as citizens.

The corporate citizen theory of corporate responsibility

The corporate citizen theory builds on the stakeholder and agent theories and adds to them an awareness of the civic context in which corporations exist.[27] This view imagines corporations as belonging to civil society with similar rights and duties as other citizens.[28] In a recent book, *Corporate Citizenship*, the authors present corporations as engaging in a variety of forms of citizenship:

We might think of corporate citizenship as forming a continuum, that stretches from "minimal" citizenship at one extreme (consisting of compliance with the laws governing the operation of the business, but nothing else),

---

[27] See Donna J. Wood and Jeanne M. Logsdon, "Business, Citizenship: From Individuals to Organizations," in *Ethics and Entrepreneurship: The Ruffin Series No. 3*, special issue of *Business Ethics Quarterly* (2002), pp. 59–94, and Jeanne M. Logsdon and Donna J. Wood, "Business Citizenship: From Domestic to Global Level of Analysis," *Business Ethics Quarterly*, vol. 12, no. 2 (April, 2002), pp. 155–87.

[28] Noel M. Tichy, Andrew R. McGill, and Lynda St. Clair (eds.), *Corporate Global Citizenship: Doing Business in the Public Eye* (San Francisco: New Lexington Press, 1997), p. 28.

to a complex relationship of interlocking rights and responsibilities at the other (between corporations and its communities, which has become an integral part of the functioning of the business).[29]

Since the citizenship theory of corporations sees corporate responsibility emerging from their location in civil society, this theory provides a strong platform for the development of a civic perspective of corporate integrity. However, this view remains extremely vague as to what these obligations are, or if they are obligations at all. Perhaps they are only charitable actions, rather than obligations. In any case, this theory, plus the corporate agent and the stakeholder theories, give us a strong foundation for continuing our movement toward a civic perspective of corporate integrity.

Figure 1.4 highlights the similarities and differences among these five different theories of corporations. It identifies their key assumptions about individuals, organizations, and society, and the view of responsibility that follows from these assumptions. Placing these different views of corporate responsibility next to the four meanings of integrity – integrity as consistency, relational awareness, inclusion, and pursuing a worthwhile purpose – it is clear that a complete theory of corporate responsibility would include those theories that emphasize community, such as the stakeholder view, and those that emphasize agency, such as the corporate agent or citizen view. A strong view of corporate integrity, in other words, does not so much leave these theories behind as gather them together.

Although the corporate citizen theory of corporations most closely matches our interest in exploring the relationships between corporations and other agents in society, the strengths of the other theories should not be forgotten. The classical view reminds us that owners and investors are interested in increasing shareholder value. The contractual approach highlights the role of social institutions as the necessary context for market transactions. The stakeholder approach allows us to see how corporate responsibility follows from existing relationships with various groups. The corporate agent approach does not contradict the strengths of these other approaches, but adds a different view of

---

[29] Malcolm McIntosh, Deborah Leipziger, Keith Jones, and Gill Coleman, *Corporate Citizenship: Successful Strategies for Responsible Companies* (London: Financial Times Management, 1998), p. xxi.

Theories of Corporations	Levels of Analysis			Notions of Responsibility
	Individual Level	Organizational Level	System Level	
Classic	Self-interested individuals	Property of owners	Invisible hand/Laws and norms	Keep promises to owner
Contractual	Self-interested individuals	Nexus of contracts	Institutional norms and rules	Honor contracts
Stakeholder	Members of stakeholder groups	Constituted by stakeholders	Network of stakeholder interests	Include stakeholder claims in decisions
Corporate agent	Persons and personnel	Decision maker with internal decision making structure	Network of systems	Make decisions that fulfill corporate function in social systems
Citizen	Persons, personnel and citizens	Corporate decision maker as citizen	Civil society	Cooperate with other agents in civil society

Figure 1.4. Models of corporate responsibility

organizations. It acknowledges their capacity to make decisions and to be held responsible for them. The fifth approach, which sees corporations as citizens, places corporations in a civic context, and it is from this context that it makes sense to consciously work on improving corporate integrity from a civic perspective. Furthermore, a civic perspective allows us to see the merits of the conflicting trends of increased corporate responsibility and increased fear of corporate dominance.

Corporate responsibility and corporate dominance

In the last twenty years, we have witnessed a dramatic proliferation of business ethics and corporate responsibility projects inside and outside of corporations. Never before have so many corporations done so much good. At the same time, we have also witnessed a growing protest against the corporate domination of noncommercial institutions from democratic governments to public schools. For some, corporate power has become a threat to civic community. For others, corporations have become the enemy, as was demonstrated by the September 11 attack on the global symbol of corporate power, the World Trade Center.

The first trend certainly looks good for business ethics. In *Value Shift*, Lynn Sharp Paine points out that what were hotly contested arguments just a few years ago, such as the idea that corporations should be considered as moral agents, have now been settled.[30] As the title of her book suggests, there has been a "value shift." One easily finds evidence to support her claim. Over 1,500 corporations have signed on with the United Nations "Global Compact," a set of ethical principles concerning human rights, labor, and the environment.[31] In the United States, the Ethics Officer Association now has more than 900 members.[32] Ethics centers have sprung up all over the world. The Association for Professional and Practical Ethics now has over 800 members.[33] The Markkula Center for Applied Ethics has over 250 links to other ethics groups on its website.[34] One could go on and on about the surge in ethical programs and projects both inside and outside of corporations. This is certainly a welcome development.

The second trend is more troubling. Have corporations taken over, as David Korten suggested a few years ago?[35] It sometimes seems as though they have. Although there are multiple interpretations of the reasons for the United States' occupation of Iraq, few doubt the strong role of corporate interests. There are other examples as well: the corporate influence in the United States' national elections, the global privatization of basic human resources, or the transfer of pension funds to the stock market. What is most worrisome about this trend is the disempowering of democratic institutions and the undermining of our identity as citizens.

---

[30] Lynn Sharp Paine, *Value Shift: Why Companies Must Merge Social and Financial Imperatives to Achieve Superior Performance* (New York: McGraw-Hill, 2003).
[31] See www.unglobalcompact.org/Portal/Default.asp.
[32] See www.eoa.org/home.asp.
[33] See www.indiana.edu/~appe/.
[34] See www.scu.edu/ethics/links/links.cfm?cat=BUSI.
[35] David Korten, *When Corporations Rule the World* (San Francisco, CA: Berrett-Koehler, 1995).

As Ted Nace has demonstrated quite convincingly, the rise of corporate power has resulted in the "disabling of democracy."[36]

The danger here is that all the good work in business ethics and corporate responsibility might, in spite of good intentions, unwittingly support a larger movement toward what could be called the privatization of democracy. This is one interpretation of such developments as fiduciary capitalism, as I suggested earlier. Other developments seem to support this idea. Partnerships between corporations and nonprofit organizations, for example, have probably never done so much good, and yet in many cases their collaboration has resulted in decreasing public resources and public services. Furthermore, even with all the good deeds of private corporate citizens, as well as private citizens, the structures of privilege have remained in place.

In a private democracy, people see one another as consumers or investors, not citizens, and their power depends on their buying or investing capacity. It does not depend on the quality of their arguments or the soundness of their beliefs. Mark Sagoff makes a distinction between the public and private self that is quite similar to the distinction between private and public democracy.

Once the affective, that is, the economic, self becomes the source of all value, the public self becomes merely "apparent" and cannot participate in the exercise of power. Power, indeed, appears to be entirely private; it is the power to satisfy one's personal preferences. It ceases to be the power to join with others in effective power action to define and pursue collective values and shared aspirations.[37]

In a public democracy, power ultimately resides in the capacity of people to act on their shared beliefs and common hopes. People are seen as citizens with the civic right to participate in the affairs that affect how they will live together. This participation is not dependent on their investments or buying power, but on their civic membership.[38] Although consumer activism, or the use of shareholder proxies, may allow some to influence corporate conduct (some, but not all citizens),

[36] Ted Nace, *Gangs of America: The Rise of Corporate Power and the Disabling of Democracy* (San Francisco: Berrett-Koehler, 2003).

[37] Mark Sagoff, *The Economy of the Earth: Philosophy, Law, and the Environment* (Cambridge: Cambridge University Press, 1988), p. 47.

[38] See Michael Walzer, *Spheres of Justice: A Defense of Pluralism and Equality* (New York: Basic Books, 1983).

it is a poor replacement for democratic politics. As long as only the few (those with corporate investments or those who are part of consumer organizations) have a chance of changing corporate practices, the structures of economic privilege will always override the political structures of democratic representation.

It may seem that the notion of corporate citizenship could dissolve the distinction between public and private realms. The issue is not quite so simple. For example, at the 2002 meeting of the World Economic Forum in Davos Switzerland, CEOs of major international corporations signed a statement entitled, "Global Corporate Citizenship: The Leadership Challenge for CEOs and Boards." Their opening statement contains the following:

For the first time in history most of the world's population live in democratic societies and market-based economies, with the potential for increased political participation and economic prosperity. There are widespread concerns, however, that this potential is not being met; that many people are still facing high levels of inequality, insecurity and uncertainty, as well as new sources of conflict, environmental decline and lack of opportunity. World events since September 11th have reinforced the interconnected nature of these global challenges and the inter-dependence of nations and their citizens. Leaders from all countries, sectors and levels of society need to work together to address these challenges by supporting sustainable human development and ensuring that the benefits of globalization are shared more widely. It is in the interests of business that these benefits continue both for companies and for others in society.[39]

At the same time as the World Economic Forum, in Porto Alegre, Brazil, over 10,000 people attended a "World Social Forum." At this meeting, the participants defined their orientation as follows:

The World Social Forum is an open meeting place for reflective thinking, democratic debate of ideas, formulation of proposals, free exchange of experiences and interlinking for effective action, by groups and movements of civil society that are opposed to neo-liberalism and to domination of the world by capital and any form of imperialism, and are committed to building a planetary society directed towards fruitful relationships among Mankind and between it and the Earth.[40]

---

[39] See www.weforum.org/pdf/GCCI/GCC_CEOstatement.pdf.
[40] See www.wsfindia.org/charter.php.

It may appear that these two groups are talking about the same thing, and in some sense I am sure they are. The issue here, however, is not just one of selecting the right words, but of creating the right perspective for giving our words the right meaning. The meaning of words like "civic corporation" or "corporate citizen" depends on the perspective one assumes when using them. Try to imagine the perspective behind this definition of corporate citizenship in McIntosh, Leipziger, Jones, and Coleman's book on corporate citizenship.

A key feature of citizenship is that it involves a mutually reinforcing relationship between individuals and communities: individuals fulfil the responsibilities of citizenship, because some of their personal needs can only be met through communal action. Responsible citizens, for instance, dispose of their refuse in appointed places, rather than dumping it along the road or putting it on a neighbour's doorstep, because they need their neighbours to do the same. Corporate citizenship likewise suggests a two-way relationship between society and corporations; some of a corporation's needs will ultimately only be met by taking actions which are oriented toward meeting communal needs.[41]

Does this definition assume that the civic realm is something like a system of exchange where people meet each other's needs? Such an assumption would belong more to a market system than to democratic politics. Notice the difference in Benjamin Barber's definition of politics: "Politics describes a realm of action, but not all action is political. We may more properly restrict politics to *public* action: i.e., to action that is both undertaken by a public and intended to have public consequences. Politics describes the realm of *we*."[42] To be political, in other words, requires public involvement in a joint process of determining what actions should be undertaken for the whole community.

It could be, of course, that statements such as those by the CEOs at the World Economic Forum are about as far as business leaders can go into public politics. After all, they do have businesses to run. True enough. The market system is different from the public square. We need both. The question is how these should be separated from and attached to each other. Our current mixture of public and private

---

[41] McIntosh, Leipziger, Jones, and Coleman, *Corporate Citizenship*, p. xxi.
[42] Benjamin Barber, *Strong Democracy: Participatory Politics for a New Age* (Berkeley, Los Angeles, and London: University of California Press, 1984), p. 123.

means of distributing goods and services may need rebalancing, but there is widespread agreement that some balance of the public and the private, rather than one overpowering the other, is our common goal. The business interest in becoming more responsible for its place in society, and the democratic interest in resisting corporate dominance of everyday life, could both contribute to a better idea of what corporate integrity means in the years ahead. To gain access to this knowledge, we need to find a place where we can listen to both groups, which is one rationale for developing a civic perspective.

Some writers in corporate responsibility appear to be moving in this direction. In his book, *The Civic Corporation*, for example, Simon Zadek describes three stages of the development of the idea of corporate citizenship.[43] The first stage relied on the argument that corporate responsibility would have a positive impact on the bottom line. Corporations that do good, in other words, would also do well.

The second stage focused more on long-term prosperity than on short-term profits. Still, the argument repeated the slogan of the first stage: corporate citizenship was a "win-win" case for everyone. In the long run, a healthy society, as well as a sustainable environment, is necessary for business success. At both of these stages, the key conversations about corporate citizenship relied on what is called the "business case," which essentially points out that there is a "business interest" in becoming involved in corporate citizenship.[44]

Without doubt, corporations who have followed this definition have accomplished many worthwhile projects. Still, Zadek questions whether this stage of corporate activity is enough to attend to current problems. He says: "The core answer to this critical question is that corporate citizenship will only be effective if and where it evolves to a point where business becomes active in promoting and institutionalizing new global governance frameworks that effectively secure civil market behaviour." Jeanne Logsdon and Donna Wood appear to agree with Zadek. After their investigation of different views of corporate citizenship, they write:

[43] Simon Zadek, *The Civil Corporation: The New Economy of Corporate Citizenship* (London and Sterling, VA: Earthscan Publications, 2001), p. 73.
[44] See Holliday, Schmidheiny, and Watts, *Walking the Talk*.

If citizenship for business organizations is thought of as only a "voluntary" concept with a limited content of local charity or self-interested strategic advantage, it has no chance to correct power imbalances or to guard against them, and so becomes a self-defeating rule, illogical, and unworkable. Balancing the demands of liberty and justice is a task for all institutions – business, government, education, family, and religion. We believe that global business will move implacably toward the goals of liberty and justice for all – toward fulfilling their duties as business citizens – because these are the conditions necessary not only for the sustenance of human autonomy and quality of life, but also for the sustainability of capitalism itself.[45]

It does appear that we must move beyond the "business case" to develop the "now global governance frameworks" that Zadek sees as the third stage of conversations about corporate citizenship. I want to suggest the needed transition is to move from making a "business case" for corporate citizenship to making a "civic case" for corporate integrity. The civic case has its historical roots in Aristotle's civic ethics.

Aristotle's civic ethic

Although Aristotle has been a major source for contemporary ethics and especially an ethics of virtue, his belief that ethics belongs to politics has not always been emphasized. Still, as a translator of Aristotle's *Ethics* points out, for Aristotle, and for the Greeks in general, it was impossible to be virtuous outside of human society, "for actions are virtuous or not when they are performed in relation to one's fellow men; a hermit is incapable of acting virtuously."[46] For Aristotle, ethics belongs to the public realm or the polis. As Harry Radner has shown, this civic ethic emphasized obedience to civic law, the importance of justice, and a devotion to one's polis or city-state.[47] For Aristotle, ethics is subservient to politics.[48] So it would seem that

[45] Logsdon and Wood, "Business Citizenship: From Domestic to Global Level of Analysis," p. 181.

[46] Martin Ostwald, "Translator's Introduction," in Aristotle *Nicomachean Ethics*, trans. Martin Ostwald (Englewood Cliffs, NJ: Prentice Hall, 1962), p. xxiv.

[47] Harry Redner, *Ethical Life: The Past and Present of Ethical Cultures* (Lanham: Rowman and Littlefield, 2001).

[48] Aristotle, *Nicomachean Ethics*, trans. Martin Ostwald (Englewood Cliffs, NJ: Prentice Hall, 1992), pp. 4–5.

business ethicists who apply Aristotle's ethics to business today would naturally take the civic perspective I am advocating. That has not been the case. Instead, we have witnessed a privatization of Aristotle's political ethics.

The Aristotelian Edwin Hartman, for example, focuses on the quality of human communities, but then, instead of using Aristotle's civic ethic to describe a civic corporate community, he transfers Aristotle's political perspective to the manager.

> The reasons Aristotle gave for saying that politics is the culmination of ethics are today reasons for saying that business ethics is the culmination of ethics. So when we think about creating the good life, in which well-being and morality overlap in the individual, we might well think first not of the politician but of the manager, and we might well use the tools and insights of business ethics.[49]

The difficulty here is that the manager is not presented as a citizen, as a member of the civic realm. Instead, Hartman detaches Aristotle's ethics from its civic context and develops a private ethics.

Another leading Aristotelian in business ethics, Robert Solomon, appears to ignore the distinctive values of a civic ethic and assumes that all values are business values. In his book, *Ethics and Excellence*, he writes:

> The very structure of our society, its ample leisure and personality, are created by business, by the way business spurs and makes productivity possible and the way it distributes the goods throughout society and the world. Indeed, the values of our society – for better or worse – are essentially business values, the values of "free enterprise," the values of necessity and novelty and innovation and personal initiative. But that does not mean that it is "everyone for himself or herself," a "dog-eat-dog world," or a world in which "everything goes." To the contrary, it is a world defined by tacit understandings and implicit rules, a practice defined, like all practices, by mutual understandings and underlying trust, and justified not by its profits but by the general prosperity it brings about.[50]

It may be that business values are stronger in the United States than in other countries, but business values do not totally dominate its

---

[49] Hartman, *Organizational Ethics,* pp. 7–8.
[50] Robert C. Solomon, *Ethics and Excellence,* pp. 123–4.

culture.[51] Self-government, for example, is a republican value founded on democratic constitutions, not corporate generosity or even ideas of corporate citizenship. Our liberties, furthermore, are not protected by corporations, but by vibrant democratic governments from the local neighborhood level to the city, regional, state, national, international, and global level. Finally, even if the United States culture is dominated by business values, that does not mean this domination is acceptable.

Aristotelian business ethics should be returned to the civic sphere. The contributions of Aristotelian scholars such as Solomon and Hartman would then become even more valuable. Robert Solomon, for example, has written, "According to Aristotle, one has to think of oneself as a member of the larger community – the polis for him, the corporation, the neighborhood, the city or the country (and the world) for us – and strive to excel, to bring out what is best in ourselves and our shared enterprise."[52] I agree with him. I would simply add that we should think not only of individuals as members of corporate and political communities, but also of corporations as members of civic and natural communities.

In contrast to both Hartman and Solomon, Aristotle did not apply his political ethics to the small-scale economy of his day. The economy was not seen as part of the polis. Today we do not have this option. The size and influence of corporations make them part of our political life whether we like it or not. The question is how the economic should fit with the political. I suggest that the economic and political relationship should be seen contextually. A civic perspective, with its emphasis on membership (the literal meaning of citizen is a member of a city), would see corporations as members of the civic realm, not separate from it. Figure 1.5 demonstrates the difference between picturing relations in terms of overlapping circles and picturing relations contextually.

In the first set of circles, the economy is pictured as overshadowing the political. This can represent the contest between private and public democracy. The second set of circles sees the economic sphere inside the political. The economy belongs to the political and corporations are

---

[51] See Michael J. Sandel, *Democracy's Discontent: America in Search of a Public Philosophy* (Cambridge, MA: Harvard University Press, 1996). Chapter 5 will say more about the values of republican citizenship.
[52] Solomon, *Ethics and Excellence*, p. 103.

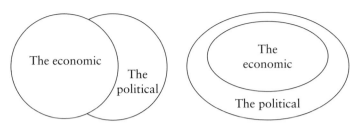

Figure 1.5. Relationships between the economic and the political

members of the civic sphere.[53] This means, as Peter Ulrich has proposed, we begin to see one another first of all as citizens.

The economic players, in all of their roles, must first of all be approached as citizens who acknowledge certain moral duties; as reflective consumers and capital investors, as critically loyal "organization citizens" in the working world, and as citizens of the state . . . Understood in this way, the republican ethos is indivisible. And it is also expressed in the fundamental willingness of the individual to pursue only those private goals, which are compatible with the legitimacy conditions of a well-ordered society of free and equal citizens.[54]

Corporate and noncorporate citizens can engage in conversations with one another about what "a well-ordered society of free and equal citizens" would look like when corporations are seen as part of civil society. Some owners of corporations, of course, may not have any interest in recognizing their participation in civil society. Some corporate practices violate the principles necessary for a well-ordered society of free and equal citizens. If these corporations cannot be constrained by the rule of law, then they should not be licensed to operate, just as governments do not allow businesses to operate that are involved in trafficking harmful drugs. After all, corporations belong to civil society; civil society does not belong to corporations. On the other hand, many corporations are already practicing integrity in civil

[53] Zadek does use concentric circles to illustrate the relationship among economic, social, and environmental spheres, but he does not name any of these circles the civic or the governmental. See Zadek, *The Civil Corporation*, p. 112.

[54] Peter Ulrich, "Ethics and Economics," in *Ethics in the Economy: Handbook of Business Ethics*, ed. Laszlo Zsolnai (Oxford: Peter Lang, 2004), p. 28.

society, and their work will be called upon in the following chapters. The work of designing one's part in civil society so that it fits with other's parts is the work of designing corporate integrity. The work of design (and redesign) involves the examination and transformation of ongoing communication patterns.

Corporations as ongoing communication patterns

The first image of corporations in our minds may not be of communication patterns. After all, they do have offices and buildings. There are raw materials that are transformed into products. There is a material world. This material world, however, is made accessible and useable because of how we talk about it. At one time trees were sacred. Now they are resources. Even humans have become "resources." They have become "resources" because there is a terminology to speak of them as such. The term "human resources" belongs to a particular corporate or business vocabulary that today makes sense in the workplace, but would not make sense in a nursery or a funeral parlour. It makes sense at work because it belongs to a larger pattern of communication.

Looking at corporations as a series of communication patterns makes it clear that they are fundamentally social constructions.[55] The notion that they are "property," for example, depends on assumptions about ownership and property rights, on legal protections of such rights, and a population that continues to honor a particular set of definitions. It could be otherwise.

At the same time, communication patterns are not all that easy to change, because we are usually unaware of them, just as a fish seems unaware of the water in which it swims. We usually only think about what we want to say, not about what in the situation provoked our

---

[55] Defining corporations as ongoing communications has a strong affinity with Kaptein and Wempe's definition of corporations: "A corporation is a social entity that presents itself both internally and externally through various 'expressions.' A corporation expresses itself through the behavior of its managers and employees, in its verbal and visual messages, and its symbols. The patterns in these expressions make it possible for internal and external parties to recognize and distinguish corporations from others. The identity of a corporation is manifested in a multitude of expressions that can be understood as a coherent whole" (Kaptein and Wempe, *The Balanced Company*, p. 146).

Post Office Model   Contextual Model

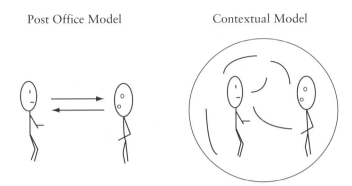

Figure 1.6. Two models of communication

thinking, or the language that provided the words and sentence structures, or the culture that configured things in one way rather than another. And yet these patterns create most of our reality. To more fully understand the linguistic texture of our lives, we need to see communication from a contextual perspective. Doing so reveals communication as something in which we live rather than as something we use. Figure 1.6 illustrates this difference by contrasting a contextual model of communication with a "post office" model.[56]

In the post office model, one isolated individual has an idea in his head, puts it in some form, and then sends it to another. The other receives the "message," decodes it, and sends back a response. It is like sending and receiving mail. Communication is a process of "getting one's views across," or "exchanging ideas." In the contextual model of communication, on the other hand, individuals participate in communication, and the context is seen as an integral part of the communicative process.[57] The space between persons, which seems like an empty space in the post office model, becomes laden with meaning in the contextual model. Speakers and listeners are seen as continually relying on, as well as continually maintaining and changing, their context.

A good example of participating in a communicative context is our participation in the English language. As those who have learned a second language know, a particular language is somehow "there," and

[56] W. Barnett Pearce, *Communication and the Human Condition*
    (Carbondale and Edwardsville: Southern Illinois University Press, 1989).
[57] Ibid., p. 192.

one learns the language by participating in it. A clear sign of linguistic competence in a second language, in fact, is the ability to think "in" that language.

The difference between these two models also highlights two aspects of human relationships. The post office model could imagine a connection between individuals but not much of its texture. The contextual model allows an awareness of this texture by providing access to the ways in which individuals belong to the relationship. Belonging to the same context not only makes sense in family and civic relationships, but also in relationships at work. As we shall see, conversations based on the assumption of belonging or joint membership can be quite different than conversations based solely on agreements or contracts.

Thinking about corporations or businesses as belonging to a textured context is rather strange for some business students. In my classes, to introduce students to contextual thinking, I ask them to imagine starting a business on the Moon, and then to list what they would need. They usually begin the list with such items as a business plan, money, products, markets, and consumers. All are important items for running a business. Sometimes they have trouble thinking of much else. After a while, someone will mention oxygen or water, and then all the environmental and infrastructural aspects of the business context come to mind. Sometimes, but not always, a student will refer to the need for government and law enforcement. Only rarely will a student mention the need for a moral community, where people trust one another, keep their promises, and work to continually create and re-create a meaningful life. They have never yet said that they would also need a shared language and common assumptions that the language would carry from one day to the next, and yet without this language the intangible aspects of business would fall apart and the material aspects would remain inaccessible.

Only by becoming aware of these different dimensions of business will it be possible to change them. And there is more. We live not only in a multidimensional world, but also a historical world. As the philosopher, Hans-George Gadamer has written:

In fact history does not belong to us; we belong to it. Long before we understand ourselves through the process of self-examination, we understand ourselves in a self-evident way in the family, society, and state in which we live.

The focus of subjectivity is a distorting mirror. The self-awareness of the individual is only a flickering in the closed circuits of historical life. That is why the prejudices of the individual, far more than his judgments, constitute the historical reality of his being.[58]

Gadamer is not using "prejudice" here in a pejorative way. To say we all have prejudices is simply to say that we belong to our time and place rather then to someone else's. Furthermore, because we live in a pluralistic culture, we continually encounter different prejudices, which enable us to become aware of our own. We are not stuck with our biases, because through dialogue with others we can become aware of them and change them. The same is true with corporate communication patterns. We can gain awareness of these patterns by engaging in dialogue with persons outside of these patterns, and we can change them by redesigning them. Creating corporate integrity, in other words, depends on our capacity to design the right kind of communication patterns.

In his book *From Good to Great*, Jim Collins suggests that companies that have made the leap from a good to a great company did not first develop a mission and then get people committed to it, but rather first found the "right" people, and then worked with them to develop the mission.

The executives who ignited the transformations from good to great did not first figure out where to drive the bus and then get people to take it there. No, they *first* got the right people on the bus (and the wrong people off the bus) and *then* figured out where to drive it. They said in essence, "Look, I don't really know where we should take this bus. But I know this much: If we get the right people on the bus, the right people in the right seats, and the wrong people off the bus, then we'll figure out how to take it someplace great."[59]

Although Collins may have a point about finding the "right" people, it is also true that whoever you put in the bus, it is still a bus. Creating corporate integrity today is about redesigning the bus. How should we arrange the seats? Should we have seats? What kind of relationships should the bus design promote? What kind of bus fits with the civic

---

[58] Hans-Georg Gadamer, *Truth and Method*, rev. trans. J. Weinsheimer and D. Marshall (New York: Crossroad, 1989), pp. 276–7.
[59] Jim Collins, *From Good to Great; Why Some Companies Make the Leap ... and Others Don't* (New York: Harper Business, 2001), p. 41.

and natural environment? Who should have a say in the bus's design? The right bus, at least from a civic perspective, is just as important as the right people. If the bus has integrity, then it will be appropriate for citizens to ride and safe to travel in our civic and natural environment.

In actual corporations, of course, we are not designing buses but rather communication patterns. The right people will be those who are able to increase our awareness of the relationships in which we live, and facilitate an understanding of how changing our communication patterns will change our relationships. They will be people willing to engage in dialogue with others. The philosopher Martin Buber wrote about dialogue, "There are no gifted or ungifted here, only those who give themselves and those who withhold themselves."[60] As chapter 2 will show, the capacity for dialogue is an essential element in the creation of corporate integrity. When we can engage in dialogue, we can begin to explore and change the communication patterns on each of the five dimensions of corporate integrity. The next five chapters will examine these dimensions, and provide the conceptual frameworks and methods for exploring the following questions:

- How should we design our corporate conversations for openness to differences and disagreement?
- How should we design our corporate conversations to ensure relationships that promote secure reciprocal participation?
- How should we design our corporate conversations to align decisions with worthwhile corporate purposes?
- How should we design our corporate conversations to cooperate with other civic agencies?
- How should we design our corporate conversations to promote natural prosperity?

From theory to practice

Questions for study and reflection

1. How would you prioritize the four meanings of integrity?
2. How would you define the necessary context for business practices today?

[60] Martin Buber, *Between Man and Man*, trans. R. Gregor-Smith (London and New York: Routledge, 2002), p. 40.

3. Which of the five challenges to corporate integrity are usual topics in your conversations?
4. What theories of corporate responsibility do you see corporations practicing today?
5. What do you see as the relevant differences between the business case and the civic case for corporate responsibility?
6. What becomes noticeable in your everyday conversations when you switch from a post office model to a contextual model of communication?

Guidelines for the assessment worksheets in the appendix

To assess your experiences with conversations about the five dimensions of corporate integrity, use Worksheet #1 to see how these dimensions have been explicitly or implicitly addressed in recent conversations.

Use Worksheet #2 to assess how conversations at work have changed, have not changed, or need to change to improve corporate integrity. Consider both verbal and nonverbal communication patterns.

Worksheet #3 offers a chance to examine some corporate ethics and corporate responsibility statements. Among the many websites with links to such statements are the Institute for Business Ethics site, www.ibe.org.uk; the Makkula Center for Applied Ethics site, www.scu.edu/ethics; and the World Business Council for Sustainable Development site, www.wbcsd.org.

2 | *Cultural integrity as openness*

A s stated in the preface, the designing of corporate integrity employs a civic perspective, focuses on relationships, and uses a method of examining and changing communication patterns. This chapter outlines the method. From the post office model of communication, examining and improving communication appears fairly simple. Just say things more clearly or get better feedback. From the contextual perspective, things get a bit more complicated. How can you change what is going on when you are part of it? It certainly is not possible without awareness, and awareness requires the possibility of reflection. Reflection occurs when we switch from automatic pilot, so to speak, to a conscious appreciation of what is going on. Such appreciation does not take us out of communication patterns, but it does change our attitude toward them. Once we have achieved this new awareness, we can examine and even change them.

In most situations, people do what they think is right considering the world they think they live in. Once we have figured out how things work in a particular setting, most of us get by fairly well. What is right is dictated by the situation. This sounds like moral relativism, which assumes that what is right depends on culture. The method presented here assumes that persons do act in the various communication patterns that constitute their culture. So, on the one hand, the method does not rely on some abstract, universal position from which one can judge the validity of different cultural norms. On the other hand, the acknowledgment that "most people do what they think is right considering the world they think they live in" does not determine what is actually the right thing to do. Without reflection, no one knows whether they are right or not. We just assume we are. So the method here is primarily a process of moving beyond cultural relativism to the type of reflection that enables participants to reflect on existing communication patterns and then to design new patterns that enable individuals and communities to live with integrity. Exactly what integrity requires will differ on each dimension of corporate life, which will be spelled out in the following chapters.

For reflection and redesign to occur, there must be some openness to differences and disagreements, and some capacity for changing communication patterns. The availability of such resources largely depends on one's culture. Culture provides the stories and images we use to interpret the world. It provides the terminology that details the meaning of things. As Kenneth Burke wrote some time ago: "Men seek for vocabularies that will be faithful *reflections* of reality. To this end, they must develop vocabularies that are *selections* of reality. And any selection of reality must, in certain circumstances, function as a *deflection* of reality."[1] This is just as true of corporate cultures as it is of tribal or national cultures. If a corporate culture turns critics into heretics, for example, then it will be difficult to design corporate integrity on any of the dimensions of corporate life. A corporate culture open to differences and disagreements, on the other hand, creates the possibility for both assessing and improving integrity throughout a corporate system.

This chapter provides a typology of communicative cultures that illustrates how different cultures can handle differences and disagreements. It then develops different strategies for increasing the possibilities of cultural openness when it is lacking. The key strategy is the practice of dialogue. Finally it explores the modernistic, technological challenge to taking the time for dialogical practices. The first step is to understand W. Barnett Pearce's typology of communicative cultures.

Pearce's typology of different cultures

In his *Communication and the Human Condition*, Pearce analyzes culture from a social constructionist perspective, a perspective that looks at how interpretative practices create and maintain social practices.[2] This perspective corresponds to the notion developed in chapter 1 of organizations as ongoing verbal and nonverbal communication patterns. Some communication patterns, of course, are more fundamental than others, and the cultural patterns set the context for all the others. Pearce has sorted out four different types of cultural patterns

---

[1] Kenneth Burke, *A Grammar of Motives* (Berkeley and Los Angeles: University of California Press, 1969), p. 59. Italics in original.
[2] Pearce, *Communication and the Human Condition*.

that differ in terms of how they establish coherence, coordination, and mystery, how they treat others and their resources, and how they interpret the temporal logic of their actions. The following brief summary of these three factors will help us understand how Pearce uses them to develop his four cultural types.

The triad of coherence, coordination, and mystery

All human communities must have something that holds them together. They must also have some way of working together. Pearce calls these requirements coherence and coordination. To these two requirements, he adds a third: access to mystery.

The way communication works is grounded in three universal aspects of the human condition: persons interpret their environment and their experience; they interact with their fellows; and they remind themselves that there is more to life than the immediate moment. I call these, respectively, coherence, coordination, and mystery. These are not "options" in which persons may or may not engage, or variables that may be present to some extent; rather, they are constitutive aspects of what it means to be human. All human beings – everywhere and always – communicate by coordinating, achieving coherence, and experiencing mystery.[3]

So all cultural communication must provide patterns for coordinating activities, achieving coherence and experiencing mystery, but different cultures do this in different ways. Different cultures also have different communicative patterns for recognizing people who do not belong to their cultures and for interpreting the traditions that have been handed down to them. Pearce calls these two cultural factors the treatment of others and the treatment of resources.

Treatment of others and treatment of resources

The treatment of resources refers to how people relate to such things as their stories, myths, and rituals that provide coherence, and the patterns and activities that provide coordination. Some cultural communicators take their resources as given and uncritically embrace them. They are "true believers." Other cultural communicators take a more

---

[3] Ibid., p. 31.

critical view of their resources and may exchange them for new resources that seem more efficient or satisfying. Pearce interprets this as putting one's resources at risk. To put one's resources at risk requires an awareness of a gap between traditional stories and contemporary context. This space allows questions to arise about the relevance or legitimacy of one's traditions. Such questions are risky because the exposure of this gap may not be bridged by a new connection to one's tradition. In such cases, believers may lose their faith.

The treatment of others refers to how cultural communicators respond to people who do not belong to their group. Communicators that treat others as they would treat themselves assume that others have access to the same resources as they do. They treat them as they would want to be treated, or as everyone else is treated in their group. Communicators that treat others as different from themselves assume others have different resources – different traditions. Pearce calls the first option "treating others as natives," and the second "treating others as non-natives." Figure 2.1 gives typical examples of the four possibilities when the treatment of resources is connected with the treatment of others.

	Do not risk resources	*Put resources at risk*
Treat others as natives	(1) Parents talking to their small children	(2) Students learning new theories
Treat others as non-natives	(3) Religious fundamentalists	(4) Inter-religious dialogues

Figure 2.1. Treatment of others and resources

Parents talking to their small children could belong in the first square, because in such conversations parents rarely invite the children to question the truth of their stories (they do not put their resources at risk) and they usually assume that the children belong to their culture. Students leading new theories might fit in the second square, because students do question tradition, but assume that everyone is involved in a similar process of learning. In the third square I have placed religious fundamentalists, because they treat others who do not share their beliefs as different from them (non-natives), but like the children in square 1, they do not question their own beliefs. Finally, I placed ecumenical religious leaders in the fourth square, because they not only see others as different, but also are willing to suspend their beliefs or to put them at risk.

To better understand these four possibilities, you could reflect on your communicative practices. Can you think of a conversation where everyone was treated as belonging to the group, and no one questioned how things should be done? That would be the first square. What about a conversation like the first one except that people questioned and were willing to discard "old" ways of doing things for "new" ways? That would fit the second square. The third square would be a conversation where some treated others as outsiders, and defended their way of seeing things as the "right" way. Finally, the fourth square would refer to an episode where you experienced people acknowledging each other's differences and examining their version of the way things should be. Most of us have experienced all of these types of conversations, and their strengths and weaknesses. When we reflect on these different experiences, they may also fit with one of Pearce's different temporal logics, his third communicative factor.

Temporal logic

All communication, according to Pearce, has some temporal orientation, which he refers to as the "logic of meaning and action."[4] For Pearce the logic or force of a statement depends on whether its motivation is grounded in the past, present, or future. To see what Pearce means here, examine the answers to the following question: "Why did you take that job?"

"Because that is what people have always done."
"Because a person like me in a situation like this must do that."
"Because I wanted to develop my potential."
"In order to get what I want."

Pearce sees these four reasons representing different time orientations. "Because that is what people have always done" appeals to the past as a reason for action. He labels this "prefigurative force" because it shows a motive informed by the way things have always been done. Pearce calls the second reason "contextual force" because it derives its obligation from the definition of the situation, or the way things should be done in such cases. It relies upon the present instead of the past, but sees the present as a particular type of situation with its own prescribed

---

[4] Ibid., p. 40.

behavior. The third temporal logic also centers on the present. Instead of seeing what the situation requires, it looks at the situation's potential for change, or to what Pearce calls its "implicative force." The final logic appeals to the future state of affairs that one wants to achieve, which Pearce calls the "practical force." Figure 2.2 shows the four "logics," the kind of reasons they employ, and their temporal orientation.

Logical force:	Pre-figurative	Contextual	Implicative	Practical
Kinds of reasons	It has always been so	To affirm my situation	To change my situation	In order to
Temporal logic	Past	Present	Present	Future

Figure 2.2. Temporal logics

The different temporal references, which loosely correspond to the four different logics, provide a useful scale for distinguishing between different communicative forms. Can you remember times when you felt pressured to do something in a certain way and the reason referred to the past, the present, or the future? Many of us have probably experienced all four logics. Together the categories of coherence, coordination, and mystery, the questions about the treatment of others and resources, and the temporal orientation, provide a holistic framework for distinguishing among Pearce's four different communicative cultures, which can be used to understand different types of communicative patterns at work.

Four communicative culture types

To understand Pearce's four cultural types, we need to practice what Pearce calls a fifth temporal logic: the reflexive. Reflexive logic begins when communicators become aware of their communicative process. It allows them to inspect their communicative patterns. This section reviews Pearce's framework for such inspection, beginning with monocultural communication.

Monocultural communication

Monocultural communicators use their community's stories to provide coherence and coordination. These stories are experienced as true and sacred, without question. Outsiders are treated as "natives," as though they share the same stories and have the same knowledge as cultural members. Monocultural communicators do not see others as different from themselves. The logical force of monocultural communication is "prefigurative"; people rely upon the past to interpret right actions. In terms of Pearce's different factors, monocultural communications have the characteristics illustrated in figure 2.3.

Coherence	*Coordination*	*Mystery*	*Treatment of others*	*Treatment of resources*	*Temporal logic*
Belief in stories	Shared beliefs	Embedded in stories	As natives	Not at risk	Past

Figure 2.3. Monocultural communication

Monocultural patterns are typical of traditional cultures where people treat others as members, and no one seriously questions the community's basic beliefs. In work settings, this communicative type assumes that the right thing to do is what has always been done. People exhibit tendencies toward such communicative practices when they automatically expect others to share their values or beliefs, and when they treat people who disagree with them as ignorant or immature.

In modern society, there are two distinct types of monocultural communicators: original monoculturalists and what could be called "reactionary monoculturalists." The original monoculturalists would be members of tribal or traditional cultures where people transfer their assumptions to the next generation as though they were the only reality. In these communities, everyone unquestionably accepts the beliefs of the group and overlooks any differences between members and non-members. A young child's world exemplifies this original form of monocultural communication. In the first stages of development, children receive and become enmeshed in the world presented by their families. For them, the "world" they receive is the only world they know.

Religious fundamentalists who react against modern pluralism could be an example of reactionary monoculturalists. Such groups can be interpreted as wishing for the reestablishment of one set of beliefs that everyone accepts. They may believe that coordination is only possible when it is based on coherence. The challenge for such groups, however, is that not everyone agrees with their set of beliefs. So, in many cases, instead of becoming monocultural communicators who treat everyone the same, they divide the world into "us" and "them." This characteristic is the basic feature of ethnocentric communicators.

Ethnocentric communication

Ethnocentric communicators imitate the monocultural communicators in not placing their resources at risk. They never question their own norms or assumptions. They differ from the monocultural communicators in their treatment of others. Others are treated as "non-natives." This leads the ethnocentric communicator to see others not only as different, but also most often as inferior. Ethnocentric stories usually account not only for the differences, but also for the "fact" that their resources are right, because the others are wrong. The mystery that gives the monocultural stories their sacred status provides a similar status to the ethnocentric communicators' division between them and us. Throughout the Cold War, for example, the communication patterns of "anti-Communists" exhibited an ethnocentric culture. They used Communism to define themselves as "anti-Communist," but never allowed the socialist critique to question their own capitalistic ideology. They also used religion to distinguish between the godless Communists and the God-fearing Christians. In the work setting, competitive practices sometimes lead to ethnocentric patterns, especially when people believe that any gain by their competitors results in their loss.

The division between them and us leaves ethnocentric communicators believing that there is only one right way of doing things – their way. This easily develops what Pearce calls "Unwanted Repetitive Patterns" (URPs), where people become locked into structures of communication that always lead to the same unsatisfactory results.[5] Even though people may wish to break out of such patterns, in most cases, the patterns are stronger than individual intentions, and the patterns pull the participants back into the same old place they were trying to avoid. Because of the ethnocentric culture's emphasis on correct behavioral patterns, they employ a temporal logic that is prefigurative and contextual: "In this situation, this is the proper way to respond." Figure 2.4 summarizes the ethnocentric culture's characteristics.

---

[5] Ibid., p. 128.

Coherence	Coordination	Mystery	Treatment of others	Treatment of resources	Temporal logic
Belief in us/them stories	Shared stories	Embedded in stories	As non-natives	Not at risk	Past and present

Figure 2.4. Ethnocentric communication

If we take a step back from the dynamics of ethnocentric communication, we can see that it sometimes draws on the cooperation of both the "us" and the "them" to maintain its communicative patterns. This is perhaps easier to see in competitive sports. In a tennis match, for example, the "us" and "them" sets up the competitiveness that makes the game interesting. This competition only "works," however, because the players cooperate in knowing and following the written and unwritten rules of tennis. Their cooperation, in other words, provides the context for competition. This combination of competition and cooperation also explains everyday transactions in the economy, even though the cooperation is not always recognized.

In terms of the structures of privilege and power in society, ethnocentric communication can serve quite different purposes. Although ethnocentric behavior usually brings to mind how members of dominant groups separate themselves from subordinate groups such as the colonizers and the colonized, sometimes a subordinate group uses ethnocentric behavior to empower itself. One can interpret the women's movement in the 1970s, for example, as using ethnocentric communication as a means of liberating women from male domination. Like other liberation movements, women protected their resources, rather than put them at risk, and treated men as non-natives. Their new stories supported the division between "us" and "them" in order to recover their own cultural history that male storytellers had ignored or silenced.

When groups do use ethnocentric communication for social and political empowerment, and are successful, they soon face the challenge of any ethnocentric group; namely, how to avoid the trap of repeating patterns of interaction that may have been appropriate for one time, but now block further development. Even liberation movements can become trapped in patterns that prevent them from changing with changing situations. To find a cultural communicative pattern that embraces change, we need to move to the third cultural type: modernistic.

Modernistic communication

In sharp contrast to the monocultural and ethnocentric communicators' protection of resources, modernistic communicators are willing to
put their resources at risk. They can evaluate and discard their stories
and traditions, because these traditions have lost their sacred status.
The world has become "disenchanted."[6] It has lost its mystery. This
disenchantment began in Western European culture in the seventeenth
century with the rise of experimental science, the use of technology to
control natural resources, and the privatization of religion. Instead of
the natural and the traditional being seen as a "home" for humans, it
became a "house" for reconstruction.

The "disenchantment" also affected attitudes toward traditional
authority. One of the more revealing formulations of this change was
the eighteenth-century "battle between the ancient and the moderns."
The argument concerned whether moderns should continue to submit
to the "superior wisdom" of ancient and classical thought, or whether
they could develop methods of analysis that would critically examine
classical texts. In other words, should the classical texts judge us or
should we judge them? The establishment of modern textual criticism,
which followed the rise of the empirical sciences, won the battle. New
knowledge became superior to old knowledge.

Modernistic communicators achieve coherence by stressing the new
and their belief in progress. This fits with their willingness to put their
resources at risk. Since what is new is better, they can discard their old
stories and beliefs without regret. Coordination relies somewhat upon
the common search for what is new, but also upon the possibility of
continual renegotiation of relationships and tasks.[7] The dot.com economy of a few years ago expressed the core of modernistic culture,
especially in terms of the modernistic fascination with the new.

Like the ethnocentrics, modernistic communicators treat others as
non-natives, but not with the implication that different is inferior.
Modernistic communicators are open to new experiences and relish
other customs and beliefs. From this perspective, it follows that the
logic that guides the moderns is not prefigurative or contextual, but
rather implicative and practical. What is new is better, and whatever

[6] Ibid., p. 137.
[7] Ibid., p. 147.

Coherence	Coordination	Mystery	Treatment of others	Treatment of resources	Temporal logic
Belief in progress	Stress on change	Disenchantment of world	Not as natives	Put at risk	Future

Figure 2.5. Modernistic communication

works is fine. A summary of the modernistic culture is set out in figure 2.5.

Pearce points out that modernistic cultures have not pleased everyone. While some bask in the adventure of modernity (Pearce calls these "happy modernists"), others have become exhausted and disillusioned.[8] For the disillusioned, what first appeared as something "new" later seemed like more of the same. Also, the disenchantment of nature and the distancing from tradition left some modernistic communicators with an impoverished language for expressing their hopes and dreams.

Dissatisfaction with modernistic culture, which is a growing theme in Western culture today, has elicited two responses. Some have attempted to retrieve a monocultural or ethnocentric base. These groups, such as religious fundamentalists and neo-conservatives, reassert traditional values and seek to establish coherence through preaching that everyone should believe in the same stories and values. Others have moved beyond the modernistic framework and entered what Pearce calls a cosmopolitan form of communication, his fourth type.

Cosmopolitan communication

The distinctive feature of cosmopolitan communication is that it gives primacy to coordination rather than coherence. The other three cultures sought coordination through coherence. Cosmopolitan communicators rely on sophisticated practices of coordination that allow participants to value other resources and at the same time to maintain a connection to the truth of their resources. As Pearce says, cosmopolitan communication "consists of a willingness and ability to construct ways of comparing and thus rendering rational the differences among the stories and practices of various social realities."[9]

[8] Ibid., p. 147.
[9] Ibid., p. 171.

The emphasis on coordination allows the cosmopolitan to see others both as natives – we all have stories – and as non-natives – we have different stories. Between the stories, so to speak, resides the mystery, which for the cosmopolitan means that there is always more than anyone can say. Mystery allows for different stories to exhibit their completeness without denying the completeness of other stories, because mystery signifies a larger inclusive wholeness that is greater than any one culture's completeness.

Coherence	Coordination	Mystery	Treatment of others	Treatment of resources	Temporal logic
Reliance on coordination	Changing patterns	More than can be said	As natives and non-natives	Put at risk and protect	Future and reflective

Figure 2.6. Cosmopolitan communication

The logic of cosmopolitan communication is both practical and reflexive, which means that its logic partly depends on an awareness of the process itself.[10] So cosmopolitan communication has the characteristics shown in figure 2.6. Perhaps the most significant aspect of cosmopolitan communication is its reflexive nature. It enables participants to become aware of the communication patterns in which they are involved and, from this awareness, acquire the possibility to change them. A reflexive perspective also enables us to understand the significant differences among the four cultural types. Figure 2.7 summarizes the differences. To understand the significance of these different communicative cultures for the life of corporations, let us assume that we were to attend a conference on corporate resources.

A corporate resources conference

When we enter the conference hall, we see four different corporate exhibits. The first one, Exhibit A, has a storyboard at the back of its exhibit, which shows their company's growth from a small company to a large corporation. The hosts in the booth all have company sweaters and seem to have somewhat identical smiles. You can tell they are a group of true believers.

[10] Ibid., p. 181.

	Monocultural	*Ethnocentric*	*Modernistic*	*Cosmopolitan*
Coherence	Belief in stories	Belief in us/them stories	Faith in progress, and the new	Primacy given to coordination rather than coherence
Coordination	Coordination is achieved through coherence	Enacting repetitive patterns	Stress on change, progress, and the new	Capacity to change communication patterns
Mystery	Embedded in stories	Supports us/them stories	Disenchantment of the world	Awareness of "more than can be said."
Treatment of others	Others as native	Not as native	Not as native	Both as native and not as native
Treatment of resources	Resources not put at risk	Not at risk	Put at risk	Both at risk and not at risk
Temporal logic	Prefigurative and contextual	Prefigurative and contextual	Implicative practical reflexive	Practical and reflexive

Figure 2.7. Matrix of pearce's four types of communication

As we move to the Exhibit B, we find another storyboard, but it contains not only the story of the company, but also the story of its key competitors, which, as you could guess, appear as inferior companies. There are also charts and graphs that show the superiority of their corporation over the competition. Also, the hosts have drawn a path through the exhibit to show visitors how they should visit it. There is, after all, one right way to do things. The hosts here are true believers, but they seem much more competitive than those at the first exhibit.

We leave Exhibit B without agreeing to take their survey, since it seemed that the answers would be either right or wrong, and move to a larger booth, Exhibit C. It is filled with the latest gadgets. There is no storyboard, but instead a symbol of progress on the back wall. The hosts are busy on their laptops. You can watch a short Powerpoint presentation of their next projects. As you examine the technology on display, you overhear two of the hosts arguing over whether a faster computer is really necessary or not. Instead of getting involved in the argument, you move to the fourth booth: Exhibit D.

Exhibit D is filled with chairs in small circles, with groups of people sharing their stories and experiences in working with corporate resources. Older people are sharing their experiences with younger people, and the younger people are questioning whether things have changed. You are invited to enter the conversation and to respond to the ideas presented so far. It is hard to distinguish the hosts from the visitors, since everyone seems to be participating in the conversation, which appears to be about how to maintain continuity in the context of change.

After visiting all four exhibits, and knowing something about the different types of conversations each one would initiate, we notice that they have very different capacities for dealing with differences and disagreements. Although Pearce did not explore this aspect of his four cultural types, how each cultural type deals with differences and disagreements allows us to understand the challenges we face when confronting different types of corporate communication patterns.

Cultural responses to differences and disagreements

In our pluralistic society, we are continually faced with cultural diversity. In many cases, we have an opportunity to recognize differences and from these differences to learn more about others and ourselves. Differences, in other words, do not necessarily mean disagreements. We can sometimes just be different. If we have to make a decision, however, then differences can lead to disagreements. In such cases, we need to learn how to use disagreements to help us make the best decision possible. Our openness to both differences and disagreements depends on the type of culture in which we participate, and in different settings we may participate in different cultures.

Of the four types, monocultural communicators have the most difficulty in even recognizing differences. Since monoculturalists see others as "natives," they see others as just like them. From the perspective that everyone is essentially similar, they would see disagreement as a lack of training or common sense. In monocultural settings, you either "get it" or you do not.

Ethnocentric communicators take a quite different view. They see differences as disagreements, and therefore as a confirmation of their stories of "us" and "them." They also tend to think in "either / or" terms. "They" are either with us or against us. Disagreement for ethnocentric communicators initiates a win/lose contest that motivates them to protect their resources. Disagreements, in other words, appear as conflicts between right and wrong, and since most differences also become interpreted as disagreements, differences are also seen as "right or wrong."

Modernist communicators or modernists appreciate differences and respond to them with enthusiasm, especially if the difference represents something "new" to them; at least until its "newness" wears off. Something like the consummate consumer, they tend to devour everything new and then move on to the next experience. They see disagreement as distinct from differences. Modernists see disagreements as problems to be solved and the sooner the better. Given their interest in progress and the new, they tend to discount disagreements and interpret them as barriers to innovation and future projects.

The fourth communicative type, the cosmopolitan communicator, sees disagreement as an opportunity for learning of different ways of constructing reality, and interprets disagreement as a resource as long as it does not completely block coordination. Disagreements about what should be done are seen as conflicts between different views of what is right. In such cases, they explore the background of the different views and try to increase their knowledge to see which "right" might be more appropriate, or if there might be a third way of resolving the conflict. Figure 2.8 presents the four different cultures and their key responses to others, resources, differences, and disagreements.

When you look at this figure, where would you put the communicative patterns of groups in which you are a member? Some of us may find that in different workplaces, or in different geographical regions, we handle differences and disagreements differently.

If we understand integrity as wholeness, then the cosmopolitan pattern of communication expresses the most integrity. It recognizes and takes seriously all parts of a whole, which the other three do not. By acknowledging that most people do what they think is right, rather than wrong, they accept that disagreements about conduct can be resources for learning. This does not mean, however, that cosmopolitan communicators believe that all values and ethical principles are relative. It does mean that they distinguish between principles and actions. Furthermore, they are willing to stand for the inclusiveness of communication practices, which rests on the principle of respect for others. At the same time,

	Treatment of Others	Treatment of Resources	Treatment of Differences	Treatment of Disagreements
Monocultural communicators	As natives	Protects them	Ignores	Lack of common sense
Ethnocentric communicators	As non-natives	Protects them	Combats	Right vs. wrong
Modernistic communicators	As non-natives	Puts them at risk	Uses	Discounts
Cosmopolitan communicators	As natives and non-natives	Protects and risks them	Recognizes	Right vs. right

Figure 2.8. Differences among the four communicative types

cosmopolitan communicators are open to engaging with others to find the best solution when they disagree about the right one.

Cosmopolitan communication, however, is an ideal type. We usually find ourselves involved in patterns that are less than ideal. So the important question is, when we find ourselves in any of the three other communicative patterns, how can we increase the conversation's openness to differences and disagreements? How can we, in other words, increase its integrity? One way is by developing different strategies for moving toward cosmopolitan communication.

Strategies for moving toward cosmopolitan communication

Because monocultural, ethnocentric, and modernistic communicators have different ways of preventing openness to differences and disagreement, each one calls for a particular response. Monocultural communicators need more curiosity about others. Ethnocentric communicators need to realize there are more resources available than they imagine, and modernistic communicators need to become more aware of boundaries (see figure 2.9).

Promoting curiosity in monocultural contexts

Curiosity will enable monoculturalists to move out of their "prefigurative" mode of thinking that assumes that other people's experiences are

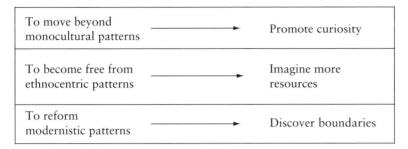

Figure 2.9. Strategies for moving toward cosmopolitan communicative culture

simply repetitions of their experiences or the experiences of their group. It is not as easy as one might think. Some time ago, for example, I was working with a white male CEO of a credit union on issues of diversity in the workplace. He had begun as a clerk in a bank and over the years had worked his way to the top. Now some women and people of color were saying that he did not understand their experience. He felt he did. After all, he had been in their positions himself. In a typical monocultural fashion, he felt that everyone was just like him. In fact, he was proud that he tried to treat others as he wanted to be treated. The fact, however, is that women and people of color had different work experiences than he did. They never had a chance to tell him, however, because he thought he already knew what they had experienced. After several sessions, he said to me, "I get it. My employees have different experiences at work than I had." This was quite a revelation to him. Instead of assuming he knew all he needed to know, he wondered if there was something he should know that he did not. He demonstrated that change is possible, but not to be taken for granted. Curiosity sometimes causes anxiety, and not only for monocultural communicators.

The ethnocentric also lacks curiosity, but for different reasons. Curiosity about others may grant a legitimacy that is threatening to the ethnocentric communicator's status. This interpretation relies on a win/lose mentality that assumes a limited amount of resources. If others gain something, ethnocentric communicators believe they have therefore lost something. Andrew Schmookler has called this the "myth of scarcity."[11] The myth of scarcity assumes every transaction is a

[11] Andrew Schmookler, *Out of Weakness: Healing the Wounds That Drive Us to War* (New York: Bantam Books, 1988).

zero-sum game. Not everyone can gain something at the same time. To move ethnocentric communicators beyond this mentality, they need to imagine the possibility of an overall increase in resources, the second strategy for moving toward cosmopolitan communication.

Imagining more resources in ethnocentric contexts

In some situations there are limited resources. If we divide up 500 dollars, for example, my share will decrease if your share increases. However, there are circumstances where one person's gain is not another's loss. For example, if you increase your communication skills, that does not decrease mine. In fact, I may even learn from you, and both of us end up with more than we had before. Ethnocentric communicators have difficulty comprehending this, because they are so used to framing things in terms of scarce resources.

The National Rifle Association is a good example of ethnocentric communication. It fights against every type of gun control, even the control of assault weapons, based on the notion that if "they" win, then "we" lose. The conversations between workers and environmentalists had a similar pattern in the 1980s. Any "victory" for the environment would decrease jobs. This was true in some cases, of course, but not in every case. Today, in fact, workers and environmentalists have joined together in some instances either to create jobs that protect the environment, or to protect workers' health by protecting the environment.[12] Once conversations overcome the myth of scarcity, communicators can enter into collaborative conversations that facilitate the articulation of common problems and common solutions. In order for ethnocentric communicators to join such projects, they need to imagine that there are more resources available than they first thought. Even though it may sound counterintuitive, it is less helpful to criticize an ethnocentric's positions than to change the perception of resources. Once they believe there are enough or even an abundance of resources, they can be more open to differences and disagreements. A stronger focus upon resources can also enable modernistic communicators to become

---

[12] For recent projects in combining corporate and environmental interests, see Livio D. DeSimone and Frank Popoff, *Eco-Efficiency: The Business Link to Sustainable Development* (Cambridge, MA: MIT Press, 2000).

more aware of personal and social boundaries, the third strategy for moving toward cosmopolitan communication.

Setting boundaries for modernistic contexts

A distinction between resources and practices can clarify the dilemma of modernistic communicative cultures. Resources are the stories, rituals, and tacit knowledge that provide communicative coherence. Practices, on the other hand, are activities that both rely on and express these resources. Modernistic communicators tend to focus on the practices and ignore the resources that give the practices meaning. They easily slip into a consumer mode where they see practices as "interesting experiences" that they can duplicate without attention to the resources that the practices express. Moderns may try Zen meditation as a "practice," for example, with very little understanding of the contextual resources that Zen practices express.

This approach to differences creates a superficial curiosity that turns everything into something "interesting." In radical contrast to the ethnocentric, which operates under the myth of scarcity, moderns operate under the myth of unlimited possibilities. Therefore, they tend to miss the boundaries between different cultures. They tend to approach cultural differences as one would approach buying a new suit: you try on different ones until you find the one you like. Really understanding cultural differences, however, is more like understanding a foreign language, which can be understood only by learning the particular cultural resources the language expresses. For the modernists to be open to differences, they must become aware of the deeper resources that practices express and let these resources become boundaries that prevent them from flattening everything to their particular tastes. Then they can actually acknowledge differences rather than merely find them "interesting."

The three strategies – promoting curiosity, increasing resources, and setting boundaries – all belong to cosmopolitan communication. They help to increase openness and therefore to foster integrity. Without curiosity, no one will ask questions. Without imagining more resources, there is little room to inquire about others. Without boundaries, the responses to those inquiries will never be adequately heard. These three strategies provide corporate leaders with reliable methods for responding to communication patterns that prevent or severely limit the development of integrity on the interpersonal, organizational, civic, and environmental dimensions of organizational communication. On every dimension of organizational life, integrity requires curiosity, some sense of security, and an awareness of appropriate boundaries.

Although these three strategies can be used as individual methods for facilitating change, they are most effective when seen as part of the practice of dialogue. Dialogue is more than a strategy for change. It is a form of life, lived through words, that enables participants to move toward a new understanding of themselves and their communities. In a sense, the dynamics of dialogue give power to strategies for change by creating the space for transforming how we speak with each other. To understand dialogue's capacity for changing communication patterns, we first need to know its characteristics.

Characteristics of the dialogical process

The unique characteristic of dialogue resides in the quality of the relationship that emerges through the conversation. William Isaacs, in his book on dialogue, goes so far as to say that the meaning of the Greek "logos," in "dia-logic" is best translated into English as "relationship."[13] A dialogical relationship, in fact, is not only the first characteristic of dialogue, but also the precondition for all the other characteristics. The Jewish theologian Martin Buber has grasped the essence of the dialogical relationship perhaps better than anyone else. He calls it the realm of the "between."

The fundamental fact of human existence is neither the individual as such nor the aggregate as such. Each, considered by itself, is a mighty abstraction ... What is peculiarly characteristic of the human world is above all that something takes place between one being and another the like of which can be found nowhere in nature ... I call this sphere, which is established with the existence of man as man but which is conceptually still uncomprehended, the sphere of "between." Thought being realized in very different degrees, it is the primal category of human reality.[14]

---

[13] William Isaacs, *Dialogue and the Art of Thinking Together* (New York: Currency, 1999), p. 19.
[14] Buber, *Between Man and Man*, pp. 240–1.

This "between" occurs when individuals turn toward one another, and acknowledge each other's presence. For Buber it holds the mystery of human existence. I think it has a strong parallel to Pearce's understanding of mystery in cosmopolitan communication as that which is "more" than anyone can say.

In his first major work on exploring this relational aspect of human existence, Buber names it an I–Thou relationship.[15] For him, pronouns always come in pairs. "There is no I taken in itself, but only an I of the primary word I–Thou, and I of the primary word I–It."[16] In other words, the "I" is always part of a relationship. If I am related as an "I–it" then the other becomes something and the "I" becomes an individual. If I am related as an "I–Thou," then I become a person related to other persons.[17]

The dialogical relationship occurs when the people involved turn to one another, acknowledge each other as a particular person – as a "you" – and respond to each other. "You" is the pronoun of address. Instead of remaining enclosed in one's isolated "I" and seeing others as "he" or "she," the dialogical process lifts its participants into the realm of a mutual "you," as they become responsive to each other's address.

For Buber, an awareness of the "between" is already a form of dialogue, because it emerges from a turning toward the other as a person. The conversation, in a sense, is then guided by the participation in the between. How we participate in such a dialogical practice will be determined by our expectations of what is possible, and what is possible depends on how well our dialogical practices connect with and express the human resources for transformation and renewal. Although dialogue does not follow any recipe, it does have some general characteristics. These following characteristics illustrate the possibilities of dialogue:

- seeing others as different
- asking questions of inquiry
- acknowledging another's resources
- exploring the unknown

---

[15] Martin Buber, *I and Thou*, trans. R. Gregor-Smith (New York: Charles Scribner's Sons, 1958).
[16] Ibid., p. 4.
[17] Ibid., p. 62.

- developing thought
- gaining self-understanding.

Although these different characteristics are all interrelated, perhaps the most important is the possibility of seeing others as different.

Seeing others as different

As long as we assume that others are like us, have the same background, and share the same values, we talk to them as though we were talking to someone like us. In effect, we end up talking to ourselves. This is the condition of the monocultural communicator. Curiosity belongs to dialogue too. In fact, dialogue requires that we see each other as particular persons. As Martin Buber has said,

> The chief presupposition for the rise of genuine dialogue is that each should regard his partner as the very one he is. I become aware of him, aware that he is different, essentially different from myself, in the definite, unique way which is peculiar to him, and I accept whom I thus see, so that in full earnestness I can direct what I say to him as the person he is.[18]

To become aware of others, we do not want to merely develop a particular image of the other, but rather to hear the other as a distinct voice – a voice that expresses another and not myself. An important key to begin this type of listening is to ask the right kind of questions: questions of inquiry.

Asking questions of inquiry

Not all questions are alike. Sometimes we ask questions of judgment and other times questions of inquiry. When we ask questions of judgment, we already know the answer and want to see if another does too. When a father asks his child the way to the store, he wants to make sure that the child knows how to get to the store. Or when a manager asks his team about the mission of the company, he wants to know if they share his vision. These questions certainly have their legitimacy, but they do not promote dialogue. Questions of inquiry do. Questions of inquiry are asked by someone who does not know the answer.

---

[18] Martin Buber, *On Intersubjectivity and Cultural Creativity*, ed. S. N. Eisenstadt (Chicago and London: University of Chicago Press, 1992), p. 73.

Questions of inquiry promote dialogue because they move one toward the unknown. They are followed not by judgment, but by listening. By listening to the other as other, it is possible to hear what one has not heard before.

Acknowledging another's resources

Once people begin to listen to one another, they hear of experiences, talents, skills, and aspirations that they do not have. When dialogue partners begin to acknowledge each other's resources, the myth of scarcity that shaped the ethnocentric communicators' responses begins to dissolve, not because everyone knows everything, but because no one knows it all. For example, in a conversation between a young male worker and an older female worker, we might expect such statements as these:

- She knows what it is like to be a woman in a male-dominated workplace and I do not.
- He knows what it is like to grow up in the 1970s and I do not.
- She knows what it is like to manage twenty people in an accounting office, and I do not.
- She knows what it is like to be laid off, and I do not.

The acknowledgment of what one does not know should not be underestimated. It is an essential aspect of dialogue. When we move into a stance of not knowing, we are then ready to formulate real questions of inquiry, and to listen to what others have to say. Moving into this type of relationship with another addresses the boundary issue of the modernistic communicator, who tends to override boundaries between persons. The acknowledgment of differences leads to honoring the concreteness of the other, which in turn reveals the mystery of human connections. Acknowledging another's resources does not require that we depreciate ours. Not at all. Instead of a scarcity of resources, we discover an abundance, some of which we had not known. In dialogue we share not only what we know, but also the unknown.

Exploring the unknown

Dialogue is not only about learning from each other, but also about learning more about some topic or thing. Asking questions of inquiry and acknowledging the other also applies to discovering the meaning of things. Once we acknowledge differences among persons involved in a dialogue, we can become authentic listeners – listening for something we have not heard before, which can initiate the creation of new knowledge with others. At the heart of dialogue is the *development* of thought.

Developing thought

The type of thinking that generates dialogue does not remain bounded by what one has already thought, but rather moves into what remains un-thought. Remember Pearce's notion of mystery as "more" than the present moment? He also defines mystery as the awareness of the "open-endedness of the world."[19] There is always more than one particular conceptuality, more contextual resources, more ways of seeing issues, and more ways of speaking about them. This more is offered to the dialogical partners as they engage in a common endeavor to understand the issue before them. The dialogical process calls us to respond to what has become "thought-provoking." This movement carries us into an unfamiliar region of thought where we can think what we have not thought before. In this process, we learn not only more about things, but also about ourselves.

Gaining self-understanding

The final part of the process is that we see ourselves reflected in the dialogical process. In such reflection, we begin to understand more about ourselves. Perhaps most significantly, we see ourselves *in* the communication we have co-created. As Gadamer has written: "To reach an understanding with one's partner in a dialogue is not merely a matter of total self-expression and the successful assertion of one's own point of view, but a transformation into a communion, in which we do not remain what we were."[20] This formation of community moves us into a culture of cosmopolitan communication, where we can acknowledge differences and develop new forms of coordination.

[19] Pearce, *Communication*, p. 84.
[20] Gadamer, *Truth and Method*, p. 341.

It may seem that these characteristics of the dialogical process are possible only in academic or religious settings, but not in the workplace. Can anyone really expect such communication practices at work? Can one imagine the development of corporate integrity without such practices? That is the real question. If we are committed to improving corporate integrity, and if an essential aspect of integrity is cultural openness to differences and disagreements, then how can we not practice dialogue at work? That does not mean that we can enter into dialogue without paying attention to the work context, or without examining if the world of work needs to be changed before dialogue can occur. Especially when we think of how modern technology dominates many workplaces, we cannot simply assume that everyone is ready for a meaningful conversation. To understand how dialogue might be possible at work, we need to examine the world of work and its relationship with the different communicative cultures.

The world of work and communicative cultures

There are, of course, many different worlds of work, from the world of the poet to the world of the soldier. The world of work that presents a barrier for many people who would like to engage in dialogue at work is a world dominated by what has been called "calculative thinking,"[21] or "technological rationality."[22] Both of these phrases refer to conversations aimed at controlling things in the most efficient and effective manner possible. Such conversations construct a world dominated by techniques or methods such as the assembly line or programmed learning. Technology is used to increase efficiency and effectiveness, as well as to realize imaginary projects. It is the world that continues to produce the better mousetrap.

In terms of Pearce's four communicative cultures, this world of technology fits most closely with modernistic culture. Remember that modernistic culture was defined as seeing new as better, and having a pragmatic view of the future. Historically, this culture developed in tandem with the development of modern science and technology. New

---

[21] Martin Heidegger, *Discourse on Thinking*, trans. J. Anderson and E. H. Freund (New York: Harper and Row, 1966).
[22] Andrew Feenberg, *Questioning Technology* (London and New York: Routledge, 1999).

gadgets or processes, especially if they increase efficiency, replaced old ways of doing things. Technological development, the belief in progress, the value of efficiency, and capitalism were experienced as interwoven aspects of modernism.

Sometimes the whole modernistic package has been seen as the distinguishing characteristic of businesses and the modern economy. This has been especially true of the technological value of efficiency. William C. Frederick, for example, has characterized business in terms of the value of efficiency or what he calls the "value of economizing."[23] He argues that economizing is a fundamental evolutionary process, and that businesses exist to economize. Although efficiency is important for business, equating business and the market economy with technological efficiency tends to replace empirical evidence with abstract theories. The fact is that our economy today is not particularly efficient. How efficient is it to use a 5,000 lb SUV, for example, to transport a 180 lb person around town? Compared to the efficiency of nature, which is 100 percent efficient, the US economy has been estimated to be only 6 percent efficient.[24] More about this later in chapter 6. Another important observation, which the identifying of businesses with efficiency overlooks, is that other organizations besides businesses, such as the military, public health systems, or university research institutes, have also been carriers of technological innovation and efficiency. Much technological innovation has actually occurred in state-financed institutions of higher education, and only later distributed through the market. To see businesses or the economy as the only "engine" for technological innovation simply ignores the historical record. Finally, a third important observation is that even though many businesses' communication patterns are premised on the values of efficiency and innovation, which belong to modernistic communicative culture, the underlying corporate culture is often not modernistic but monocultural or even ethnocentric. In the United States, at least, the relationship

---

[23] William C. Frederick, *Values, Nature, and Culture in the American Corporation* (New York: Oxford University Press, 1995), p. 9. Muel Kaptein and Johan Wempe, *The Balanced Company*, also see efficiency as the reason for the existence of corporations.

[24] Paul Hawken, Amory Lovins, and Hunter L. Lovins, *Natural Capitalism: Creating the Next Industrial Revolution* (Boston: Little Brown and Company, 1999), p. 14.

between workers and managers is often based on master-and-servant relationships, which gives managers the right to terminate employees without cause. Modernistic cultures, on the other hand, are much more based on equality and individual human rights. Sometimes corporate cultures are ethnocentric, especially toward their competitors. These differences between the world of technology and corporate culture are not only signs of a lack of consistency within an organization, but also a sign of a distinction that can make a difference. If the world of technology can exist in different corporate cultures, it becomes possible to develop a cosmopolitan communicative culture, and the conditions for dialogue, as the culture for a technological world.

The world of technology, in other words, can be seen as referring to something besides culture, even if it is embedded in a culture. One way to think about the distinction is to use the term "world" to refer to the things that we use in getting things done. This world includes devices, tools, and methods or strategies. In such a scheme, culture would refer to the assumptions or beliefs, the presuppositions that give a particular interpretation of the "world." Let us imagine that you have lost your job, your house has burned down, and someone ran into your car. It would be safe to say that your "world" has come crashing down. Your culture, on the other hand, remains intact, or at least it could. You might interpret these events as payment for past deeds, or merely bad luck. That does not mean that world and culture are not intertwined with each other. It does mean they are not the same. Without such a distinction, modernistic culture remains the only context for modern technology. With the distinction, other cultures could provide such a context. Separating the world of technology from modernistic culture provides the possibility of creating a culture that highlights the social and environmental boundaries that modernistic culture overlooks. This requires a conversation that explores the relationships between the world of technology and cultural pluralism.

The world of technology and cultural pluralism

In some ways, we already experience cultural pluralism in the world of technology. Imagine for a minute sitting in the waiting area of an international airport – the world of air travel. As you sit there, you observe people from a multitude of different cultures participating in this "world." A Buddhist monk and a secular computer programmer, for example, may sit next to each other waiting to board their flight. They are both in the "world of air travel," and yet could belong to quite different cultures. Even though the world of modern air travel developed out of modernistic culture, and could not have emerged from any traditional culture, people who belong to traditional cultures can participate in this world without discarding their culture, or so it seems.

The relationship between world and culture is actually very complex. The methods of our modern technological world are not only methods of doing things, but also methods of thinking about things. It is easy to get caught up in the mystique of technological control. But it is not necessary. As Feenberg and others have argued, technological development always belongs to a social history, and by becoming aware of its history, we can see that just as history could have been otherwise, we also can make different choices today.[25] Richard Sclove makes a similar point in terms of the relationship between technology and democracy. While he agrees with technological critics who claim that technological developments have led to nondemocratic structures, he does not believe this is inevitable. He believes that technology can be made to fit with democratic institutions.[26] The question is whether one can maintain a communicative culture that continues to offer resources for making our age a human age rather than merely a technological one.

A good example of the kind of choices we face today is how we respond to the impact of modern technology on our experience of time.[27] In traditional cultures things happened in their own time. A family dinner, for example, could last for hours. In the world of modern technology, the drive is to eliminate time. The less time something takes the better. If we could do something in no time at all, that would be perfect. Instead of a family dinner, why not go to a fast-food takeout? From the technological point of view, the goal of eating is to acquire needed nutrients, and the less time one spends acquiring the nutrients the better. Fast food is efficient and effective. It gets the job done. A family dinner includes storytelling, the give and take of different opinions, and the sharing of food and gossip. Although nutrients

---

[25] Feenberg, *Questioning Technology*, p. 83.
[26] Richard Sclove, *Democracy and Technology* (New York and London: The Guilford Press, 1995).
[27] Lorenzo Simpson, *Technology, Time and the Conversations of Modernity* (New York: Routledge, 1995).

are received, the meaning of the dinner resides in the quality of the time together, not in being as efficient as possible.

Can a family eat fast food on a regular basis and still maintain the shared time of a traditional family dinner? Or, do fast-food outlets bring with them a worldly tempo that automatically wipes out more traditional ways of doing things? Not necessarily. In Europe, for example, one finds a "slow-food" movement, dedicated to restoring the time it takes to enjoy eating together. Headquartered in Bar, Italy, the movement has over 60,000 members, who have become interested not only in enjoying the pleasure of eating well, but also related environmental issues.[28] People in Italy have also begun a slow-town movement, which again is aimed at restoring human time in a techno-logical world.[29] These and similar efforts demonstrate that people can become aware of different ways to structure time, which in turn provide them with different ways of living together.[30] In other words, the modern world of work is not like the weather: we can do something about it, because we created it. An awareness of the difference between culture and the world may increase our capacity to evaluate each one in terms of what kind of life we want to develop together.

If we take a step back, many of us may remember curious mixtures of modern technology and traditional cultures. Religious fundamen-talists, for example, use the latest information technology to reach their millions of contributors, without any apparent experience of rhetorical conflict. In many businesses, one finds a similar disparity. Businesses may use technological and financial language to define their future prospects, and yet use traditional vocabularies to structure employer and employee relations. The next chapter on interpersonal relationships will examine such disparities. For now, the distinction between corporate culture and technological world has provided a space to improve a corporation's integrity by increasing its capacity to respond to differences and disagreements by designing occasions for dialogue.

---

[28] See www.slowfood.com/eng.

[29] See www.matogmer.no/slow_cities_citta-slow.

[30] The simplicity movement in the United States is another example of people finding an alternative to modernism. See Lisa H. Newton, *Ethics and Sustainability: Sustainable Development and the Moral Life* (Upper Saddle River, NJ: Prentice Hall, 2003).

Designing cultural integrity through dialogue

The philosopher of technology, Lorenzo Simpson, asked the following question: "What is the relationship between our allegiance to techno-logical rationality and our options regarding the ways in which we can talk about ourselves, the kind of stories that we can tell about our-selves, in short, the shape of the human conversation?"[31] Answer: "We can have a conversation grounded in dialogical practices that is open to differences and disagreements and explores the meaning of integrity at work." This conversation does not need to be divorced from modern technology, but instead it needs to provide a conversational framework for talking about the use of technology.

The task at least should now be clear: we need to move beyond modernistic communicative patterns that mindlessly support techno-logical trends to a cosmopolitan communicative culture that can be responsive to the different voices and disagreements that constitute the life of corporations today. The linkage of three elements – modernistic cultures' belief in the new, technology's drive toward efficiency, and modern capitalism's emphasis on maximization of profit above all else – has created a strong ideology. Although it is not invincible, it is formidable. A key weakness of the ideology, of course, is that it lacks integrity. It only sees a part of the whole, and takes this part (its dynamics) as the whole. Like modernism, it is unconscious of appro-priate boundaries. Therefore, we need leaders who can facilitate the movement beyond modernism to cosmopolitan communications.

For corporations to have integrity at the cultural level, we need to design ongoing conversations that are open to differences and disagree-ments. Although the world of technology may not foster such a culture, neither does modern technology make an open culture impossible. It is possible if we understand the barriers to openness, such as the lack of curiosity, the fear of scarcity, and the absence of boundaries, and have some capacity for overcoming them. Our capacity for overcoming these barriers resides not so much in us as individuals, but rather in a dialogical process with co-workers. Through dialogue, participants can become aware of the communication patterns that need changing, and experience with others the types of inclusive and open conversa-tions that promote a cosmopolitan culture.

[31] Simpson, *Technology, Time,* p. 3.

From some perspectives, such as the economic or financial perspective, the effort to create such a culture may not seem worth it. It means focusing on things other than productivity and profitability. Many would argue, of course, that enlarging a corporation's horizon of concern might well have a positive effect on profitability, and in many cases that may be true. My focus here, however, is not to make a business case for cultural openness, but a civic case. Citizens should be interested in how social organizations handle differences and disagreements, since citizens not only work in them but are also impacted by them.

In the long run, only cosmopolitan communicative cultures support democratic institutions and practices. Citizens should not have to leave their civic rights at the corporate gate. Citizens inside and outside the corporate gates should not have to endure corporate conduct that is based on ignorance, fear, or mindlessness.

For corporations the question of integrity is not answerable with a simple yes or no. The appropriate answer is more or less. Corporate integrity is always a process of creation. Pearce's notion of cosmopolitan communication gives us a vision of corporate cultural integrity. His cultural framework and the strategies for improving communication integrity provide a useful method for meeting the challenges of integrity on the interpersonal, organizational, civic and natural dimensions of corporate life.

From theory to practice

Questions for study and reflection

1. What are the key differences among Pearce's four communicative cultures?
2. What provides coherence, coordination, and mystery in your workplace, your family, and your neighborhood?
3. What are some of the reasons for treating people the same, and what are some reasons for treating people differently?
4. What usually happens to disagreement in the groups in which you are a member?
5. How do you interpret the relationship between the world of work and your cultural heritage? And the heritage of others?
6. What are some of the barriers you have experienced to engaging in dialogue? How could they be overcome?

Guidelines for the assessment worksheets in the appendix

To explore the communicative cultures in which you participate, use Worksheet #4 to first list different communication partners and then evaluate the conversations in terms of Pearce's temporal logic. After filling in the worksheet, you can share with others why the patterns are different with different people, and how they could become more cosmopolitan.

Worksheet #5 allows you and members of your group to assess their individual capacity to engage in dialogue. What most people discover is that they have quite different experiences with different people. When you have finished, imagine if those who received lower scores were to fill out this worksheet. Do you think they would have some communication partners with high scores too? If so, then the different numbers do not reflect individual capacity, but rather communication patterns. What would have to occur for these patterns to allow individuals to perform closer to their capacity?

Finally, you may want to do Worksheet #6 on images of relationships before you read chapter 3, so the example of how others have used it will not stifle your imagination. Fill in each of the squares with drawings of how you imagine the various relationships. Remember to *draw* the images rather than use words.

3 | *Interpersonal integrity as relational wholeness*

The previous chapter presented a method for examining and changing communication patterns and examined the meaning of cultural integrity as openness to differences and disagreements. This chapter also performs two related functions. It demonstrates the significance of the book's focus on relationships and, at the same time, explores the interpersonal challenge of relational wholeness.

From a contextual model of communication, relationships among employees and between employees and employers are constituted through multiple verbal and nonverbal communication patterns. These patterns provide the context for addressing, or avoiding, a number of issues that affect the quality of the work community, such as health and pension benefits, job security, due process, occupational safety, fair wages, racism, gender differences, equal opportunity, balancing work and family obligations, privacy, monitoring, honesty, trust, conflicts of interest, and employee participation. Conversations about any of these issues rely on a number of ethical principles and standards of justice, which are sometimes included in corporate mission statements and codes of conduct. In other cases, those responding to these issues can bring ethical principles into the conversation. Whether any ethical analysis actually occurs, as well as what counts as ethically relevant, depends on the communication patterns that provide the expectations and limits of what should be discussed in specific situations. A conversation on due process, for example, would not even occur in a work setting dominated by the master-and-servant image of relationship. Its occurrence requires at least some notion of workers as having civic rights. The same is true with most other employee/employer issues. The kind of questions we ask and the kind of resources that have moral force, in other words, largely depend on our understanding of work relationships.

Current work relationships are quite varied, ranging from master-and-servant relationships ("I am the boss, and you do what I say") to partnership relationships ("Let's decide what we can do here"). Some of these relationships are more appropriate for adequately addressing current relational issues between employees and employers than others, because some of them come closer to the second dimension of corporate integrity: relational wholeness. The purpose of this chapter is to discover which ones.

Instead of beginning the investigation with some image of an isolated individual, and then exploring what type of relationships will accommodate that image, the contextual model of communication requires that the investigation begin with human relationships. To see workers holistically, in other words, requires that we begin with the relationships in which individuals receive their identity and then use the core meaning of these relationships to gain an adequate understanding of relationships at work. Although there is certainly a variety of non-work relationships that may be significant for different individuals, for most of us, the two basic relationships are family and civic, so the following exploration of interpersonal integrity will use family and civic relationships to understand the integrity of work relationships. Before this exploration begins, we need to understand the meaning of the phrase "images of relationships."

Images of relationships

You may wonder how it is possible to really examine relationships at work or any other place. After all, has anyone ever seen a relationship? Only individuals, and their actions and reactions, are directly observable. I sometimes wonder how different the world would be if relationships were visible and individuals were invisible. At least the contextual communicative model would be easier to understand. As it is, we must rely not on our observations, but on our understanding of relationships, which largely depends on the images or mental models that gives meaning to various human interactions. Carol Gilligan's research on images of relationships confirms this theory.

Carol Gilligan's work on images of relationships

The phrase "images of relationships" is the title of the second chapter of Carol Gilligan's *In a Different Voice*.[1] In this chapter she presents her

---

[1] Carol Gilligan, *In a Different Voice* (Cambridge, MA: Harvard University Press, 1993).

research on the different responses sixth-grade boys and girls made to the particular ethical question of whether to steal the medicine that one's spouse needed, when there was not enough money to buy it, and the need was great. The boys felt that Heinz (he was the husband) should steal the medicine. Even though it was wrong to steal, they felt it was even more wrong to let someone die. Gilligan sees the boys as interpreting the image of the relationship between Heinz and the druggist as a relationship of conflict. They then transpose this conflict as a conflict between different ethical principles: do not steal and do not let people die. The principle of saving a life overrides the principle of respecting someone's property. Heinz should steal the drugs.

The girls interpreted the case differently. First of all, they disagreed with the boys. They believed Heinz should not steal. Their reasoning was also quite different. Instead of interpreting the issue as a conflict between individuals, they saw the issue as the lack of a strong enough connection between the druggist and Heinz's wife. Their solution was to make clear to the druggist the gravity of the situation, and then to allow people to make appropriate responses. The girls did not see the dilemma as a conflict between different principles, but as what Gilligan calls a failure of response. There was someone in need and people were failing to respond appropriately.

Gilligan concludes from these differences between the male and female framing of the issue, as well as from her other research, that there is a difference between a masculine ethic that focuses more on ethical principles and a feministic ethic that focuses more on relationships and care.[2] Her work was instrumental in laying the foundation for the development of a feminist ethic: a key resource for this book's relational focus. In my work with images of relationships, I have found that both men and women are interested in good relationships. For several years, I have asked students to explore their images of relationships through a drawing exercise.

An exercise in drawing images of relationships

In classes for graduate students and adult learners, students have filled out a worksheet that has places for them to draw their realistic, official,

---

[2] For a balanced analysis of feminist ethics, see Daryl Koehn, *Rethinking Feminist Ethics: Care, Trust, and Empathy* (London and New York: Routledge, 1998).

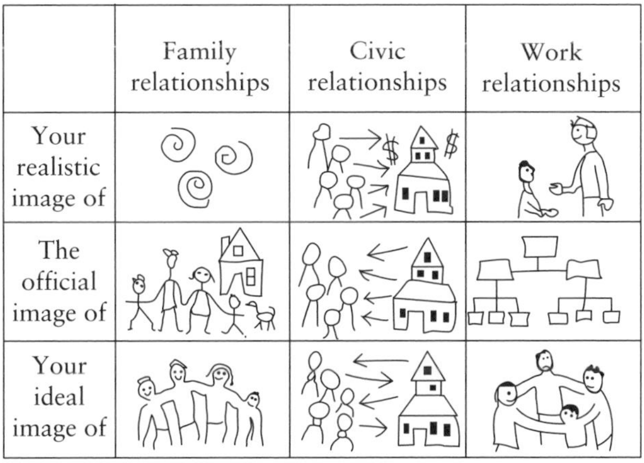

	Family relationships	Civic relationships	Work relationships
Your realistic image of			
The official image of			
Your ideal image of			

Figure 3.1. Images of relationships

and ideal images of family, civic, and work relationships. The realistic refers to the image from their experiences, the official refers to the image projected by their culture, and the ideal refers to the image of relationship they would desire. Sometime, of course, the realistic, official, and ideal are the same. More often they are quite different. The set of images in figure 3.1 is typical.

As you can see, the family, civic, and work images move from images of separation and inequality, in the realistic row, to images of more connection and equality in the idealistic row. In the family column the realistic image shows each member spinning in her or his own circle, the official image shows a family with their house and dog, and the ideal image shows a set of family members connected to each other. The civic realistic image shows citizens giving things to government, without any return, the official image shows people receiving things from government, and the ideal image shows citizens giving and receiving. In the work column, the realistic image shows a significant difference in size between persons, perhaps representing the differences between managers and workers. The official image shows a traditional organizational chart, and the ideal image pictures persons working together, as happens in work teams. Most students wish that their work relationships were more strongly connected than they think they are.

Some might say that it is impossible to move from the realistic to the idealistic images at work, because the workplace is structured to get things done, not to develop interpersonal relations. At one level, this is true; the workplace is a different world than the home, or the civic sphere. At the same time, a reasonable conclusion from chapter 2 is that people can have different images of relationships and live with different cultural assumptions in the same "world." Human relationships at work are not only determined by the current state of technology. Cultural communicative patterns, and the images or mental models that influence our interpretations and expectations of each other, also determine them.

If we let our realistic images control our expectations, then we may miss possibilities for moving relationships toward our ideals. On the other hand, if we only focus on ideal images, we will probably miss opportunities to create effective change. What we need are images that show us our current conditions as well as images that show us what change is possible. To provide these resources, the following exploration will first examine four different official images of work relationships, all of which are practiced today. It will then explore ideal family and civic images, since it is the ideal images that come closest to relational wholeness in each of these spheres. Finally, the exploration will match the different work images of relationships with the ideal family and civic relationships to select which official images could serve as an ideal image. This will give us not only an image of work relationships, but also a conceptual understanding of how conversations at work should be designed so that interpersonal relationships have integrity. The first step is to examine different official images of work relationships.

Official images of work relationships

In the Western tradition, and especially in the United States, a number of official relational images have been institutionalized in both law and business practices. Four worth exploring are the master-and-servant image, the market image, the team image, and the entrepreneurial image.

The master-and-servant image

In her book, *Belated Feudalism*, Karen Orren has shown that well into the early decades of the twentieth century the master-and-servant relationship served as the dominant image of work relations in the

United States.[3] Developed during the feudal period, the master-and-servant relationship belonged to common law, and served as the legal precedent for the adjudication of labor management relationships. As Orren points out, the founding of the United States extended liberty to persons in many areas of life, but not to the workplace. "The employee lived in a divided political world. One section was governed by public representatives of his own choosing. The other was sealed in the somber and mystifying routines of the courtroom."[4] The "other" included laws concerning the workplace. (It also included laws about family life.) In other words, even though workers were recognized as citizens in the political sphere, they remained servants at work.

A central doctrine of the master-and-servant common law tradition was the notion of obedience. Orren quotes a 1877 treatise: "A servant, strictly speaking, is a person who, by contract or operation of law, is for a limited period subject to the control or authority of another person in a particular trade, business or occupation."[5] There was no distinction made here between a worker and the work. The worker had the status of doing work. A worker works. Until late in the nineteenth century, if a worker was not working – did not have a job – he could be arrested for vagrancy. In contrast to almost all other criminal law, vagrancy focused on one's status rather than on one's action. Being a servant to a master was not just a contract; it was an identity.

In response to the collective action of workers, Congress eventually removed labor law from the exclusive jurisdiction of the courts. Orren argues that this transformation of labor law changed not only the workplace, but also the relations between the courts and the legislature. "The old established orders of persons (master and servant, parent and child, vendor and purchaser, etc.) were reconstituted as fields of activity (labor law, family law, consumer law, etc.) reachable and malleable through legislation."[6] With the passage of laws that gave workers the right to organize and to engage in collective bargaining, workers were seen for the first time as citizens.

---

[3] Karen Orren, *Belated Feudalism: Labor, the Law, and Liberal Development in the United States* (Cambridge and New York: Cambridge University Press, 1991).
[4] Ibid., p. 92.
[5] Ibid., p. 95.
[6] Ibid., p. 213.

In the United States today there are two types of labor laws: laws based on the master-and-servant image, such as the doctrine of employment at will, and laws that protect workers' civic rights, such as laws against racial discrimination. Although the acknowledgment of citizens' rights in the workplace occurred over a half century ago, it has not become a dominant image of work relationships. Instead, the market image was placed alongside the master-and-servant image of relationships.

The market image

Within the first decades of the twentieth century, the dominant labor unions in the United States turned away from issues of workers' rights, and focused almost exclusively on wages and benefits, which resulted in seeing the relationship between management and labor as one of exchange. Each side would work in its self-interest to make the best deal in a given situation. Today, many workers and managers, whether members of unions or not, see the workplace as a marketplace where they trade their respective goods, depending on the dynamics of supply and demand. One gets work by entering the "job market." A "good job" pays well, has benefits, and opens a career path. As though it was a commodity, one "shops" for work and then gets a job by exchanging one's skills, talents, and time for wages.

In the 1980s and 1990s, the Total Quality Management (TQM) movement strengthened the market image of work by persuading managers to interpret all work relationships as customer relations. TQM also required teamwork, which will be examined shortly, but its unique feature was to see others, both inside and outside the organization, as customers.[7] The workplace itself became a "marketplace."

In contrast to the master-and-servant image, where the servant is obedient to the master, the market image portrays persons as freely exchanging their "wares" with one another. Allen Cohen and David Bradford, for example, consider all transactions in organizations as exchanges between people. They claim that exchanges, or what they call the "Law of Reciprocity" is "the fundamental truth that everyone who does anything for someone else expects to be paid back eventually

[7] Marshall Sashkin and Kenneth J. Kiser, *Putting Total Quality Management to Work* (San Francisco: Berrett-Koehler, 1993).

in one form or another."[8] Cohen and Bradford are certainly correct that the workplace is not a place where people do something for nothing. On the other hand, neither should work relationships be understood merely as a bargain of work for money. The idea of reciprocity has a much richer meaning.

Lawrence C. Becker sees reciprocity as a deontic virtue.[9] For him, a virtue is a disposition to act in a certain manner, and a deontic virtue is a disposition to obey a moral obligation. In the case of reciprocity, the obligation is to return good for good, but not necessarily for evil.

Social life is thick with exchanges – transactions that involve, for each party, both receipts and disbursements. Some of these exchanges are economic; others concern things that the parties are unwilling to treat as commodities. (Acts of love, for example.) For all of these exchanges, in all societies of record, there is apparently a norm of reciprocity, the form of which can be stated thus: Good is to be returned for good, but not necessarily for evil.[10]

As a moral or deontic virtue, reciprocity is more than deciding what one must pay to get someone's services. It begins with the recognition that someone has contributed something worthwhile, and then making an appropriate and fitting response in return. The exchange, in other words, is based on a balancing of mutual benefits.[11] In this sense, reciprocity can be seen not only as a virtue of moral agents, which is Becker's idea, but also of work relationships. From a contextual approach to communication, individuals participate in relationships of reciprocity, and these relationships promote the virtue of individual reciprocity. Reciprocity, in other words, is based not only on fair exchanges, but also on cooperation.

When reciprocity is not practiced at work, the practice of exchange has few resources to develop relationships, because exchanges too easily back people into a post office model of communication, where people are seen as disconnected from one another. The relationships of cooperation that serve as the context for good exchanges become unavailable. Without this cooperation, however, the social bonds

---

[8] Allen Cohen and David Bradford, *Influence Without Authority* (New York: John Wiley, 1991), pp. 28–9.
[9] Lawrence C. Becker, *Reciprocity* (Chicago and London: University of Chicago Press, 1986).
[10] Ibid., p. 81.
[11] Ibid., p. 112.

that undergird exchanges will eventually unravel. Different self-interests will become conflicting interests. Just as plants rely on light to grow, but cannot create light, so exchanges rely on cooperation, but cannot create it. The problem with the market image of work relationships is that it does not signify the implicit cooperation on which it depends. Only the third image, the image of team relationships, adequately reveals the need for cooperation in the workplace.

The teamwork image

The teamwork image explicitly acknowledges a relationship of cooperation by referring to employee participation in such endeavors as clarifying a common vision, developing new strategies, and solving problems. Teamwork, of course, has many different meanings, as Marvin Weisbord points out:

Team building has come to mean everything from interpersonal encounter among co-workers (a format I do not recommend), to joint work on tasks of mutual importance for the future (a format I strongly support). The earliest modes used an exchange of interpersonal feedback as the key building block. In my practice now I am more committed to helping each team member take a public stand on critical issues the team faces, the ones most likely to shape the future. The most powerful team building occurs in the mutual revisiting of an organization's future, its central tasks, the design of its jobs, politics, and systems – and how people move toward or away from these tasks.[12]

Weisbord's experience suggests that although work teams can facilitate personal development, that should not be their primary focus. Rather, the primary focus should be mutual participation in the building of an organization that achieves its goals. Workers invest in the activities of the company, and as a by-product they develop as persons. Peter Senge envisions effective teams as "learning teams."[13]

The team image can give us access to rich resources for learning, for engaging in dialogue, and for discovering new strategies of cooperation. Through the active participation of its members, the

---

[12] Marvin Weisbord, *Productive Workplaces: Organizing and Managing for Dignity, Meaning, and Community* (San Francisco, CA: Jossey-Bass, 1987), p. 288.
[13] Peter M. Senge, *The Fifth Discipline: The Art and Practice of the Learning Organization* (New York: Doubleday Currency, 1990), p. 236.

organization itself can become a learning organization and a learning community. At the same time, the team image sometimes appears to cover up what the market image expresses: the need for reciprocity. Senge's discussion of learning teams, for example, as well as his overall strategy for developing learning organizations, tends to ignore the questions of fair wages. James O'Toole offers some sound advice:

For participation to be effective and legitimate two things must occur; first, employees must participate in the decisions that affect their own work. Second, employees must participate in the financial rewards that come as a result of their efforts . . . Thus, if treating employees as stakeholders is to be anything more than meaningless rhetoric, it all comes down to the two most sensitive issues in management: *power and bucks.*[14]

The image of reciprocal relationships can handle the "bucks" issue, but the "power" issue must wait for the civic image of deliberation. First, however, comes the exploration of the fourth image: the entrepreneurial.

The entrepreneurial image

An entrepreneur is the initiator of new ideas, products, and processes that keep the economy growing. In a way, the success of private enterprise depends on such individuals. It is possible to encounter self-appointed entrepreneurs who see themselves as driven by greed and ego, but those are not their key characteristics. In their philosophical exploration of entrepreneurship, Charles Spinosa, Fernando Flores, and Hubert Dreyfus present the entrepreneur as one of three types of "history makers." The other two types are individuals involved in democratic action, such as the founder of Mothers Against Drunk Drivers (MADD), and cultural figures who create solidarity around a common concern, such as Martin Luther King Jr.[15] All three have in common the skill of noticing something uncommon – an anomaly – and forging a business, civic, or communal response to it. "Being captivated by an anomaly amounts to becoming sensitive to the fact that one's

---

[14] James O'Toole, *Vanguard Management: Redesigning the Corporate Future* (Garden City, NY: Doubleday, 1985), pp. 99–100. Emphasis in original.

[15] Charles Spinosa, Fernando Flores, and Hubert Dreyfus, *Disclosing New Worlds: Entrepreneurship, Democratic Action, and the Cultivation of Solidarity* (Cambridge, MA and London: MIT Press, 1997).

preanomaly understanding of what it made sense to do in the situation was more limited than the understanding one's activity now reveals. So instead of just responding sensitively to solicitations of the situation, one responds with heightened sensitivity."[16] In other words, the entrepreneur sees some unrealized possibility and is drawn to disclose it, to realize it.

According to our view, the true entrepreneur is not primarily engaged in competition (although it is, of course, free market competition that makes entrepreneurial activity possible). The true entrepreneur is involved in holding on to an anomaly and producing something that reduces a disharmony by changing the style of a disclosive space. As long as she remains innovative in this way, she will have no competitors. She will instead be engaged in the rewarding and meaningful activity of developing a new enterprise. Her main competition will be not other businesses but the old style of life she is changing.[17]

This description of the entrepreneur fits well with the modernistic culture covered in the previous chapter. The entrepreneur exemplifies the faith in the new over the old, and appears willing to disregard the past for the sake of the future.

Does this mean that Spinosa, Flores, and Dreyfus have simply gone to heroic lengths to characterize the modern individual as virtuous? It does seem as though they see the entrepreneur as an isolated individual or what could be called an unrelated self. This interpretation, however, could be improved by remembering the two aspects of the self: the relational self and the self as agent. Spinosa, Flores, and Dreyfus's portrait of the entrepreneur is a picture of the self as agent. From this view of the self, they have captured an important aspect of individual creativity. Entrepreneurs, however, are not only active; they are also inactive, just like the rest of us. Entrepreneurs, in other words, also exist as members of work, family, and civic communities.

These different images of work relationships elicit a couple of questions. "What difference does it make which image is operative in an organization's communication patterns?" and "Which image or images most closely conform to the notion of integrity as relational wholeness?" An exploration of family and civic images will help

---

[16] Ibid., p. 66.
[17] Ibid., p. 173.

answer the second question. To answer the first, imagine how these four images would influence a performance review of a worker by her supervisor.

Relational images and performance reviews

Performance reviews are typically conversations between supervisors and supervisees about the supervisee's performance. Our first image, the master-and-servant image, carries with it the medieval notion of "employment at will," which gives employers the privilege of terminating employees without due process. The employer is the "boss." Given this relational image, one can imagine that a performance review conversation would be rather one-sided. The supervisor would control the conversation, and the supervisee would take a subordinate position of trying to figure out how to please the "master." This pattern may seem familiar to many, since the master-and-servant image continues to shape many work conversations.

The market image of relationships, on the other hand, could promote a more equal exchange. It would all depend on the relative needs of each party, what they have to trade, the larger market conditions of supply and demand, and so on. The exchange would consist of bargaining, with each party trying to make the best deal for themselves. This relational image by itself tends to turn people into commodities that can be traded, but it also acknowledges the importance of fair dealing.

The team image would promote a more cooperative conversation, since the participants would see each other as working together. In more mature organizations, the conversations could become a dialogue focused on mutual learning. Performance reviews based on this image would encourage the supervisor and subordinate to work together to develop mutual expectations for future performance. They would also explore how they could improve their interactions for the sake of team performance.

The fourth relational image, the entrepreneurial, would probably frame performance reviews as occasions for networking and sharing new ideas. There would be less emphasis on working together than on the team image, since the image of the entrepreneur highlights individual creativity. The expectation of something new happening could make the conversation very lively, and the relationship very modern, with a focus on new possibilities.

Each of the four images of relationships has both an explicit and an implicit basis that maintain the relationships. The explicit relationship for the master and servant is status or social class. The implicit relationship is one of control and domination. The master's privilege, of course, is that he can ignore the domination, since he takes for granted his elevated status. "That's the way things are supposed to be." The market image's explicit relationship is one of competitive exchanges. Its implicit relationship is cooperation. The team image is almost the opposite of the market image. It makes the cooperation explicit and the competition or exchange implicit. Finally, the explicit focus for the entrepreneurial image of relationships is an unrelated self. This self, however, must also rely on an implicit set of supportive relationships.

Official work relationship	Explicit relationship	Implicit relationship
Master-and-servant	Status or social class	Privilege/domination
Market	Competition	Cooperation
Team	Joint action	Adequate exchanges
Entrepreneurial	Unrelated self	Hidden support

Figure 3.2. Explicit and implicit aspects of work relationships

Figure 3.2 summarizes the differences among the four images of work relationships. Which of these four images are appropriate for the development of corporate integrity? The answer depends on which images are capable of including the core meaning of family and civic relationships. To get to these core meanings, I will first explore the ideal images of family relationships and then the ideal images of civic relationships.

Ideal images of family relationships

Even though people have quite different experiences of family relationships, as the exercise on drawing realistic, official, and idealistic images of relationships demonstrated, many of us have similar ideal images. One image that would refer to everyone's experience (almost everyone anyway) and also implies an ideal family relationship is the image of the caring mother-and-child relationship.

The mother-and-child image

In spite of the different situations in which we enter the world, we all begin as infants. If we are lucky, our early experience matches the image of a caring interaction between a mother and a child. The "mother" may be male or female, but traditionally we talk of someone "mothering" the child. That seems obvious. Not so obvious, but just as significant, is the child's reaching out for the mother. John Bowlby, one of the key early contributors in the field of attachment theory, puts it this way: "Human infants, we can safely conclude, like infants of other species, are preprogrammed to develop in a socially cooperative way; whether they do so or not turns in high degree on how they are treated."[18] Bowlby's conclusion means that humans are not preprogrammed to be greedy or selfish, as some might think. Instead, they are wired to develop in and through cooperative relationships. This cooperation is based on mutual dependency. Infants are dependent on caregivers, and caregivers are dependent on infants to receive their care. The dynamics of the relationship can be quite different in different cases, as the clinician, Daniel Siegel, has observed:

The nature of an infant's attachment to the parent (or other primary caregiver) will become internalized as a working model of attachment. If this model represents security, the baby will be able to explore the world and to separate and mature in a healthy way. If the attachment relationship is problematic, the internal working model of attachment will not give the infant a sense of a secure base and the development of normal behaviors (such as play, exploration, and social interactions) will be impaired. Of course, if circumstances change, a securely attached infant or young child can become insecurely attached and an insecure attachment can become secure.[19]

The major factor that determines an infant's behavior, in other words, is not the infant's character, but instead the quality of the relationship (or relationships, since there could be more than one caregiver)

[18] John Bowlby, *A Secure Base: Parent–Child Attachment and Healthy Human Development* (New York: Basic Books, 1988), p. 9.
[19] Daniel Siegel, *The Developing Mind: Towards a Neurobiology of Interpersonal Experience* (New York: The Guilford Press, 1999), p. 72.

in which the infant develops. While the first relationships establish a person's relational or attachment style, so to speak, later significant relationships throughout one's life may change it. Every significant relationship has the possibility of becoming a "secure base" for the participants, which will facilitate their individual flourishing. As Bowlby suggests: "Although the capacity for developmental change is diminished with age, change continues throughout the life cycle so that changes for better or for worse are always possible."[20]

The secure base that the mother and child image projects is not limited to child and parent relationships, but is actually a necessary condition for significant adult relationships as well. Susan Johnson, a couples and family therapist, has written extensively on the application of Bowlby's attachment theory to understanding adult relationships.[21] The following summary of three of her five "basic tenets" of attachment theory shows the similarities she recognizes between parent-and-child relationships and romantic relationships between adults.

- Seeking and maintaining contact with others is a primary motivating principle in human beings. Dependency is an innate part of being human, rather than a childhood trait that we grow out of as we mature.
- Such contact is an innate survival mechanism. The presence of an attachment figure provides comfort and security, while perceived inaccessibility of such a figure creates distress.
- The building blocks of secure bonds are emotional accessibility and responsiveness, whether the relationship is between child and parent or between two adult partners.[22]

What Johnson and others have witnessed is the repetition of specific patterns of attachment behaviors as people move from one significant relationship to another. Even when the behavior appears to indicate avoidance of conflict in relationships, it is based not only on past relational experiences, but also on the general human need to be in relation with others. Dependency, in other words, is not something we

[20] Bowlby, *A Secure Base*, p. 136.
[21] Susan Johnson, *Creating Connection: The Practice of Emotionally Focused Marital Therapy* (New York: Brunner/Mazel, 1996).
[22] Ibid., pp. 18–19.

outgrow. It is part of the human condition. Adult family relationships, of course, look different than parent-and-child relationships, so we need another image to grasp this aspect of family experiences. I propose the image of the family dinner. Family dinners nourish the body, the whole person, and, most importantly, the whole family.

The family dinner image

People in different cultures have very different traditions regarding family meals. Still, it seems safe to say that the ideal purpose of family dinners, which is not always realized, is to enjoy and to enhance family relationships. The family dinner can become a "secure base" for people around the table. When people have meaningful family dinners, participants are in tune with the security and pleasure of simply being together. Their dependency on each other can easily go unnoticed, because it is mutual. It provides the secure base from which each person can express his or her own individuality. Family members may even encounter disagreements and have to work on mutual understanding. The point is that their individuality is grounded in mutual dependency, not in a separate isolated independence. A family of one cannot exist. Secure relationships, in other words, create secure, strong, and flexible individuals.

At its best, the family dinner becomes a place to engage in the dialogue practices listed in chapter 1. Family dinners are also places for storytelling, whether the dinner is for two or twenty. Through storytelling, family members participate in the meanings that the stories make available. When we participate as listeners, we learn about the larger context to which we belong. When we participate as storytellers, we develop our identity in the face of others who listen to us. In this process, our self-identity becomes embedded in narrative. The multitude of different and even sometimes conflicting family stories about what has happened, is happening, and will happen provide access to the resources for meaning. A family realizes its possibilities in and from its stories. The image of relationship that emerges here is of people who carefully engage in mutual storytelling, and who nurture the possibilities of continuing the unfinished stories that project each one's own best possibilities. This image resonates and defines the traditional image of family relationships as loving relationships or as relationships of care. But how useful is this image in understanding the appropriate character for work relationships?

Family relationships and the work setting

Most of us would agree that the type of emotional bond created in strong family relationships is not an appropriate ideal in the work setting. True, there are occasions when people do develop attachment relationships at work that closely parallel family relationships, but that does not mean that corporations should design interpersonal conversational patterns that depend on such emotional attachments. At the same time, attachment images of family relations reveal something about ourselves that should not be ignored. The work of John Bowlby and others suggests that human beings are fundamentally communal or relational animals. We need to have secure relationships.

Bowlby's research supports the feminist position proposed by Virginia Held and others that the mother-and-child image more correctly represents our human nature than the image of the "economic man."[23] This certainly would be contrary to much of the Western, patriarchal tradition, and yet it does seem to conform to our deepest experiences. We all began as infants, and survived only because of the care we received from others. We begin connected to others, not separated from them. The desire for a secure connection at work may take different forms in different work settings, but at the very least it will be a desire for membership and for a sense of belonging.

The philosophical tradition that stands behind the notion of the economic man comes partly out of the social contract theories developed in the seventeenth century. These theories usually pictured humans as individually free before they were social. Individuals then chose to form a commonwealth or community to protect their individual freedoms. In this tradition, individuals come first, then community. Modern psychology, as well as feminist ethics, has provided a different sequence, and one that corresponds much more to human experience. Individuals develop in and through relationships. Furthermore, this development depends on the security of family relationships. The human need for security is not limited to family relationships, however,

---

[23] Virginia Held, *Feminist Morality: Transforming Culture, Society, and Politics* (Chicago and London: University of Chicago Press, 1993).

but extends to all human relationships, including relationships at work. Just how that need should be recognized at work is another question, which will be addressed after the core meaning of civic relationships completes the context for relational wholeness at work.

Ideal images of civic relationships

While humans have always been members of families, they have not always been members of civic communities in which they could be citizens. In a kingdom, for example, people are subjects, not citizens. Dictatorships can also prevent the practice of citizenship. Some democracies have denied citizenship to women, slaves, and non-natives. So what makes one a citizen rather than a subject? Perhaps the most important difference is that a citizen has a say in determining the qualifications for citizenship, and a subject does not. If you do not have a say, then you are subject to other people's decisions. To participate in, or at least to have your views represented in, the process of making decisions about the communities to which you belong is the first condition of citizenship.

This first condition already implies a second condition: a citizen is a member of a political community among and with others. No one can be a citizen by himself. It is a relational term. What should be the character of this relationship among citizens? Benjamin Barber's distinction between thin and strong democracy lays out two quite different options.[24]

Thin and strong democracy

Barber's notion of a "thin" democracy refers to the liberal political tradition that emphasizes individual rights and limited government. It is the same tradition that supports the notion of an "economic man." This liberal tradition, as developed by philosophers such as John Locke, holds that individuals should be free to choose their own ends and to follow their own life plans.

---

[24] Benjamin Barber, *Strong Democracy: Participatory Politics for a New Age* (Berkeley, Los Angeles, and London: University of California Press, 1984).

Perhaps as a consequence of their focus on individual freedom and rights, liberal democrats have what Barber calls an anarchist disposition toward community involvement: "The aim [of liberals] is not to share in power or to be part of a community but to contain power and community and to judge them by how they affect freedom and private interest."[25] Individuals may develop relationships, when they choose, but liberal democrats see individuals as essentially isolated and independent. This stands in marked contrast to the dependent relationship between mother and child, as well as to the contextual model of communication presented in the first chapter.

Still, this liberal tradition remains the dominant ideology in the United States today. As Michael Sandel points out, however, this has not always been the case.[26] In the early history of the United States, and actually until the last century, there also existed a republican theory of citizenship. Championed by people like Thomas Jefferson, supporters of the republican view argued that the key to democracy was citizen deliberation, and through deliberation, the cultivation of civic virtue. The idea was to promote what Sandel calls "the self-governing republic." Sandel draws the following contrast between the liberal and the republican views of liberty:

On the liberal view, liberty is defined in opposition to democracy, as a constraint on self-government. I am free insofar as I am a bearer of rights that guarantee my immunity from certain majority decisions. On the republican view, liberty is understood as a consequence of self-government. I am free insofar as I am a member of a political community that controls its own fate, and a participant in the decisions that govern its affairs.[27]

This republican view is similar to Barber's notion of strong democracy. Barber also believes that political freedom is not primarily freedom *from* community, but rather freedom *for* the development of community. For him, the thin and strong versions of democracy have very different views of citizenship. He says that for "thin" liberals "Citizenship is an artificial role that the natural man prudently adopts in order to safeguard his

---

[25] Ibid., p. 7.
[26] Michael J. Sandel, *Democracy's Discontent: America in Search of a Public Philosophy* (Cambridge, MA and London: The Belknap Press of Harvard University, 1996), p. 25.
[27] Ibid., pp. 25–6.

solitary humanity."[28] Contrast that to the strong view of citizenship: "Citizens are neighbors bound together neither by block nor by contract but by their common concerns and common participation in the search for common solutions to common conflicts."[29] Republican citizenship, in other words, is a common activity.

An examination of the notion of self-government can clarify the difference between these two views of citizenship. For the liberal, self-government means something like self-control, or the freedom to govern oneself. The republican tradition, on the other hand, thinks of self-government as a collective activity of deciding with others how to arrange their lives together. One cannot make such arrangements alone, unless one can control everyone else. In modern democracies, only by participating in collective actions, or at least by having one's views represented in the making of collective decisions, can individuals participate in self-government. This requires what Barber calls the transformation of private interests into public goods, which occurs through the practice of citizens engaging in what he calls "public thinking."

[Public thinking] moves us perforce from particularistic and immediate considerations of our own and our groups' interests, examined in a narrow temporal framework ("Will there be enough gasoline for my summer vacation trip?" for example), to general and long-term considerations of the nature of the communities we live in and of how well our life plans fit in with that nature ("Is dependence on oil a symbol of an overly materialistic, insufficiently self-sufficient society?" for example).[30]

Participation in "public thinking" is quite different from the liberal's view of political activity. For the liberal, the essence of political activity is symbolized by the secret ballot. In the context of tyrannical governments, the secret ballot can be a powerful tool for the protection of democratic rights. In democratic republics, however, the secret ballot hardly suffices for self-government. As Barber points out, the secret ballot is really a "private" act. We do not have to explain or justify our decision. This is a silent democracy. In contrast, the image of a strong democracy highlights conversations that create a public conversation. "The affective power of talk is, then, the power to stretch the human

---

[28] Ibid., p. 8.
[29] Ibid., p. 219.
[30] Ibid., pp. 196–7.

imagination so that the I of private self-interest can be reconceptualized and reconstituted as a we that makes possible civility and common political action."[31] The notion of strong democracy elicits possibilities for common endeavors that can draw out the essential resources for our political life. It corresponds to a key image of civic relationships: the town hall meeting.

The town hall meeting

Imagine a town hall meeting. Community members fill the meeting hall to address some common need. They may see each other as family member, employee or employer, member of a religious community, and so on, but here, at this meeting, each one has an equal right to speak. The meeting may even be guided by Robert's Rules of Order, to ensure that everyone has access to the floor. The speakers may have different ideas about what is at stake and what they should do. Differences in age and experience, as well as status in the community, may influence the persuasiveness of each person's voice. At the same time, the meeting's structure allows all voices to be heard. As the deliberation continues, the group could come to an agreement about what is best for the community. Together, they have engaged in the practice of self-government.

Not all town meetings, of course, fit this image. The history of democracy is also a history of some people excluding others, and of structures of privilege overriding equal participation. Sometimes what is taken as a public agreement turns out to be a private deal. Furthermore, some would say that while town meetings may be useful for making neighborhoods safe, they are of little use for addressing national or global problems. To ensure that the town hall meeting is not only an ideal but also a possible image of civic relationships, it must meet certain conditions of public deliberation.

The conditions for public deliberation

In his book on public deliberation, James Bohman defines public deliberation as "a dialogical process of exchanging reasons for the

---

[31] Ibid., pp. 189–90.

purpose of resolving problematic situations that cannot be settled without interpersonal coordination and cooperation."[32] For this dialogical process to occur, Bohman suggests that three conditions must be in place, which he defines as non-tyranny, equality, and publicity.[33] The condition of non-tyranny means that the outcome of the deliberative process is not decided by a person's status or wealth, but by the quality of the reasons developed through the process of deliberation. The process, in other words is not controlled by powers extraneous to the deliberative process itself.

The condition of non-tyranny has been central to pubic deliberation since its early practice in classical Athens. Athenian democracy, of course, was far from perfect. Women, slaves, and non-Greeks were excluded. Still, in many ways the Athenian practice of deliberation initiated a practice of self-governing that one finds in few cultures. Its genius was locating political power in the process of deliberation itself. The philosopher Hannah Arendt has expressed this idea of political power as follows:

Power is actualized only where word and deed have not parted company, where words are not empty and deeds not brutal, where words are not used to veil intentions but to disclose realities, and deeds are not used to violate and destroy but to establish relations and create new realities ... Power is always, as we would say, a power potential and not an unchangeable, measureable, and reliable entity like force or strength. While strength is the natural quality of an individual seen in isolation, power springs up between men when they are together and vanishes the moment they disperse.[34]

This understanding of power as a kind of empowerment provides an answer to James O'Toole's earlier question about the role of power in teams. The real power of teams is their capacity for creating new ideas through deliberation. Such power, however, will emerge only if force and strength are not allowed to dominate their conversations.

This view of power has not been the most popular notion of power, even in politics. For much of the twentieth century, a more popular

---

[32] James Bohman, *Public Deliberation: Pluralism, Complexity, and Democracy* (Cambridge, MA: MIT Press, 1996), p. 27.

[33] Ibid., p. 35.

[34] Hannah Arendt, *The Human Condition* (Garden City, NY: Doubleday, 1959), p. 179.

view was that political power belonged to the wealthy or the aristo-crats. Reinhold Niebuhr, a major contributor to a "realistic" view of politics, wrote in 1939: "The political power in any society is held by the group which commands the most significant type of non-political power, whether it be military prowess, priestly prestige, economic ownership, or the ability to manipulate the technical processes of the community."[35] For Niebuhr, the powerbrokers were those who "had" power, either through position or property, rather than those who participate in a process where, as Arendt said, "word and deed have not parted company." Actually, there are different types of power, and they need to be distinguished from each other.

John Kenneth Galbraith's typology of power can be useful here.[36] He distinguishes among three different types of power, which he calls condign, compensatory and conditioned. Condign power relies on the threat of punishment, and it has its basis in one's status or what Galbraith calls "personality." It is the kind of power that matches the master-and-servant image of work relations. Compensatory power relies on the control of resources, and has its basis in the ownership of property. Relationships of exchange rely on compensatory power. Galbraith's third type of power, conditioned power, depends on the organization of beliefs. This is the power of the lobbyist or the deal-maker who instead of using threats (condign power) or promises tit for tat (compensatory power) persuades by drawing on and reinforcing a set of beliefs. Persuasion can be powerful when it calls forth and activates people's deeply held beliefs. In a deliberative process, where people are open to the possibilities of moving forward with shared commitments and joint action, and when word and deed have not parted company, this type of power comes into play. It is the power one finds in highly functional teams. This type of power, of course, depends on the process of deliberation remaining free from the tyranny of status or property.

Bohman's second condition, the condition of equality, is much easier to develop if the deliberative context is non-tyrannical. Everyday life, of course, is rife with inequalities, some of which can be justified and

---

[35] Reinhold Niebuhr, *Reinhold Niebuhr on Politics,* ed. Harry R. Davis and Robert R. Good (New York: Charles Scribner's Sons, 1960), pp. 93–4.
[36] John Kenneth Galbraith, *The Anatomy of Power* (Boston: Houghton Mifflin, 1983).

some that cannot. When these inequalities dominate the deliberative process, they smother the democratic possibilities of self-government. When these inequalities are bracketed for the sake of democratic action, then decisions will be based on the best reasons available, because everyone has equal access to the public forum. In the deliberative process every citizen should have an equal right to speak and to be taken seriously.

The third condition, publicity, is perhaps the most intriguing. It is what makes public deliberation *public*. At the center of public discourse is the practice of developing reasons for different positions or policy proposals and making them available to others. Making one's reasons available to others does not presume that others will agree, but rather that they will understand. Listeners should be able to say, "If I saw the situation as this speaker does, then I would agree with her conclusions." In some cases, making one's view public requires a bit of translation. Martin Luther King Jr. was a master in such translations. As a Christian, he believed in equal opportunity because of the Christian doctrine that everyone is a child of God. In the public realm, he spoke of civil rights. One could agree with him without becoming a Christian, because he translated his private beliefs into a public language. Public deliberation requires public reasons.

When these three conditions are met, the right of citizens to participate, or to have their views represented, empowers democracy itself. This power can create changes that improve the life of communities and individuals. People find themselves participating in collective self-government. The governance of most corporations, of course, is not based on the "thin" democracy of one person one vote. Neither are most religious or educational organizations. That does not mean, however, that people lose their right to participate in these communities when they enter them. Some version of strong democracy should be established in the workplace, because the workplace does not exist beyond civil society, but belongs to it. Chapter 5 will explore the broader ramifications of this idea.

In terms of relational wholeness, excluding the civic relationship from our considerations of work relationships is just as impossible as excluding the family relationship. Work relationships of inclusion must recognize the human need for security and the right to participate.

The need for security and the right to participate

The conclusion that work relationships should honor people's need for security and their right to participate may not receive immediate agreement, for what may look like good reasons. Why not let the home and family life take care of security? In fact, some might argue that the insecure worker sometimes works harder and faster than someone who is secure. I agree that there are such cases. The question here, however, is how we should consider relationships in terms of relational wholeness. The fact is that people do exist in relationships at work. So the question is not whether to have relationships, but rather what kind of relationships to have. This is a question that can receive different answers, and which answer we give will influence an organization's level of maturity. As Robert Kegan suggests:

In any case, the decision any workplace must make (resignedly or unselfconsciously) is identical to that which faces a community, family, a marriage, or any long-term human context which like it or not, becomes a culture for a person's growth. The decision is simply this: to which is it more committed – the present evolutionary state of its constituents, or the bigger picture of the person as the process of evolution itself?[37]

According to Kegan, if the organization chooses the current state of its employees' development, then the employees' desire to grow will probably drive them out of the company to another place where they can pursue their lifeplans. If the organization, on the other hand, chooses to see its employees as people involved in a process of growth and learning, then they will need to provide the security that facilitates such growth, similar to how a family relationship provides a secure base for exploration and innovation.

Georg von Krogh, Kazuo Ichijo, and Ikujiro Nonaka, in their book on enabling knowledge creation, take a position very similar to Robert Kegan's.[38] Based on their research of successful, global companies such as Unilever and Narvesen, they argue that companies that provide

---

[37] Robert Kegan, *The Evolving Self: Problem and Process in Human Development* (Cambridge, MA: Harvard University Press, 1982), p. 248.

[38] Georg Von Krogh, Kazuo Ichijo, and Ikujiro Nonaka, *Enabling Knowledge Creation: How to Unlock the Mystery of Tacit Knowledge and Release the Power of Innovation* (New York: Oxford University Press, 2000).

a caring context will benefit from individuals creating and refining innovative knowledge.

When care runs high in an organization, the individual member works in a context in which colleagues show genuine interest in her progress. She can trust her colleagues and will receive active help. She can access expertise wherever required and can afford to experiment. She knows her colleagues will welcome such courage and judge the outcome of open-ended knowledge creation leniently. When colleagues are supportive, individual participants are more likely to articulate their knowledge spontaneously, using new metaphors and analogies. And because a high-care organization allows for the expression of emotions, "fuzzy" logic, and ideas that are not rigidly specified, individuals will also share their tacit knowledge at the same time that they refine it. They will create knowledge while bestowing it on others, and their colleagues will do the same.[39]

Although Von Krogh, Ichijo, and Nonaka's research provides a business case for providing a secure base for individuals, it also makes sense in terms of a civic case for corporate integrity. Ignoring people's need for security simply prevents the achievement of relational wholeness. Acknowledging basic human needs, on the other hand, will facilitate the design of communication patterns that allow people to live more confidently with one another and to flourish more fully as individuals. As citizens, we do have an interest in organizations creating such possibilities in the workplace because our work lives do influence our lives outside of work. So, yes, a secure home is certainly desirable, but it does not mean that the need for security can be ignored at work.

Some people could also disagree with the idea that workers have the right to participate. They might remind us of the distinction between the public and private spheres. Is not "private enterprise" beyond the reach of "public deliberation"? In the master-and-servant tradition, business was more private, under the control of the master, except that government protected the master's property, provided the necessary infrastructure, education, and so on. In any case, in the United States, early in the twentieth century, democratically elected officials began to recognize workers as citizens, which made the workplace public in the sense that workers' rights were protected there. The civil rights movement in the 1960s made corporate life even more

---

[39] Ibid., p. 57.

public when the government required corporations to develop hiring and promotion programs that gave all citizens an equal opportunity for jobs they were qualified to hold. Corporations were given a public responsibility not to run their businesses according to private privilege, but according to public opportunity. Business law today contains two legal traditions – the older master-and-servant tradition and the more recent democratic tradition. These traditions sometimes conflict with one another, such as in conflicts between the doctrine of at-will employment and the right to due process.[40] Still, just as persons now have their rights as citizens protected in the home, their civil rights should also be protected at work.

If corporations exist in the civic sphere, and if workers are citizens in that sphere, then why not give workers the benefit of the doubt and consider them as citizens at work as well? This would mean that workers would be treated as citizens unless there were good reasons for not doing so. The burden of proof, in other words, rests with those who would deny citizenship, not with those of us who advocate it. Until such reasons are forthcoming, the relationships at work should be recognized as civic relationships.

Recognizing the civic aspect of work relationships, however, does not require that corporations set up voting booths. Instead of trying to follow the image of a "thin" democracy, it makes more sense to include the key factor of a strong democracy: namely, participation and public deliberation. Although worker participation may take different forms, from employee ownership, to collective bargaining, to autonomous teams, to online employee feedback programs, the principle remains the same: people should have opportunities to deliberate with others about the arrangements of their work life. So the arguments that security should remain at home, and not be part of workplace relationships, or that workers should not be treated as citizens in the workplace, are not really that persuasive. Much more persuasive is the claim that the human need for security and the civic right to participate should be taken into consideration in designing corporate verbal and nonverbal conversational patterns.

---

[40] Patricia H. Werhane and Tara J. Radin, "Employment at Will and Due Process," in *Ethical Theory and Business*, sixth edition, ed. Tom Beauchamp and Norman Bowie (Upper Saddle River, NJ: Prentice-Hall, 2001), pp. 266–94.

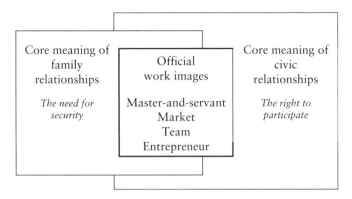

Figure 3.3. The family and civic context for work relationships

Figure 3.3 summarizes the exploration of the core meaning of the ideal images of family and civic relationships and shows how these meanings provide a context for selecting the appropriate images of work relationships. This figure illustrates two conclusions that can be drawn from the arguments of the previous sections. First of all, since the sphere of civic relationships provides the context for work relationships, and since civic relationships are key to our modern identity, relational wholeness at work must in some fashion recognize the civic right to participate. Second, since the family image of relationships expresses a basic human desire for a secure relational base, relational wholeness at work must somehow recognize the human need for security. Given these two core requirements for interpersonal integrity – the need for security and the right to participation – which of the four images of work relationships could be most easily molded into an image of an ideal work relationship?

In terms of the human need for security the team image probably most closely resembles the family image's notion of a secure base. The master-and-servant image might provide security, but it would be paternalistic, rather than being based on mutual dependency. The market image is more complex. To the degree that it turns people into commodities, it would not develop human relationships at all. On the other hand, one may find security in exchanges based on reciprocity. If one can count on receiving the benefit of the doubt, for example, or equal treatment, then the exchanges may rest in a cooperative set of assumptions that provides a caring context. The same could be true for the entrepreneurial image of work relationships. If it shows an awareness of the dependency of human relations, then it might well have a place in organizations. If it totally ignores the relational security it actually relies on, then it would not contribute to corporate integrity.

So it seems that any of the four images of relationships could be fashioned to provide an appropriate type of security, but the team image probably comes the closest because it is most likely to enable its members to explicitly recognize each other's need to belong to a work community. It has the strongest capacity, in other words, for the mutual recognition of dependency.

What about the civic right to participate? The master-and-servant relationship must be rejected, because it sees workers as servants rather than citizens. The market image is more complicated. One could interpret this image from a liberal perspective and say that as long as people have choices, there is nothing to worry about. As we have already said, however, exchanges are only part of the picture. Another part is the cooperative context for the exchange. Who determines that? Self-government, as was stated before, is not so much about governing one's self as about participating in governing the arrangements in which one lives, or, in this case, in which one makes exchanges. If the agreements that enable exchanges to occur are mutually developed and reciprocal, then the exchange relations could fit the civic standard of deliberation. The entrepreneurial image of relationships should be interpreted in a similar fashion. Its integrity depends on whether there are occasions for civic deliberation about what arrangements are best to get the work done.

Designing occasions for deliberation is easiest when people are working in teams. As members of teams, employees can develop reliable relationships that are in alignment with the family images of relationships, as well as conversations of mutual participation, which can recognize workers as citizens. Furthermore, these conversations could clearly honor the principle of reciprocity. Remember that reciprocity requires good for good. It refers to just relationships of exchange. Reciprocity expresses one distinguishing mark of work relationships that separates them from family and civic relationships. So if we add reciprocity to the notions of secure and civic, meeting the challenge of interpersonal integrity would require conversations that promote secure civic reciprocal relationships.

Relationships of secure civic reciprocity

The notion of secure civic reciprocity in the world of work provides a way to practice the notion of openness that was developed in the previous chapter on communicative culture. Openness to differences and disagreements in conversations that expect secure, civic reciprocity should facilitate the collaboration among co-workers and managers that is required to successfully address complex employer and employee issues. In fact, for some issues, developing a shared understanding among corporate members that relationships should strive for secure civic reciprocity might already provide a way of resolving them.

Remember the previous review of employee performance evaluations? How would they proceed if guided by the notion of secure civic reciprocity? First of all, they would occur in conditions of safety rather than intimidation. The need for security would imply that both employee and employer could trust each other to be honest, forthright, and collaborative. Also, both would participate, assuming that their relationship was not only defined by work roles and responsibilities, but also by civic standards of non-tyranny, equality and publicity. Finally, the conclusion they drew would show a spirit of reciprocity, with rewards matching performance, accountability matching control, and requirements matching capacity. If conversations followed these guidelines, they would exhibit relational wholeness and therefore promote corporate integrity.

Relational wholeness, as the practice of secure civic reciprocity, actually provides a strong guide for many current workplace issues. Issues that arise from the practice of white privilege, or from patterns of discrimination against people of color and women, could be addressed if people felt safe to tell the truth, to learn from each other, and to recognize each other as members of the same civic society. The need for security is probably nowhere more important than in the exercise of one's civic right to participate. Likewise, the right to participate is perhaps nowhere more important than in determining what is necessary for the development of safety. If I am a manager, I may feel safe when I am in control, but not when the process of deliberation moves in directions beyond my control. Where is my safety then? If I have not joined in the process of developing good reasons for a proposal, including my good reasons, then I may find myself sabotaging the process because I was not ready to follow the development of thought. So the need for security and the right to participate are closely interrelated. When they exist together, much of the work of resolving conflicts has already been done, but not all of it.

For example, not only workers but also corporations have an interest in security. How do you balance the security needs of the corporation that could be met with more monitoring and the security needs of workers, which could require privacy? The standard of corporate integrity does not provide a complete guide here. Other guides, such as treating people with respect, or treating others as you would like to be treated, might also be helpful. What corporate integrity can contribute, however, is to show what kind of interpersonal relationships should exist among those involved in determining how to balance the employees' and the corporation's need for security. If all participants not only feel safe to enter into deliberation with others, but also can trust that their security will be considered, then the work of bringing together particular observations, examining different values, and exploring different assumptions can begin. If the conditions of non-tyranny, equality, and publicity are present, the conversation actually has a good chance not only of resolving the dilemma, but also of increasing the corporation's integrity.

Conversations about downsizing and transferring jobs oversees represent even more difficult conversations. How can we design such conversations with integrity? It would seem laying off employees violates the need for security and participation, as well as ignoring how workers are a part of the whole that constitutes a corporation. In some cases, such actions probably destroy company integrity, especially when the senior leadership profits from downsizing at the expense of workers. On the other hand, when business conditions require change, and all members of the work community bear the burden of the change, with as much security given to the most vulnerable as possible, then a corporation may actually create integrity during its most difficult times. Such a conversation would need to create a safe place where various stakeholders could become involved in the process of public deliberation about their common challenges and possible joint solutions.

The purpose of creating a standard for interpersonal relationships at work was not to say exactly what managers and workers should do in particular situations, but rather to provide a guideline to use in deciding what to do. Most conversations at work are not about interpersonal relationships, and yet all conversations at work depend on implicit images of interpersonal relationships. Designing corporate integrity on the interpersonal level requires not only an awareness of these implicit images, but also an awareness of persons as belonging to different types of relationships. These conversations could end with quite different conclusions, depending on the situation, but the process should be designed so people feel safe, they see themselves treated as citizens, and the exchanges are reciprocal. Chapter 7 on organizational leadership returns to these same challenges, when it explores the relationship between leaders and followers.

The challenge of developing secure civic reciprocal relationships may seem unrealistic for some corporations. Others have already designed such relationships. In any case, whether it is a realistic goal depends on what corporations are for. Why do they exist? The next chapter addresses that question. It will show that relationships that are secure, civic, and reciprocal fit with pursuing a corporation's worthwhile purposes.

From theory to practice

Questions for study and reflection

1. Do you agree with Gilligan about gender differences in the interpretation of situations?
2. Of the four images of work relationships, which ones have influenced the communication patterns of your work experiences?
3. How would you characterize the explicit and implicit relationships at your workplace?
4. Why are family and civic relationships important for understanding relationships at work?
5. How would the idea of secure civic reciprocity in work relationships affect conversations about the employee/employer issues listed at the beginning of this chapter?
6. What needs to be done to improve the integrity of relationships at work?

Guidelines for the assessment worksheets in the appendix

If you have not used Worksheet #6 on images of relationships before reading the chapter, you can use it now to assess your realistic and idealistic expectations of what is possible in your relationships with others.

Worksheet #7 allows an assessment of the conditions for public deliberation. You can either choose a particular conversation or a more general communication pattern to evaluate.

4 | *Organizational integrity as pursuing a worthwhile purpose*

The exploration of the two dimensions of corporate integrity reviewed so far have shown that corporate communication patterns should be designed for the inclusion of differences and disagreement and for relationships of secure civic reciprocity. These conclusions were drawn from answering the first two challenges of integrity, which required cultural openness and relational wholeness. Do these types of relationships really fit with the purpose of corporations? This chapter demonstrates that they do. The demonstration, of course, belongs to the book's overall approach of working from a civic perspective, focusing on relationships, and using a method of examining and changing communication patterns. The difference in this chapter is that organizations are also seen as agents. This means that integrity requires a consistency between their purpose and their actions. To understand the integrity challenge on this dimension of corporate life, it is necessary to understand what it means for corporations to pursue a worthwhile purpose.

"Why should corporations exist?" "What are they good for?" These questions will elicit different answers depending on the perspective from which they are addressed. An economic or financial perspective, for example, would give a quite different answer than a managerial perspective, or the civic perspective. Whether the question addresses the individual, organizational, or social level of analysis will also make a difference. This chapter primarily focuses on the organizational level, not because the other two are insignificant, but because that is where the challenge of organizational integrity exists: the question of a worthwhile purpose. The organizational level of analysis also allows a comparison between different types of organizations, such as for-profits and nonprofits. In terms of the significance of pursuing a worthwhile purpose, common assumptions about nonprofits can help us explore our assumptions about for-profits, especially when both types of organizations are interpreted from a civic perspective.

The civic perspective, of course, is not the only perspective. In the review of theories of corporate responsibility in chapter 1, the civic perspective was presented as the logical next step after the notion of corporate citizenship. Taking this step, however, does not occur in a vacuum. It occurs in a context of, and in the contest of, different perspectives. To ensure that the civic perspective is the best one for designing conversations that promote organizational integrity, it is important to understand what these other perspectives offer, especially the economic and the managerial perspectives. The following review of these two perspectives will clarify the reasons for using a civic perspective to design conversations about a corporation's purpose.

The economic perspective of corporate purpose

Although economics is not limited to a neo-classical perspective, this perspective does dominate most conversations in the United States and to a large extent the rest of the developed world. Expressed in a language of costs and benefits, economizing is the language of most MBA programs, almost all shareholders, and certainly the financial departments of corporations. For many economists, the worth of something is not connected to purpose but to price. Consumers determine something's worth by how much they will pay for it. There is some truth to this view, but it is not the whole truth. What turns this view into a set of half-truths is that it takes one aspect of human behavior (individuals acting on preferences) and treats it as if it could define all human behavior. Some of the results from this overgeneralization are that individuals are seen only as consumers with preferences rather than also as citizens with shared beliefs. Also, individual preferences are seen as constant rather than changeable by changes in society or culture, not to mention advertising. So the contextual and relational aspects of human existence are mostly ignored. Perhaps the most irritating half-truth is the assumption that whatever people prefer is "rational." This means that many people are supposedly rational in the United States and elsewhere when they eat themselves into obesity and poor health, engage in unsustainable consumption, and continue to increase family debt. Not a very persuasive explanation of current social trends.

The truth about prices is that they can facilitate an effective relationship between producers and consumers in determining how to allocate those resources that should be distributed through the market system. Some services, such as fire protection, for example, are not distributed through the market system, but rather through city services. Still, the market system does distribute many products and services that do have value and are worthwhile. Some are intrinsically valuable things that do have a price, but their value is not determined by their price (novels). Others are things that should have a minimum value regardless of price, but a higher price will mean a higher value (a small life insurance plan versus a larger life insurance plan). Many things should be seen as worthwhile, and their price merely reflects consumer tastes and decisions about how to allocate their resources (different types of automobiles). Price, in other words, allows consumers to choose among alternatives, and these choices provide valuable information about the range of products and services to provide. The *quality* of the products and services, however, should not solely depend on consumer preferences, as will become clear by the end of the chapter.

From an economic perspective, the mission of a corporation is quite clear. Businesses, after all, are called "for-profit" organizations. If businesses are "for-profit" then what language could be more appropriate than the language of finance to talk about corporate purpose? The problem is that the "for-profit" terminology, especially as many neo-classical economists use it, belongs to a world of individuals and systems, not a world of individuals, systems, *and* organizations. If the question of corporate purpose is about the purpose of organizations, then classical economics does not have a vocabulary to even talk about it. In his *The Wealth of Nations*, for example, Adam Smith, speaks of two (not three) players in the development of wealth: individuals and the market.

Every individual is continually exerting himself to find out the most advantageous employment for whatever capital he can command. It is to his own advantage, indeed, and not that of the society, which he has in view. But the study of his own advantage naturally, or rather necessarily leads him to prefer that employment which is most advantageous for the society ... He generally, indeed, neither intends to promote the public interest, nor knows how much he is promoting it. By preferring the support of domestic to that of foreign industry, he intends only his own security; and by directing that industry in such a manner as its produce may be of the greatest value, he intends only his own gain, and he is in this, as in many other cases, led by an invisible hand to promote an end which was no part of his intention.[1]

There is nothing about organizations in this famous passage. If there are any doubts about the absence of organizations in the classical view, then turn to R. N. Coase's famous 1937 essay on the firm. In this essay, Coase tries to answer the question of why firms exist. Why not have all economic transactions guided by price? He answers his own question by saying that coordinating some activities through organizational structures costs less than coordinating them through prices.[2] Although this answer has been debated and modified, even more interesting than his answer is the fact that he asked the question. If classical economics had had a theory of organizations, he would not have asked the question as he did.

Even though the economic landscape is filled with organizations today, the dominant economic conversations, at least in the United States, continue to repeat the individualism of previous historical periods. Milton Friedman writes, in his *Capitalism and Freedom*:

Despite the important role of enterprises and of money in our actual economy, and despite the numerous and complex problems they raise, the central characteristic of the market technique of achieving co-ordination is fully displayed in the simple exchange economy that contains neither enterprises nor money. As in that simple model, so in the complex enterprise and money-exchange economy, co-operation is strictly individual and voluntarily provided: (a) that enterprises are private, so that the ultimate contracting parties are individuals and (b) that individuals are effectively free to enter or not to enter into any particular exchange, so that every transaction is strictly voluntary.[3]

The notion of corporations as organizations having purposes just does not fit with neo-classical economic conversations because they do not have a vocabulary for the organizational dimension of corporations.

---

[1] Adam Smith, *The Wealth of Nations*, ed. E. Cannan (New York: The Modern Library, 1937), pp. 421–2.

[2] R. H. Coase, "The Nature of the Firm: Origin (1937)," in *The Nature of the Firm: Origins, Evolution, and Development* ed. Oliver E. Williamson and Sidney G. Winter (New York and Oxford: Oxford University Press, 1993), pp. 18–33.

[3] Milton Friedman, *Capitalism and Freedom* (Chicago: University of Chicago Press, 1962), p. 14.

Current work in institutional economics, on the other hand, has at least developed a place for organizations in its language. Douglass North, for example, sees organizations within the context of various types of "institutions." The institutions provide the "rules of the game in a society," and organizations capitalize on these rules to their advantage.

Organizations include political bodies (political parties, the Senate, a city council, a regulatory agency), economic bodies (firms, trade unions, family farms, cooperatives), social bodies (churches, clubs, athletic associations), and educational bodies (schools, universities, vocational training centers). They are groups of individuals bound by some purpose to achieve objectives ... Both what organizations come into existence and how they evolve are fundamentally influenced by the institutional framework.[4]

While North does recognize the existence of organizations, it remains unclear if his vocabulary is refined enough to clearly distinguish between individuals and organizations. For example, he defines economic organizations as "purposive entities designed by their creators to maximize wealth, income, or other objectives defined by the opportunities afforded by the institutional structure of the society."[5] Are the purposes of his "purposive entities" really different than the purpose of the entrepreneurs who created them? If not, then corporate purpose is simply an individual's purpose applied to an organization.

The lack of a clear distinction between individual and organizational levels of analysis has led many to simply assume that corporations have the same motives as investors; namely, to maximize shareholder value. People also assume that corporations have a similar social function as wealthy individuals to increase total social prosperity. Sometimes the economic perspective emphasizes the micro view, increasing the wealth of individuals, and sometimes the macro view, increasing social prosperity. In either case, the emphasis is on the result or consequence of achieving a goal, rather than the goal itself.

Kaptein and Wempe's theory of corporate integrity, which ultimately sees it as the balancing of the different claims of stakeholders, suffers from a similar focus on consequences rather than purposes.[6]

---

[4] Douglass C. North, *Institutions, Institutional Change and Economic Performance* (Cambridge: Cambridge University Press, 1990), p. 5.
[5] Ibid., p. 73.
[6] Kaptein and Wempe, *The Balanced Company*, p. 272.

This conclusion follows quite logically from their assumption that the reason for a corporation's existence is efficiency.[7] Following Ronald Coase's rationale for the existence of firms, their framework cannot entertain the notion that corporations are types of organizations that have their own purposes in society. To be fair to Kaptein and Wempe, it is true that they do mention that corporations "exist to produce goods and services in the most efficient way possible," but the emphasis on efficiency so dominates their approach to corporate integrity that the final purpose or mission of corporations is not the production of goods and services, but the balancing of stakeholder claims for everyone's mutual advantage.[8] In such a scheme, the management of consequences becomes the corporation's mission.

What is left out in conversations that begin with the classical or even Coase's economic interpretation of corporations is the meso or organizational understanding of purpose. The source of much of the confusion could be that such terms as "for-profit," which originally referred to individuals, are now commonly used to define business organizations.

In *The American Heritage Dictionary*, "for-profit" is defined as: "Established or operated with the intention of making a profit: a for-profit hospital."[9] Key to this definition is the notion of intention. To say that individuals intend to establish or operate a hospital for profit, however, is not the same as to say that the hospital, as an organization, intends to make a profit. If a human person has intentions, it usually means that the person is motivated to do something. Behind the motivation are desires, which originate from our situated embodied existence. Organizations are not situated in a similar way. They are not part of the animal kingdom. They cannot be motivated by profit, because they do not have motives. Profit may motivate an individual to start a company or to work for one; it cannot "motivate" a corporation. This is not to say that all entrepreneurs are motivated by profit. As Amartya Sen reminds us, non-profit motives have played a large part in the creation of successful businesses.[10] Still, the main point here is that even though our everyday talk continues to call organizations

---

[7] Ibid., p. 164.
[8] Ibid., p. 165.
[9] *American Heritage Dictionary of the English Language*, p. 715.
[10] Amartya Sen, "Does Business Ethics Make Economic Sense?" *Business Ethics Quarterly*, vol. 3, no. 1 (January, 1993), p. 50.

"for-profit" or "nonprofit," this terminology actually refers to an individual's not a corporation's purpose.

A second reason for not transferring an individual's profit motives to an organization is that motives or intentions do not create a good standard for evaluating conduct, at least not in the world of work. Say that I am deeply motivated by profit and decide to become a medical doctor. Should not the quality of my work be judged by my performance as a doctor, rather than my motivation for becoming a doctor? Furthermore, even if I did become wealthy, that would not necessarily mean I was a "good" doctor. Good personal character and professional competence, of course, are both morally relevant, but they are not the same. The same is true for corporations. People may establish corporations for various reasons, but our evaluation of them as organizations should take into account what they were designed to do.

A key reason for considering the purpose of corporations is that a corporation's worthwhile purpose serves as a guide for making good decisions. The idea here is that if the purpose is good, and a proposed action aligns with that purpose, then the action has integrity in the sense that it fits with the corporation's good purpose. This is the meaning of integrity as consistency between what one strives for and what one does. Profit, however, does not have a normative quality that allows it to serve as a reliable guide for deciding what to do. Who wants to praise a company for having integrity simply because it made a lot of money? It all depends on how the money was made. Profit does play a crucial role in organizations, but that is true of both for-profits and nonprofits. Actually the difference between what we call for-profit and nonprofit organizations is not as great as the language of economics would lead one to believe, at least not on the organizational level of analysis, as later sections will demonstrate.

This economic perspective fails to fully consider the reality of organizations and how they differ from individuals. Furthermore, it does not include a concept of purpose that would serve as a "good" guide for evaluating the integrity of corporate decisions. The management perspective overcomes the first failure, and comes close to rectifying the second.

The management perspective of corporate purpose

There are managers today who approach corporations from the economic perspective, and manage as if corporations existed solely to make money, sometimes for themselves. Stock options have tempted some managers to focus on increasing the value of their stocks rather than realizing the purpose of the corporation. This view, however, is not universal. Other managers believe that the way to a successful company is to pursue a corporate purpose that attracts talent and commitment, provides focus and direction, and makes people proud of the projects in which they invest their time and energy.

In their book, *Built to Last*, Collins and Porras portray eighteen highly successful companies, each of which had some purpose other than profit.[11] David Packard, the co-founder of one of these companies, Hewlett-Packard, expresses a view that represents what can be named the management perspective of corporate purpose:

I think many people assume, wrongly, that a company exists simply to make money. While this is an important result of a company's existence, we have to go deeper and find the real reasons for our being. As we investigate this, we inevitably come to the conclusion that a group of people get together and exist as an institution that we call a company so they are able to accomplish something collectively that they could not accomplish separately – they make a contribution to society, a phrase which sounds trite but is fundamental.[12]

Another of the companies selected by Collins and Porras, Johnson and Johnson, has a credo that has become a model for responsible management. The credo expresses Johnson and Johnson's understanding of itself as a purposeful organization (see figure 4.1).

Although this credo does not directly speak of the company's purpose, it clearly gives Johnson and Johnson a distinct identity. Instead of seeing itself as an "economic organization," as the language of finance categorizes businesses, it sees itself in terms of the concrete groups of people that have a stake in its conduct: its stakeholders. If any stakeholder defines the corporate purpose more than the others, it is the people who use its products and services. Profit is a result of serving all the stakeholders well. This does not mean that profit is not important for the management perspective. It does mean that the difference between managing for-profit and nonprofit organizations is not as great as one might think. I discovered this a few years ago at a conference for travel agency managers.

---

[11] James C. Collins and Jerry I. Porras, *Built to Last: Successful Habits of Visionary Companies* (New York: HarperBusiness, 1997).
[12] Ibid., p. 56.

Our Credo
We believe our first responsibility is to the doctors, nurses and patients,
to mothers and fathers and all others who use our products and services.
In meeting their needs everything we do must be of high quality.
We must constantly strive to reduce our costs
in order to maintain reasonable prices.
Customers' orders must be serviced promptly and accurately.
Our suppliers and distributors must have an opportunity
to make a fair profit.

We are responsible to our employees,
the men and women who work with us throughout the world.
Everyone must be considered as an individual.
We must respect their dignity and recognize their merit.
They must have a sense of security in their jobs.
Compensation must be fair and adequate,
and working conditions clean, orderly and safe.
We must be mindful of ways to help our employees fulfill
their family responsibilities.

Employees must feel free to make suggestions and complaints.
There must be equal opportunity for employment, development
and advancement for those qualified.
We must provide competent management,
and their actions must be just and ethical.

We are responsible to the communities in which we live and work
and to the world community as well.
We must be good citizens – support good works and charities
and bear our fair share of taxes.
We must encourage civic improvements and better health and education.
We must maintain in good order
the property we are privileged to use,
protecting the environment and natural resources.

Our final responsibility is to our stockholders.
Business must make a sound profit.
We must experiment with new ideas.
Research must be carried on, innovative programs developed
and mistakes paid for.
New equipment must be purchased, new facilities provided
and new products launched.
Reserves must be created to provide for adverse times.
When we operate according to these principles,
the stockholders should realize a fair return.

Figure 4.1. Johnson and Johnson credo (with permission). (See www.jnj.com/careers/ourcredo.html)

For-profit and nonprofit management

At the "2000 Travel Learning Conference," a conference for nonprofit travel agencies, I facilitated two workshops on the difference between managing nonprofit and for-profit travel agencies and centers. Managers from both for-profit and nonprofit organizations were present. Two questions guided our conversations. First, "How important is it to work for a nonprofit (or for-profit) organization?" For some, working in a nonprofit was very important. They saw themselves as having other motives than profit or money. For most of the "for-profit" people, this was not a particularly interesting question. The second question was: "How would you describe the difference between how nonprofits and for-profits relate to stakeholders (customers, workers, suppliers, owners, and the larger community)?" In response to this question, both groups gave very similar answers. Both types of managers aimed to satisfy their customers. Each felt a responsibility to treat employees well, wanted good relationships with their suppliers, and felt obligated to return something to their communities. Each manager had boards of directors that wanted their organizations to meet high standards of performance. In other words, as Jon Van Til has argued, managers face very similar challenges in nonprofit and for-profit organizations.

Skills in leadership, resource mobilization, and management have become essential for the contemporary professional whether she or he is employed by a nonprofit corporation, a university, a church, a governmental agency, or a business organization. Differences in tradition and mission remain, of course, among these organizations, but they do not allow escape from the basic triad of skills. We live in an organizational society, and, increasingly, if we are to advance or even persist, we will be required to show our skills in collaborative leadership, business-like resource development, and effective organizational management. In a very real sense, we have all become, at least in part, businesspersons. It is just that many of us pursue our business in the organizational milieu of the third sector [the nonprofit sector].[13]

As I mentioned earlier, some participants in the workshop claimed that motivation does make a difference. Nonprofit managers, they

[13] Jon Van Til, *Growing Civil Society: From Nonprofit Sector to Third Space* (Bloomington and Indianapolis: Indiana University Press, 2000), p. 112.

claimed, are not driven by the profit motive as for-profit managers are. Lester Salamon seems to take a similar view in terms of why individuals choose either nonprofits or for-profits: "Nonprofit organizations facilitate the exercise of individual initiative for the public good just as the business corporation facilitates the exercise of individual initiative for the private good."[14] In some cases, this may be true. But some for-profit managers at the travel conference refuted this claim. They said they were just as interested in providing excellent services as managers of nonprofits. Even if there is a difference here, it is a difference about individuals, not organizations. As I stated earlier, such terms as "for-profit" and "profit motive" refer to individual, not organizational, characteristics. Companies, like other human organizations, are designed for certain purposes, and their purposes give them direction. Still, profit does play an important role in managing organizations. In fact it plays several roles.

The uses of profit in organizations

Many people use profit as a measure of success and effective management. A company that makes a profit is seen as probably well managed, which would mean that resources are effectively used and waste is minimized. Paying attention to costs and benefits could promote a stewardship of human and natural resources. From a management perspective, of course, this use of profit refers not to what one should do (purpose), but to how one should do it. This is true for both for-profit and nonprofit corporations.

Making a profit also increases a corporation's capital for growth and development, and this in turn can create wealth. Managers, as well as citizens, are certainly interested in the process of wealth creation, but in many ways this is more of a social/systemic process than the result of any one corporation. The key here is whether the wealth, to use Georges Enderle's terminology, is accumulated wealth or created wealth.[15] The accumulation of wealth refers to transferring wealth

---

[14] Lester M. Salamon, *America's Nonprofit Sector: A Primer*, second edition (New York: The Foundation Center, 1999), p. 14.
[15] Georges Enderle, "Business Ethics and Wealth Creation: Is There a Catholic Deficit?" Occasional Papers of the Erasmus Institute, 2004 Series, no.1, University of Notre Dame.

from one holder to another, such as when the Europeans accumulated the wealth of the American peoples in the sixteenth century. Wealth creation, on the other hand, increases wealth through innovation and ingenuity, such as employing technological knowledge to improve efficiency. These two types of wealth, however, are seldom totally separated, and when we consider the current state of the natural environment, which has been a major source for wealth and prosperity, it becomes clear that wealth creation needs some new thinking. Chapter 6 takes up this issue. In terms of organizational integrity, wealth creation has the same limitation as profit in terms of serving as a standard for conduct. Whether a corporation creates wealth or not does not tell us whether its actions were right or wrong. This does not mean that profit and wealth creation are unimportant; they just should not function as the organizational purpose of a corporation.

Some managers do spend much of their time worrying about profits, and in some schools of business that worry seems to occupy most of the curriculum. This is like worrying about the consequences of doing something, instead of worrying about what to do. They are both important, of course, but one needs to keep the order straight. Finance departments have the responsibility of managing consequences, and they should be supported in doing that, but not be allowed to manage the whole corporation. Some managers still know that.

Richard R. Ellsworth, for example, argues: "The leader is responsible for defining a purpose that has a significant positive effect on corporate performance, on employees, on the satisfaction of human needs, and thus on society."[16] For Ellsworth, the key issue is whether the capital market or the product market drives the business. Does business exist to raise money from the capital market or to produce products for the product market? He writes:

Purposes of increasing shareholder wealth and serving customers' needs are manifested in fundamentally different priorities in goals. One set of goals reflects the capital market, the other the product market. One set emphasizes financial returns, the other growth and innovation. For the long-term health of the company, financial goals should be the results of – not the drivers of – product-market strategies.[17]

[16] Richard R. Ellsworth, *Leading with Purpose: The New Corporate Realities* (Stanford, CA: Stanford University Press, 2002), p. 20.
[17] Ibid., pp. 121–2.

When corporations do make a profit, managers then face the question of how they should distribute it. "Who is the profit for?" Most corporations distribute some to R&D, some to company expansion, some to training, and some to investors as dividends. Profits, in other words, do not belong to the investors, but to the corporation itself. Of course managers are accountable for their decisions, but they are accountable to more than shareholders. A holistic view of integrity would show that they are accountable to all stakeholders.

In any case, the management perspective does not ignore the role of profit, but rather puts it in its place. It is seen as a result of good management, not its goal. For individuals, as well as for social systems, profit may have other functions, but for organizations, it does not lead them, it follows. Corporations are led by their purposes. And how do we know if they have selected the right purpose? Collins and Porras have an answer for this question and their answer shows how the management perspective uses the business case for justifying various types of corporate conduct.

The business case for a positive corporate purpose

In *Built to Last*, a company's purpose equals "The organization's fundamental reasons for existence beyond just making money – a perpetual guiding star on the horizon; not to be confused with specific goals or business strategies."[18] This purpose, plus a company's core values, constitutes what Collins and Porras call a company's core ideology. As they point out, highly successful companies can have different ideologies:

- Some companies, such as Johnson and Johnson and Wal-Mart, made their *customers* central to their ideology; others, such as Sony and Ford, did not.
- Some companies, such as HP and Marriott, made concern for their *employees* central to their ideologies; others, such as Nordstrom and Disney, did not.
- Some companies, such as Ford and Disney, made their *products or services* central to their core ideology; others, such as IBM and Citicorp, did not.
- Some companies, such as Sony and Boeing, made audacious *risk taking* central to their ideology; others, such as HP and Nordstrom, did not.

---

[18] Collins and Porras, *Built to Last*, p. 73.

- Some companies, such as Motorola and 3M, made *innovation* central to their ideology; others, such as P&G and American Express, did not.[19]

So does it matter what a company's purpose is? Apparently not for Collins and Porras. They write: "The fact that both Merck and Philip Morris – companies at opposite ends of the spectrum in terms of what their products do to people – show up as visionary companies guided by strong, yet radically different ideologies, raises some interesting questions. Is there a 'right' core ideology for being a visionary company?" Their answer, "No single item shows up consistently across all the visionary companies."[20] Does this mean that any core ideology is acceptable, as long as it achieves success? Although Collins and Porras may not give a positive answer to such a question, there is nothing in their book that would prevent them from doing so.

So the management perspective leaves us with an inadequate notion of purpose in terms of evaluating the integrity of corporations, because integrity requires that a corporation aim for something good. True, a corporation may not need a worthwhile purpose to be successful, but it needs one to ensure that it has integrity. Only a worthwhile purpose can serve as a standard to evaluate the integrity of corporate decisions, as well as the integrity of a corporation's place in larger social systems. To understand this meaning of corporate purpose more fully, we must move to a civic perspective.

The civic perspective on corporate purpose

As stated in chapter 1, the civic perspective has its roots in Aristotle's civic ethics, which assumed that leading a good life was only possible in the polis or political realm. Although Aristotle did not place economic activity in this realm, neither did he face modern nonprofit and for-profit corporations. Today, there is widespread agreement that non-profits belong to the civic realm or civil society, but some questions about where for-profits belong. Chapter 5 addresses these questions. The focus here is on Aristotle's notion of purpose.

The term for purpose in Aristotle's work is *telos* or final end. For humans, this purpose is happiness, which can be understood as a

---

[19] Ibid., p. 87.
[20] Ibid.

flourishing of the self in community with others. Aristotle further defines human happiness in terms of function. This notion of function, which is also defined as an agent's "characteristic action," is especially relevant for applying Aristotle's civic ethic to the idea of corporate purpose.

For just as the goodness and performance of a flute player, a sculptor, or any kind of expert, and generally of anyone who fulfills some function or performs some action, are thought to reside in his proper function, so the goodness and performance of man would seem to reside in whatever is his proper function. Is it then possible that while a carpenter and a shoemaker have their own proper functions and spheres of action, man as man has none, but was left by nature a good-for-nothing without a function?[21]

The question is a rhetorical one. Aristotle believes that human beings have a function too: "The proper function of man, then, consists in the activity of the soul in conformity with a rational principle, or at least not without it."[22] For Aristotle, there are actually two rational principles, a practical and a theoretical. The function of the theoretical, which is beyond our interest here, is the contemplation of wisdom. The function of the practical, which does have significance here, is to realize one's happiness by figuring out how to realize one's best potential (characteristic action) in particular situations.

Aristotle's discussion of function provides a fruitful way to examine the purpose of organizations. If the function of the shipbuilder is to build good ships, or the flautist to play the flute well, as Aristotle suggests, then surely we can also ask about the function of a particular organization. Our answer may not be the same as Aristotle's, but our question sounds quite similar. The answer to Aristotle's rhetorical question, "But are you good-for-nothing?" resides in what an organization is designed to do well.

This notion of *telos* has nothing to do with efficiency or other utilitarian considerations. The common identification of utilitarianism as a teleological ethic has obscured this difference. *Telos* is not about consequences or results, but about purpose – the good that agents aim for. As Alan Gewirth has written, "The desiderative ends that figure in Aristotle's ethics are therefore not primarily desired consequences

---

[21] Aristotle, *Nicomachean Ethics*, p. 16.
[22] Ibid., p. 17.

external to actions; they consist rather in the ideal of excellence itself, as this is manifested in the spirit with which one engages in virtuous purposive conduct."[23] Although consequences are important, they do not belong to the notion of integrity as purpose does. It is the purpose that specifies the function of the agent, and those actions that belong to the excellence of this function belong to it, as a part belongs to a whole. A utilitarian approach to integrity can only balance different claims, as Kaptein and Wempe demonstrate in their book on the balanced corporation.[24] Balancing different claims may hold things together, but it does not tell us whether the things held together are worthwhile or not. Only when the purpose is clear and worthwhile is it possible to really know the costs and benefits of pursuing it.

Aristotle's civic ethic seems to easily fit with our understanding of such organizations as the Red Cross or even Greenpeace. They have "good" ends or purposes to serve others and their policies and decisions can be judged in terms of their alignment with these ends. Can the same thing be said of for-profits or business corporations? What if the meaning of purpose for nonprofits and for-profits was just as similar as the similarity in managing them? An interesting hypothesis. If nonprofits and for-profits have quite similar functions in society, then the characteristics of nonprofits could help us understand how we should interpret for-profits. Our normal expectation that nonprofits have some good purpose could also be transferred to for-profits. This would allow us, as citizens, to design conversations that would examine the function of all corporations in terms of how they should work together for the public good. The hypothesis can be tested by comparing for-profits and nonprofits.

The comparison of for-profits and nonprofits

Lester Salamon points out that there are two basic types of nonprofits: those that serve their members, such as professional associations, and those that serve the public, such as organizations involved in healthcare, education, social services, arts and recreation, advocacy and

---

[23] Alan Gewirth, "Can Any Final Ends Be Rational?" *Ethics*, vol. 102, no. 1 (October, 1991), p. 91.
[24] Kaptein and Wempe, *The Balanced Corporation*.

international aid.[25] For the "public-serving" type, which is more like for-profits, Salamon offers six defining characteristics:

1. They are organizations. He does not consider temporary groups as part of the nonprofit sector. Nonprofits are chartered under state laws – they have "nonprofit" status, and therefore have the right to make contracts and perform other functions of "legal" persons.
2. They are private, not governmental, even though they may receive government grants. Governments do not control their boards.
3. Nonprofits are "non-profit-distributing." While they may make profits, the profits cannot be distributed to their "owners." They must be reinvested into the mission of the agency.
4. They are self-governing. They have their own procedures for deciding what they should do.
5. They are voluntary in the sense that, as Salamon says, they are "non-compulsory." They usually involve some degree of voluntary participation either in the corporation's activities or in its management, such as its board.
6. Finally, they are "of public benefit." Nonprofits "serve some public purpose and contribute to the public good."[26] This final characteristic combines two elements that could lead to some confusion – public benefit and public purpose. An organization could benefit the public without having a "public purpose." Benefits refer to the consequences of actions. Purposes, on the other hand, refer to what an organization strives to achieve. Any organization could be "of public benefit," depending on the consequences of its conduct. So the more important aspect of this sixth characteristic for our analysis is the reference to "public purpose."

Do for-profits share these six characteristics? For some of the characteristics, the answer is quite clear. For-profits are also organizations and private: characteristics 1 and 2. Characteristic 3 reveals a major difference. For-profits can distribute their profits to their owners. This difference reflects a legal distinction about the ownership of corporate assets. For-profits are owned privately – that is one of the meanings of a private enterprise system. The assets of nonprofits, on the other hand, do not belong to their founders or their board. They belong to the

---

[25] Salamon, *American's Nonprofit Sector*, p. 22.
[26] Ibid., pp. 10–11.

public. That is why nonprofits do not pay income taxes on their profits. These profits never become the property of those who run the organization. While for-profits can distribute their assets to owners, nonprofits must invest their assets in similar public service projects.

What about characteristics 4, 5, and 6? Charactistics 4 and 6 relate more to the notion of purpose, which is our main concern. I will briefly examine characteristic 5 and then turn to them. Are for-profits "voluntary" like nonprofits? On one level, obviously not. People work to fulfill human needs. For most of us, work is necessary. This does not mean, however, that work relationships should be compulsory. In fact, acknowledging workers as citizens requires that workers should not be forced to work. Chapter 7 on organizational leadership will explore what this means in terms of a leader-and-follower relationship. For now, it is enough to say that workers in both nonprofit and for-profit corporations have the same civic rights. Furthermore, we should not forget that nonprofits also have employees. They hired 10.9 million in 1996. As Salamon says, "If the US nonprofit sector were a separate country, it would exceed the gross domestic products of most of the countries of the world."[27] In terms of work relationships, nonprofits face the same challenge as for-profits: designing conversations that facilitate relationships of secure civic reciprocity. If there is a difference between nonprofits and for-profits here, it refers more to the motivation of individuals than to the relationship among individuals at work. So we are left with characteristics 4 and 6. Are business corporations self-governing organizations with a public purpose? These two characteristics will be handled separately.

Business corporations as self-governing organizations

In the earlier analysis of corporate social responsibility, corporations were presented as moral agents. I argued that because corporations have their own decision making structures, have choices, and justify them with corporate reasons, it made sense to treat corporations as moral agents. So it would seem to follow that they are also "self-governing organizations." What was not addressed then, but can be addressed now, is the key argument against this view. Responding to the criticism will actually help to clarify the meaning of corporations as self-governing organizations.

---

[27] Ibid., p. 21.

The current controversy about the agency of corporations began with Peter French's book, *Collective and Corporate Responsibility*.[28] The key contribution of French's work, it seems to me, was to point out that corporations had an "Internal Decision Structure."[29] The structure is constituted by procedural rules and policies. It provides a process, in other words, for the corporation to make a decision. French, however, also argued that the corporation could be seen as an intentional person.[30] The controversy has largely been over whether French's attribution is justified. Are corporations persons with intentionality?

Although people have taken a number of positions on the moral status of corporations, perhaps the most persistent critic of French's position has been Manuel Velasquez, who has recently taken up the debate again in the *Business Ethics Quarterly*.[31] In this article, Velasquez defends what he calls the "individualist" view of responsibility, which holds that only individuals in an organization can be held morally responsible.[32] He uses the National Semiconductor case to illustrate his point. National Semiconductor had manufactured and sold to the Department of Defense twenty-six million computer chips that were used in the guidance systems of nuclear weapons, guided missiles, and rocket launchers. It turns out that these computer chips had not been as rigorously tested as was required. Furthermore, some managers falsified documents to cover up the mistake. Other managers refused to participate in the cover-up. In the end, National Semiconductor agreed to pay $1.75 million in penalties for defrauding the government. What is especially interesting in this case is that Charles Sporck, the company's CEO, refused to give the names of the individuals who were involved in the fraud. He argued that the corporation was responsible, not individuals. Velasquez quotes him as saying, "We feel it's a company responsibility, [and this is] a matter of ethics."[33] In the end, no individuals were ever held liable for the crime, only the company.

[28] Peter A. French, *Collective and Corporate Responsibility* (New York: Columbia University Press, 1984).
[29] Ibid., p. 39.
[30] Ibid., p. 89.
[31] Manuel Velasquez, "Debunking Corporate Moral Responsibility," *Business Ethics Quarterly*, vol. 13, no. 4 (2003), pp. 531–62.
[32] Ibid., p. 531.
[33] Ibid., p. 535.

It might seem that the best course of action would have been to hold both the company and individuals responsible, especially those individuals who chose to cover up the fraud. Velasquez takes another approach. He believes that only individuals should be held responsible, because only individuals have the capacity for moral agency, which requires a conscious mind.[34] Velasquez's argument, like French's original essay, focuses on the ontological status of moral agency. Human moral agency is grounded, for Velasquez, in the desires, beliefs, and motives of a conscious mind. Organizations certainly do not possess these. So Velasquez's argument seems valid as long as one requires intentionality for moral agency. The fact is, however, that moral agency can also be grounded in specific communicative practices, such as the practices of corporate decision making. Furthermore, the questions of intention or conscious mind belong much more to the post office model of communication, which sees isolated individuals disconnected from each other, than to the contextual model, which sees individuals involved in a common process of living in communicative structures. Both French's and Velasquez's grounding of corporate moral agency in a foundational theory of organizations, in other words, is unnecessary. Corporate moral agency can be grounded in the communicative practices that evolve through persons participating in the ongoing conversations that constitute an organization's existence.

If organizations' communication patterns are designed so that the people who participate in those patterns work together in a decision making process, and if the process is guided by the organization's purposes rather than the purpose of the individuals involved, then it makes sense to see the decision as a corporate decision. Just as a democratic assembly can make a decision for the community it represents, so also can a group of corporate personnel when they have the necessary corporate structures and guidelines. The notion of strong democracy, as described in the last chapter, invites citizens to participate in a process that transforms their private interests into public concerns, and to make public decisions based on what is good for all. Corporate deliberations are not much different, except that they would use corporate purposes, policies, and procedures.

---

[34] Ibid., p. 546.

One reason for insisting on the moral agency of corporations is that it allows us to expect corporations to make a response to their mistakes. What happens when we make a mistake? First of all, we get blamed for doing something wrong. This blame assumes that we could have done otherwise, and sometimes we could have if we had been more thoughtful. In any case, an appropriate response to blame is to repair the harm we have done, and then to make sure it does not happen again. National Semiconductor, for example, did repair some of the harm. The fine could be interpreted as such, but, even more significantly, they could redesign their procedures so this type of mistake would not happen again. If we only blame individuals, as Velasquez suggests, then we can only ask individuals to change, and yet, in many cases, it is the organizational verbal and nonverbal communication patterns that need to change.

Seeing organizations as multiple ongong communication patterns enables us to see how patterns enable decisions and how changing patterns could also change future decisions. Determining who is included in the process, what standards are applied, how processes are monitored, what happens to disagreement or collusion, will determine the risk of making mistakes and the chances of doing it right. In some cases, individuals can also increase their chances of doing something right by examining their patterns of conversation. Both individuals and organizations have the capacity to act as moral agents, even though organizations will always require human participants in their communicative patterns to maintain and to change them. Given this view of corporate moral agency, for-profits can be understood as self-governing organizations, which was characteristic 5 of nonprofits. Do they also have a public purpose? The answer to this question requires us to examine different meanings of the notion of purpose.

Business corporations and public purpose

The notion of purpose is used quite loosely in everyday conversations. It is attributed to things, to persons, and to organizations. To understand the significance of corporations as purposeful organizations, these different meanings must be sorted out. To distinguish between the purpose of things and of persons, examine the following statements: "The purpose of the traffic light is to control the flow of traffic." In this sentence, purpose refers to what the traffic light was designed to do. What about this sentence: "The purpose of the law is to maintain order." Purpose here could refer to either the function of law in society, or to the intention of lawmakers, or to both. In any case, the purpose of the law, and of traffic lights, is quite different than the purpose of persons. For persons, purpose serves as a guideline for their decisions. Laws and traffic lights are not decision makers, or agents, although both may help us make decisions. Actually, traffic lights can tell us what to do, but they do not make decisions themselves. In their book on corporate strategy and ethics, Freeman and Gilbert give a definition of a person's purpose that clearly distinguishes it from the purpose of things.

Persons have values, which collect themselves into purposes and give rise to projects, which, in turn we try to realize through exchange with others. Projects are fundamentally concerned with commitments to certain ends, which the individual perceives as being of value. Indeed, to describe an individual is to recognize the unique relationship between that person and his or her ends.[35]

The source of a person's purpose, in other words, is his or her commitment or intentions. Since things do not have commitments, agent-centered purposes are quite different from non-agent-centered purposes (see figure 4.2).

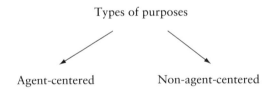

Figure 4.2. Agent and non-agent purposes

Given these two different types of purposes, the next question is whether organizations are more like laws and traffic lights or like persons in terms of their status as agents. Gilbert and Freeman believe that corporations are not like persons. For them, corporations exist only as a means for personal ends, perhaps something like laws or traffic lights.[36] There is a sense in which corporations are like laws and

---

[35] R. Edward Freeman and Daniel R. Gilbert, Jr., *Corporate Strategy and the Search for Ethics* (Englewood Cliffs, NJ: Prentice Hall, 1988), p. 117.
[36] Ibid., p. 170.

traffic lights. They are human systems designed to perform specific functions in society. At the same time, because they are also human communities designed to make decisions, they are also agents. Their capacity to make decisions has already been established in the previous discussion of the self-governing character of both nonprofit and for-profit organizations. Granting them agency, however, does not grant them personhood. One can agree, for example, with Ted Nace's argument that giving corporations the status of legal persons has given them too much legal protection, without agreeing that corporations are nothing but, as Nace says, "merely a collection of papers."[37] Corporate agency, for nonprofits and for-profits, is determined by organizational design. In contrast to individual persons, whose purpose is a choice based on their hopes and intentions, an organization's purpose resides in the good that it is designed to pursue. So, just as there are two types of purposes – agent-centered and non-agent-centered, there are also two types of agents (see figure 4.3).

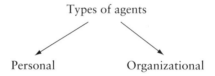

Figure 4.3. Personal and organizational agents

Although persons and organizations are different types of agents, they also have some similarities. Both of them can use their worthwhile purposes as a standard to evaluate any proposed course of action. If the purpose is good, and the means to achieve it are in alignment with it, then the means are right. Both can also enhance their integrity by clarifying their purpose and ensuring that their actions are consistent with it. An important dissimilarity is that persons can decide how to realize their purposes by themselves, whereas organizations depend on persons taking on organizational roles and working together in the organization's internal decision making structure to decide how to achieve corporate purposes. Still, talking about an organization's purpose can use the language of an agent's function much as Aristotle did when thinking about an individual's purpose.

---

[37] Ted Nace, *Gangs of America: The Rise of Corporate Power and the Disabling of Democracy* (San Francisco: Berrett-Koehler, 2003), p. 176.

When Aristotle speaks of a person's function he is not only thinking of what a person should do or achieve, but also what he or she should become. Many people today interpret this aspect of Aristotle's ethics as an "ethics of virtue."[38] For the most part, this ethical approach has been concerned not with doing, but with being – with being a virtuous person. In terms of organizations, an ethics of virtue would examine the character of the organization community, as Edwin Hartman and others have suggested. For Hartman, one of the duties of a manager is to create a "moral culture" that respects an individual's autonomy and encourages moral behavior.[39] Robert Solomon also applies the notion of virtue to corporations by interpreting them as a community. "If we consider corporations first of all as communities – not legal fictions, not monolithic entities, not faceless bureaucracies, not matrices of price/earnings ratios, net assets and liabilities – then the activities and the ethics of business become much more comprehensible and much more human."[40] The development of good corporate character – a good community – should also define a corporation's purpose. So the internal purpose of becoming a good community is somewhat different from the external purpose of producing excellent products and services (see figure 4.4).

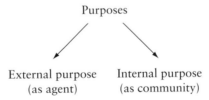

Purposes

External purpose   Internal purpose
(as agent)   (as community)

Figure 4.4. External and internal purposes

The development of a corporation's internal purpose faces the challenges of both cultural openness and relational wholeness. The corporation should become a community where individuals can develop their particular skills and capacities to contribute to its overall excellence. As corporate conversations elicit each person's contributions, they also need to promote relationships of secure civic reciprocity. The

[38] Solomon, *Ethics and Excellence*, p. 150.
[39] Hartman, *Organizational Ethics and the Good Life*, p. 146.
[40] Solomon, *Ethics and Excellence*, p. 150.

work community, in other words, has an internal purpose that matches the requirements of interpersonal integrity.

Another reason for the development of a virtuous community is that people's experiences at work will affect their attitudes toward and readiness for participation in democratic politics.[41] If the world of technology, for example, is not adequately embedded in cosmopolitan cultures and capable of supporting safe and engaging relationships, then the workplace will most likely function as a deterrent to democratic practices, not only at work, but in the civic realm as well. How we live with others at work, in other words, will affect how we live together as citizens. The pursuing of the internal purpose of a moral community that meets basic human needs and respects human rights is just as important for the civic interest in corporate integrity as the pursuing of the external purpose of delivering excellent products and services is for consumers. This is true for nonprofit and for-profit corporations.

This process of sorting out the different meanings of purpose has yielded some basic distinctions, beginning with the difference between non-agent and agent purposes, followed by the two types of agents, individuals and organizations, and ending with two kinds of organizational purposes: internal and external. Figure 4.5 shows these different meanings of purpose.

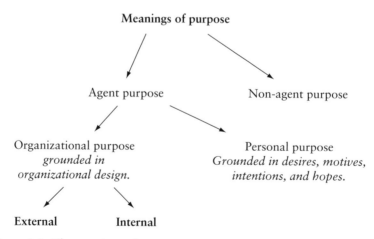

Figure 4.5. The meanings of purpose

[41] Carole Pateman, *Participation and Democratic Theory* (Cambridge: Cambridge University Press, 1970), p. 53.

Although organizational purposes belong to organizations, they cannot exist without persons who create and sustain them. Still, the purpose of both for-profits and nonprofits is grounded in what they are designed to do and become, in their functions in society. It does seem that nonprofits and for-profits can be considered as agencies pursuing worthwhile purposes. From a civic perspective, corporations do have public purposes not unlike those of nonprofits. This should not be a surprise since the civic perspective sees corporations as part of civic society and corporate members as citizens. This civic view also allows us to image not only the public purpose of individual corporations, but also how they could pursue their good purposes in cooperation with other public agencies.

Imagine that we are sitting at a town hall meeting and have taken up the topic of what the purpose of a large corporation, say a healthcare facility, should be in our area. What are the likely conclusions of such a conversation? The first conclusion will probably come fairly easily. The facility should provide the best healthcare possible for all citizens. We would also want the healthcare facility to promote secure civic reciprocal relationships in the workplace. The facility should also provide reliable reports on its economic, social, and environmental performance, as many corporations engaged in triple-line reporting are doing today. Finally, we would want the healthcare facility to cooperate with other agencies in a common effort to determine how public and private agencies can work together to meet various health needs.

Would these requirements change if the healthcare facility were a nonprofit or a for-profit corporation? Not in the least. On the organizational dimension of corporate integrity, the corporation's purpose is not determined by the source of its financing, but by its function in society.

Corporations belong to larger social systems and the quality of their products and services affects the viability of these larger systems. Pharmaceutical companies, for example, are part of a larger healthcare system, and the quality of that whole system depends in part on the quality of pharmaceutical products and services. These larger systems, whether it is the healthcare system, the transportation system, or the housing system, are complex mixes of for-profit, nonprofit, and government agencies, and all of them determine the whole. The purpose of any of these larger systems, of course, is not to make money, but to meet human needs and to enhance human life. For for-profit corporations to play their proper role in these systems, they need a worthwhile purpose, much like nonprofits do.

If the purpose of nonprofits and for-profits refers to their particular function in society rather than the role of profit (neither one are really "for" profit), then they really are quite similar. There are some differences. For-profit corporations raise funds through capital markets; nonprofit corporations raise funds through donors. This results in for-profits becoming privately owned and nonprofits becoming publicly owned. Ownership, however, does not influence purpose, at least not from a civic perspective. The private corporation's purpose is determined by its social function, and in many cases its social function depends on its place in larger social systems. A brief examination of the different types of agencies in the road and highway transportation system can illustrate this conclusion.

Private and public corporations and the road and highway transportation system

To understand the transportation system, few would recommend a visit to the large automobile corporations, such as General Motors or Mercedes Benz. These corporations are certainly part of the system, but perhaps not the most reliable authorities on its current state. Instead, one would probably go to government or nonprofit agencies, whose transportation studies are funded by taxes or donations. The process of gathering information already shows that the system consists of different agencies. This becomes even clearer when one examines who pays for the transportation system. Although it is impossible to assign specific numbers in many cases, the transportation system involves both public and private costs. In a study by the Institute of Transportation Studies of the University of California, Mark Delucchi researched the various costs of the transportation system in the United States from 1990 to 1991. The private costs, which included such items as the entire motor-vehicle car and truck fleet, insurance, and accident costs, as well as such things as travel time, came to somewhere between $807 and $919 billion.[42] There are also non-monetary costs, of course, such as deaths and suffering caused by accidents, pollution, and resource waste.

[42] Mark A. Delucchi, *The Annualized Social Cost of Motor-Vehicle Use in the U.S., 1990–1991: Summary of Theory, Data, Methods, and Results*, UCTC No. 311 (University of California, Berkeley: The University of California Transportation Center, June, 1997), p. 41.

These costs would also be billions of dollars, but are harder to measure. In contrast to these private costs, the public costs, mostly from building and maintaining the highway and road infrastructure, ranged from $131 to $240 billion.[43] The public costs were between 20 and 30 percent of the total costs. Furthermore, the public sector manages the infrastructure that the car owner requires to use her purchase from the privately owned automobile corporation.

So the transportation system, which consists of *public* freeways, roads, and streets, and *private* automobiles, relies on both public and private funds. Most of the public funds go to private firms that build the system. The purpose of these firms is to build a safe and reliable system of roads. To use this system of transportation, however, one needs to buy an automobile from a for-profit company – perhaps from Ford or Honda. Their place in the system is to provide quality cars and trucks.

Nonprofit corporations also play a significant role in this system. Groups such as Mothers against Drunk Driving, for example, have tried to decrease the number of deaths this system produces. Environmental groups have worked to decrease automobile pollution. Neighborhood groups have resisted the building of freeways through their communities. Groups such as the American Automobile Association, a nonprofit corporation, offer various services and also compete with private companies in offering automobile insurance. So this is a system dependent on government spending and law enforcement, dependent on private companies to build the roads and to provide the vehicles individuals need to use the public system, and dependent on nonprofit corporations to give voice to citizens' concerns that neither the automobile companies nor the government agencies would otherwise notice. They all belong to the same transportation system as figure 4.6 illustrates.

The role of profit here is not unimportant. The profit that the system generates enables its expansion and development. It could be seen as a public benefit that the system produces, much like pollution is a public cost. The purpose of the different agencies in the transportation system, however, is not to make a profit. It is to develop a transportation system that fits with social and environmental needs. As the next chapters will show, the dimensions of social and natural integrity will

---

[43] Ibid., p. 43.

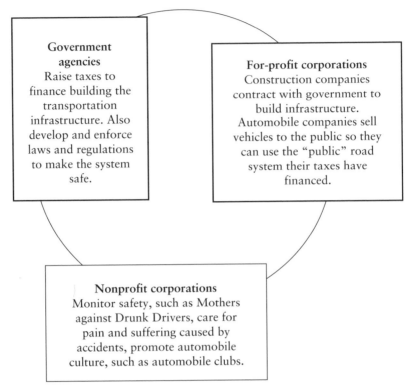

Figure 4.6. Organizational and social relationships of the transportation system

further define what types of products and services actually can fit with a future that is humane and sustainable.

Organizational integrity requires that corporations as organizations be designed to pursue worthwhile purposes. That design should be guided by what makes them worthwhile in the civic sphere. As self-governing agents, corporations should be treated as responsible agents who aim for worthwhile purposes, but, in the final analysis, the formulation of their purposes will develop in a dialogue with other agents in society, a mutual awareness of social and environmental needs, and the preferences of consumers. The economic and managerial perspectives can also contribute to developing a corporation's purpose. They can fill in what a civic perspective tends to overlook, such as a purpose that promotes wealth creation and inspires the workforce to high performance. Still, only the civic perspective is adequate for a complete evaluation of the third dimension of corporate integrity, which is grounded in a corporation's worthwhile purpose in social systems.

From theory to practice

Questions for study and reflection

1. What are the main differences between an economic, management, and civic interpretation of corporate purpose?
2. How does your company's mission or values statement compare with Johnson and Johnson's credo?
3. What do you see as the difference between nonprofits and for-profits?
4. How would you interpret the role of business from an individual, organizational, and social point of view?
5. How does an organization's purpose differ from a person's?
6. Why should corporations be held responsible for their decisions?
7. Why should citizens be interested in the internal and external purpose of corporations?

Guidelines for the assessment worksheets in the appendix

Some of the work in designing corporate integrity is the work of developing a useful vocabulary. Worksheet #8 offers an opportunity to work toward a consensus on some of the terms used in this chapter.

This chapter ends with the idea that corporations belong to larger social systems that play a role in defining their purpose. Use Worksheet #9 to explore the larger system in which a corporation you select belongs, and see how you would interpret the corporation's purpose in its larger social system.

5 | Social integrity as civic cooperation

T he previous chapter concluded that a corporation's purpose depends on its place in larger social systems. The purpose of automobile companies, for example, depends on the transportation system in which they exist. Corporations, of course, are not the only agents in these systems. Social systems also contain nonprofit corporations and government agencies. So how should these different agencies relate to each other? The idea that corporations should cooperate with communities and governments has become a standard requirement of corporate citizenship.[1] This chapter examines what cooperation would entail in the context of cities or city regions.

Although many people would agree that corporations should cooperate with various public agencies, they would not agree about the best way to talk about it. As we have seen already in previous chapters, some people make the "business case," which argues that doing good will result in doing well. Others make a case based more on reciprocity. Corporations should give something back to society for providing them with resources such as an industrious population, an educated workforce, or even the social infrastructure necessary for corporations to exist. A third argument, which was mentioned in chapter 1, is that corporations should act as citizens. This idea has been more popular in Europe than elsewhere, but it seems to be spreading. Is this the best way to talk about corporate cooperation with public agencies? The previous strategy of using our understanding of nonprofits to shed some light on our understanding of for-profits can help answer this question.

Should nonprofits be treated as corporate citizens? The distinction between thin and strong democracy, as presented in chapter 3, may be useful here. Nonprofits certainly do not practice the "thin" democracy

---

[1] Noel M. Tichy, Andrew R. McGill, and Lynda St. Clair (eds.), *Corporate Global Citizenship: Doing Business in The Public Eye* (San Francisco: New Lexington Press, 1997), p. 5.

of voting. Should nonprofits practice the strong democracy of "public thinking"? Would you agree that the Red Cross, through some type of representation, should participate in public thinking about such things as emergency services and public health? I would think so. If so, should we call the Red Cross a citizen? I doubt it. This does not mean that the Red Cross does not have a public purpose or does not exist for the public benefit. It just means it is not a citizen. It also means that we evaluate the Red Cross not in terms of how it has performed as a citizen, but instead in terms of how well it has fulfilled its public purpose. The standard, in other words, is not citizenship, but integrity. I think the same is true for for-profits or business corporations. The basis for civic cooperation, in other words, is not citizenship, but corporate integrity.

Corporate integrity does not focus so much on the identity of corporations (are they citizens or not?), as on the relationships among corporations and the other members of the whole to which they belong. Although this social whole could be defined in several ways, the definition that most clearly includes all the parts of the whole is the idea of civil society, and, even more concretely, the contemporary city. Corporations almost always exist in cities and towns. Emphasizing the corporation's urban context allows us to think of the global economy as happening in some place, rather than as merely an abstract category. Furthermore, by seeing corporations in the context of cities, we can imagine the many social and political conversations that provide the communicative context in which corporations exist. In some ways, cities and corporations are alike. They are both communities and agents. This means that corporations will have a double relationship with cities: with civic communities and with city governments. How these relationships should be designed will partly depend on the characteristics of modern cities.

Characteristics of modern cities

In the current global environment it may seem rather old-fashioned to emphasize the importance of cities. What about the notion of the information age and the idea of global networks? When you can sit at your computer in London, and someone in India provides technical support, does location have any meaning? Globalization does not occur on location, so to speak, but in networks between places. In other words, global networks provide the context for cities rather than cities providing a context for global networks. The feasibility of such a reversal depends on the connections between cities, networks, and regional places.

Cities and networks

From the perspective of virtual communication and communities, it does appear that cities have become, to use Amin and Thrift's phrase, a "field of movements."[2] Many of these movements follow the twists and turns of the global economy. Instead of being the home of corporate offices, they have become, to use another of Amin and Thrift's terms, "sites" for corporate transactions.[3] The global economy of goods, services, and information, in other words, exists as a network, located wherever people connect to it. As the urban sociologist John Friedmann has pointed out, such networks reach even farmers in Kansas:

A Kansas farmer with a university degree, hooked up to the Internet and a fax machine, with a barn full of expensive machinery, who keeps strict accounts and sells his grain on the Chicago Mark is no longer meaningfully engaged in anything we might want to call "rural life"; in an economic if not in a demographic sense, he is as fully urbanized as any medium-size manufacturer in Topeka.[4]

For the Kansas farmer, modern technology has made the economic dimension of urban life accessible. Anywhere, anytime, people can participate in the global economic network, at least in theory.

This expansion of cities into virtual space, however, is only half of the story of modern cities. The other half is that cities have become gigantic. Half of the world's population now lives in cities. The ten most populous cities in the year 2015 are projected to be: Tokyo (26.4 million), Bombay (26.1 million), Lagos (23.2 million), Dhaka (21.1 million), São Paulo (20.4 million), Karachi (19.2 million), Mexico City (19.2 million), New York (17.4 million), Calcutta (17.3 million), and

[2] Ash Amin and Nigel Thrift, *Cities: Reimagining the Urban* (Malden, MA: Blackwell Publishers, 2002), p. 83.
[3] Ibid., p. 64.
[4] John Friedmann, *The Prospect of Cities* (Minneapolis and London: University of Minnesota Press), p. 4.

Jakarta (17.3 million).[5] Cities have become the location of a majority of the global population. They have become what Allen Scott has called "city-regions."[6] Maybe some people can live away from cities and participate in virtual exchanges, but most people do not. The notion of cities as networks, in other words, may have less staying power than the notion of cities as regional places.

Cities as regional places

The fact is that although the Kansas farmer may well participate in urban life while remaining on the farm, his children have probably moved to a city. Even though the Internet and other information technology makes it possible to disregard place as an important part of the global economy, this possibility has not been widely realized. As Saskia Sassen shows in her book *The Global City*, developments in financial services as well as increases in other "producer services" (services to producers rather than consumers) have led to more centralization, rather than less.[7] Even William Mitchell, in his recent *City of Bits*, which quite uncritically extols the virtues of contemporary telecommunications and the future of a "virtual" city, acknowledges that there are "vigorous centralizing forces" even in the world of cyberspace.[8] So, even if some aspects of the work of cities do become located in cyberspace, the people who do the work tend to live in cities. In modern cities, people and their organizations depend on electricity, water, and sewer systems, as well as on laws, stakeholders, and business plans. "Virtual communication" only exists as long as no one pulls the plug. Citizens remain earthlings, and so do cities.

Cities are vibrant places that provide the structures for distributing goods and services and the context for turning dreams into reality. This

---

[5] *The New York Times 2003 Almanac*, ed. John W. Wright, NewYork: Penguin Reference Books, 2003, p. 472.
[6] Allen Scott, John Agnew, Edward W. Soja, and Michael Storper, "Global City-Regions," in *Global City-Regions*, ed. Allen Scott (Oxford: Oxford University Press, 2001).
[7] Saskia Sassen, *The Global City: New York, London, and Tokyo* (Princeton, NJ: Princeton University Press. 1991).
[8] William W. Mitchell, *City of Bits: Space, Place, and the Infobahn* (Cambridge, MA: MIT Press, 1999), p. 138.

vibrancy, however, is not shared equally. Recent studies show a grow-ing gap between the urban elite (including the Kansas farmer) and the marginalized.[9] As Saskia Sassen points out, global cities are not only great concentrations of corporate power, but also great concentrations of diverse cultures and of poverty.

These disparities, as seen and as lived, between the urban glamour zone and the urban war zone have become enormous. The extreme visibility of the differences is likely to contribute to further brutalization of the conflict: the indifference and greed of the new elites versus the hopelessness and rage of the poor.[10]

During a recent visit to Caracas, Venezuela, I saw a clear example of the kind of city she is writing about: fortresses for those with property, the lack of basic services for those without. As Friedmann says, those on the periphery are poor and powerless and are on a downward-spiraling path.[11] One finds similar trends in urban areas in the United States, even if the "periphery" is not on a city's outskirts, as in many nations, but in downtown areas. In either location, the poor can become invisible to those living in a fast lane between suburban homes and city offices. In modern city-regions, such as the San Francisco Bay Area, commuters may live in one suburb and work in another, seldom encountering the growing number of people living on the edge of the developed world. The increased physical separation of the rich and poor in the past decades has paralleled an increase in the earning gap, especially since the Reagan cutbacks on social services in the 1970s.[12] The United States now has the distinction of having the greatest income and wealth disparities of any advanced industrial nation.[13] In a few decades, when for the first time in history most of the world's people will be living in cities, and when at least one in six people will be mired in extreme poverty, uniting divided cities will

[9] Saskia Sassen, "Whose City is It? Globalization and the Formation of New Claims," in *Cities and Citizenship*, ed. James Holston (Durham, NC and London: Duke University Press, 1999).
[10] Ibid., p. 193.
[11] Friedmann, *The Prospect of Cities*, p. 13.
[12] Peter Dreier, John Mollenkoph, and Todd Swanstrom, *Place Matters: Metropolitics for the Twenty-First Century* (Lawrence, KS: University Press of Kansas, 2001).
[13] Ibid., p. 13.

become a daunting global challenge.[14] In light of our understanding of integrity as "making whole," a city's integrity will depend on how we address this problem.

From a post office model of communication, it may seem like the privileged and marginalized have little to say to each other. They live in different worlds. From the contextual model of communication, however, we are all in this together. We all belong to civil society. How can corporations pursue integrity in this situation? The answer lies in two types of relationships: the relationship between corporations and civic communities, and the relationship between corporations and city governments. Reviewing recent conversations about civic society can help us assess the first type of relationship. These conversations provide two basic alternative interpretations of the corporate/city relationship: corporations can be seen *apart from* civil society or as *a part of* civil society.

Corporations and civil society

The notion of civil society has roots deep in Western history, but the development of citizen movements in former Communist countries in Eastern Europe in the 1980s brought about the current interest in its meaning. The Solidarity movement in Poland and the Velvet Revolution in Czechoslovakia, for example, showed the power of non-government movements in developing democratic alternatives to state control.[15] The emergence of various types of associations and movements created a space for participation in democratic practices not controlled by the state. Civil society, in other words, referred to a living process of participation in democratic practices beyond and sometimes in opposition to government institutions. Robert Post and Nancy Rosenblum's definition of civil society seems to reflect these recent events: "Civil society is a zone of freedom for individuals to associate with others and for groups to shape their norms, articulate their purposes, and determine for themselves the internal structure of

---

[14] Molly O'Meara Sheehan, "Uniting Divided Cities," *State of the World, 2003: The Worldwatch Institute*, ed. Linda Starke (New York: W.W. Norton, 2003).

[15] Jean L. Cohen and Andrew Arato, *Civil Society and Political Theory* (Cambridge, MA: MIT Press, 1992).

group authority and identity."[16] When one examines the literature on civil society, there appears to be more agreement on what it is (Post and Rosenblum's definition is typical) than on who belongs to it. The most controversial issue is whether businesses and corporations should be included or not. The controversy centers on different ideas about how to relate civil society, the economy, and the state.

The civic, the economic, and the governmental

The classical liberal view sees businesses and the economy as a part of civil society. "Those who see markets as classical liberals do – as places where people voluntarily congregate to exchange products of their labor for mutual benefit – will see markets as at the heart of civil society."[17] This view has some historical validity. As Tom Palmer points out:

[Civic society] was a way of life of a particular order of society. As the church asserted its independence from the secular powers, the burghers of the cities asserted their independence from both. The knightly order and the orders of the church had their peculiar characteristics, and so did the order of the burghers that began to take definite form in the eleventh century. The foundation of the way of life of the burghers was commerce, in the form of both trade and manufacturing. In contrast with the hierarchical and mystical orders of the church, commercial orders tended to equality, liberty, and rationality.[18]

The development of civil society as a place for voluntary actions and free associations does seem to be a result of the bifurcation of power in the West. As the church and the feudal lords continually contested each other's power, a third sphere of commerce developed that was not completely controlled by either of them. This development, however, does not tell us much about how we should see civil society today, especially when we consider the enormous power of contemporary corporate actors.

---

[16] Robert C. Post and Nancy L. Rosenblum,"Introduction," in *Civil Society and Government*, ed. R. Post and N. Rosenblum(Princeton, NJ, and Oxford: Princeton University Press, 2002), p. 3.

[17] Steven Scalet and David Schmidtz, "State, Civil Society, and Classical Liberalism," in ibid., p. 28.

[18] Tom G. Palmer, "Classical Liberalism and Civic Society: Definitions, History, and Relations," in ibid., p. 48.

In contrast to the liberal view, others see corporations as well as governments as belonging to their own separate spheres, instead of belonging to civil society. Cohen and Arato, for example, write:

Political and economic society generally arise from civil society, share some of its forms of organization and communication, and are institutionalized through rights (political rights and property rights especially) continuous with the fabric of rights that secure modern civil society. But the actors of political and economic society are directly involved in state power and economic production, which they seek to control and manage. They cannot afford to subordinate strategic and instrumental criteria to the patterns of normative integration and open-ended communication characteristic of civil society.[19]

From this perspective, corporations do not belong to civil society because they operate according to different criteria than the criteria of "normative integration and open-ended communication." In regard to civic cooperation, this is a rather challenging view. If it were true, then conversations between civic and corporate leaders based on cooperation and mutual interests would seem impossible. Perhaps Cohen and Arato are referring to individual persons rather than to organizations when they write of the "actors of political and economic society." In any case, it seems just as likely today that corporations as purposeful organizations *should be required* to engage in "patterns of normative integrative and open-ended communication." It all depends on what meaning we give to the notion of existing *in* civil society.

A common way to picture the relationship between corporations, civil society and government is in terms of different sectors. There is a market sector, a government sector, and what has become known as the "third sector," which includes associations not controlled by the market or government. Or, if one includes the family, then there could be four sectors – the institutions of government, businesses, families, and civil society.[20] If one could show that the market system is actually independent of civic and government relations, then it would seem that corporations could exist as creatures of the market, and remain apart from civil society. That would not necessarily make the market "uncivil." It could make it seem natural, something like the weather.

[19] Cohen and Arato, *Civil Society and Political Theory*, p. ix.
[20] Til, *Growing Civil Society*.

Instead of depending on human imagination and creativity, as civil society does, perhaps the market relies on the dynamics of supply and demand, on scarcity and competition. Although there may be some truth to this idea, it does not really explain how markets work, as the following exercise that I use in my business ethics classes demonstrates.

The exercise begins by asking the students to imagine that we are living on an island where work has to be done and we must find someone to do it. We decide to auction off different jobs, beginning with the most urgent. Before we begin the auction, I tell them that they will need as much money to live on the island as they currently need to live in our society. The first urgent job put up for bidding is the job of developing and maintaining a sewer system. I say that whoever takes this job will get rubber boots and gloves. The bidding usually begins at a salary of about $60,000 a year but usually no one takes the job until the bidding reaches $80,000 or $90,000. I then ask for a couple of people to take care of several elderly who are bed-ridden. They need to be turned daily, or they will get bedsores, and require twenty-four-hour care. Again, none of the business majors or other students want to do this type of work for less than $80,000 or $90,000. I auction off a few other jobs, such as someone to run a slaughterhouse to prepare meat for the rest of us, someone to pick the strawberries in the fields, and someone to clean our offices and stores. All these jobs go for more than $70,000 or $80,000. Then I turn to some office jobs, such as a job keeping track of income and expenses in running our community: an accountant. Some student will usually do that for around $40,000. I also develop a job for a philosopher – some-one who sits around and thinks about things, and sometimes teaches others. Almost without exception, a student will either volunteer to do that without pay, or for a minimum wage.

Once the auction is over, I ask how they would explain the difference in wages between what they needed for unpleasant jobs and what the people who do these jobs in the United States actually receive. According to market conditions of supply and demand, and to the idea of individuals acting on their preferences, those jobs that few preferred would command a higher salary. It takes a higher salary to attract someone to do something that most preferred not to do. On the other hand, jobs that were preferred by many could secure the needed job applicant a lower salary. The choices made seem to make "economic sense." But that is not how the real economy works. In the real world slaughterhouse workers make the minimum wage and accountants make high salaries. Students are usually puzzled by this contradiction. Their economic perspective could not provide a solution. To understand the setting of wages in the United States, we need not only an economic language, but also a political language, so we can understand not only the economics, but also the politics of the market. In other words, one can only understand the behavior of individuals in the market if one sees the market as embedded in social relations.

The economy is not an independent system, but rather a subsystem embedded in other systems.[21] Furthermore, it is a subsystem that relies on other systems for its existence. As John Keene has written: "no business, global business included, can properly function as business unless it draws freely upon, and nurtures, the non-market environment of civil society in which it is more or less embedded, or seeks to embed itself."[22] Kenneth Boulding's concept of three different types of strategies for managing systems can help us picture the relationships among the economy and other social systems.

Civil society and Boulding's three types of system strategies

Kenneth Boulding's triad of threat, exchange, and integration presents three different ways to manage a system.[23] The threat strategy says either you do this or you will be punished. The exchange strategy says if you do this, then you will get this in return. And the integration strategy says that we can do it together. It may seem that these three strategies parallel the three sectors of society: the governmental (threat), economic (exchange), and civic (integration). In a sense this is true, but a closer examination shows that each of these sectors contains all three strategies. Any organization, in fact, will have all three, but not always in the same proportion.

Let us say that we want to manage a community development project and we have these three strategies at our disposal. How should we use them? We could begin with increasing the power of threat, such as increasing the police force in neighborhoods that have a high crime rate.

---

[21] Peter Ulrich, "Ethics and Economics," in *Ethics in the Economy: Handbook of Business Ethics*, ed. Laszlo Zsolnai (Oxford: Peter Lang, 2004), pp. 9–37.
[22] John Keene, *Global Civil Society?* (Cambridge: Cambridge University Press, 2003), p. 82.
[23] Kenneth Boulding, *Three Faces of Power* (New York: Sage, 1990).

Will this develop community? Not necessarily. Threat by itself may be experienced as tyranny. You cannot order people to care for their community. On the other hand, if the streets are unsafe, threat may be a way to increase safety. Threat can protect the development of community, even though it cannot facilitate that development by itself. The rule of law, in other words, is necessary, but not sufficient for building community.

Since threats cannot develop community, we could try exchanges. We can reward certain types of behavior and show that people's contributions are noticed. Although this may have short-term positive effects, people may soon believe that others are only interested in community development for the money. This could dissipate any sense of common endeavor – any sense of community. Exchanges by themselves could finally pull the community apart rather than pull it together

Only integrative strategies can lay a foundation for community. They provide a basis for people to participate in common projects and endeavors. Developing educational programs for families or facilitating neighborhood associations to address common concerns would be examples of integrative strategies. As these integrative powers are developed, the threat and exchange powers can also be introduced. The rule of law can protect community building. The power of exchange can provide rewards to those who contribute and incentives for individual performance. In many cases, exchange strategies can encourage the efficient use of resources to achieve important goals. For community building to succeed, all three organizers are necessary, but they will only be sufficient when combined in the right way.

Observing how these three strategies of threat, exchange, and integration interact in the development of communities makes it clear that seeing the economy, government, and civil society as separate sectors is quite inadequate. They are much more closely connected and interdependent. Another way to think about their relationships is to look at them contextually.

A contextual view

How should Boulding's triad of threat, exchange, and integrity be arranged contextually? Which one of the three should contain the other two? Relationships of integrity would be the obvious choice, if for no other reason than strategies of exchange and threat are self-destructive by themselves. All successful exchanges – especially competitive exchanges – require a context of cooperation to maintain the processes of exchange. Competition requires cooperation, or it turns into war. Threat also requires some integrative context or it becomes tyrannical. At the same time, the threat strategy is needed to protect the process of integration and exchange. So the proper relationships among the three strategies would be pictured as shown in figure 5.1. In this figure, the integrative strategy or set of relations provides the context for exchange relations. At the same time, the threat strategy protects both circles, but does not dominate them. This type of contextual picture could easily be transferred to a contextual picture of a civic triad that shows the connections among civil society, market exchanges, and the rule of law (see figure 5.2).

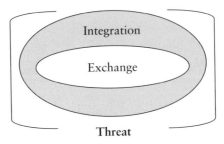

Figure 5.1. Boulding triad

Figure 5.2. A civic triad

For this figure to accurately picture the three relationships, civil society needs to be seen as both containing market exchanges and restraining the rule of law, so government does not become tyrannical, but does protect civil society and the market. Given this double duty of civil society, the picture does illustrate that market exchanges, and therefore corporations, belong to and are supported by civil society. The picture also supports the notion of a civil economy, as Severyn Bruyn has defined it:

By civil markets, we mean systems of exchange in which competing actors agree to standards for the common good and are capable of enforcing them. This means situations in which trade, professional, labor, and community associations set codes of conduct, require certification procedures, and establish neutral observers (monitors) and regulatory systems that are authorized to issue penalties for members who break contracts. For a "free market" to operate with civility, it must be based on certain principles of justice and rules of fair competition.[24]

As Bruyn points out, progress has been made in developing a civil economy, such as the establishment of the International Organization for Standardization in 1947, the United Nations Conference on Trade and Development in 1964, and the Coalition for Environmentally Responsible Economies in 1989. These developments, as well as many other forms of responsible corporate activities, provide evidence that markets can become civil, and in fact have a responsibility to work with other civic actors to maintain the civic realm.

Whether such civility will become a social norm, of course, is an open question. When one thinks contextually, it is easy to imagine the reversal of the container and the contained. Instead of civil society serving as the context for the market, the market becomes the context of civil society. All relations would then become relations of exchange and the necessary relationships of trust and integration would dissipate. When corporations control the media, the entertainment industry, the press, and many other resources significant for the maintenance of a strong civil society, we all face the risk that what was supposed to remain within the container becomes the container. To prevent this from occurring, city governments must become active guardians of democratic practices. This brings us to the second question concerning corporate city relationships – the relationship between corporations and city governments.

---

[24] Severyn T. Bruyn, *A Civil Economy: Transforming the Market in the Twenty-First Century* (Ann Arbor: University of Michigan Press, 2000), p. 207.

Corporations and city government

As expected, the relationships between corporations and city governments are quite varied and complex. To sort out some of the more prevalent types of relationships, I have developed six relational models. These models are not mutually exclusive, and some existing corporate/city relationships could contain more than one. The six are the ownership model, the unconscious model, the business leader model, the competitive market model, the philanthropic model, and the partnership model.

The ownership model

Sometimes, the corporate/city relationship has been determined simply by who owns what. Whoever owns the land controls what happens on it. The notion of a "company town" fits this type of relationship. Potlatch Lumber Company, for example, constructed the town of Potlatch, Idaho, at the turn of the nineteenth century. They built the homes, the stores, and even the churches: one church for Catholics and another for Protestants. By 1906 the population had reached 1,000. Later, in 1950, the company, now in the hands of the lumber giant Weyerhaeuser, decided to sell their town. At the time, they owned 267 houses, two apartments, thirteen business buildings, and two churches. The churches, as well as the library, fire hall and fire truck were donated to the community. Residents purchased their homes, and in 1952 Potlatch became a village. In the following year, for the first time, residents voted in an election for city council.[25]

Another company town had a somewhat different transition from company control to citizen control. In 1989 the Illinois Supreme Court ordered the Pullman Company to divest itself of all its property in Pullman, Illinois, that was not used for manufacturing purposes.[26] George Pullman, the founder of the Pullman railroad car company, had built the town for his workers, in the same way as Potlatch had been built. In this case, however, the courts were asked to address the relationship between corporate ownership and democratic control.

---

[25] See www.potlatch.com/historicalsociety/chapt_05.asp, p. 1.
[26] Michael Walzer, *Spheres of Justice: A Defense of Pluralism and Equality* (New York: Basic Books, 1983), p. 297.

The court decided that the ownership of property should not replace the citizens' rights to self-government – to democratic participation in deciding how to live together. Although one may still find "company towns" today, they serve as representatives of pre-democratic rather than democratic institutions. The second model represents somewhat of an opposite attitude toward cities. They never even appear on the business community's radar screen.

The unconscious model

Like the ownership model, the unconscious model overlooks the civic aspects of cities, not because of the corporation's interest in controlling the city, but just the opposite. In this model, the corporation does not even recognize the city's existence. One can observe various manifestations of this model, from the hostile takeover of one corporation by another to the planting of giant chain stores on the edge of cities that drain economic assets from city centers.

A notorious example of a hostile takeover was the case of Pacific Lumber Company in 1986. Pacific Lumber Company was something like the Potlatch Lumber Company just mentioned. It had a very paternalistic approach toward its workers and the local community. At the same time, it had a rather enlightened policy for cutting trees. It did not engage in clear cutting and it protected 2,000-year-old redwoods as a national treasure. These lumber assets, plus the workers' retirement fund and a strong profit margin, made it a good candidate for a hostile takeover. Charles Hurwitz and his firm Maxxam, Inc. offered $10 more a share than the shares' stated value, and the board agreed to a buyout. Afterwards, Hurwitz began a much more aggressive harvest of the forests, used the workers' pension funds to pay off some of his junk bonds, and created an enduring conflict between the lumber workers and environmentalists.[27]

Although one would not call the building of a giant Wal-Mart store on the edge of a small town a hostile takeover, its effect is somewhat similar. Such practices commercialize the relationship between cities and corporations by treating everyone only as consumers. The public

[27] Lisa H. Newton, "The Chainsaws of Greed: The Case of Pacific Lumber," in *Case Studies in Business Ethics*, fourth edition, ed. Thomas Donaldson and Al Gini (Upper Saddle River, NJ: Prentice Hall, 1996).

space of the city becomes deserted, except for antique stores, and the private space of the shopping mall becomes the place to hang out. Once again people are seen as part of the commercial enterprise, only this time as consumers rather than workers, and the city becomes a commercial resource. It is all about commerce. This is in sharp contrast to a somewhat more traditional model of the business leader, the third model.

The business leader model

The key assumption of the business leader model is that those who know how to run a business also know how to run a city. Business leaders become intensely involved in developing plans for the city and working with city leaders to implement them. Their plans, as one would expect, flow from their interests in promoting a positive business environment, which has sometimes been at the expense of city residents. The business leader model was used extensively in many urban areas in the United States during the urban renewal movement following the Second World War.

Urban renewal began in the United States when Congress passed the Housing Act of 1949 as a response to the deterioration of city centers. Urban renewal programs rested on the assumption that the path to vital cities was through commercial development. Slums were cleared, high-rise office buildings and cultural complexes were built, and the skylines of major cities in the United States were forever changed. Much of the planning was top-down, without consideration for the people who were displaced by business and cultural centers. Each city has its own story about urban renewal, but the consensus seems to be that the renewal projects worked more to the advantage of people who lived in the suburbs than those who lived in the cities. In fact, renewal projects did not so much renew housing for city residents as replace them. According to the authors of *Place Matters*, "between 1956 and 1972, urban renewal and urban freeway construction displaced an estimated 3.8 million persons from their homes."[28] Many of these people, of course, did not have the resources to move into expensive suburbs, but instead moved into low-quality city housing.

---

[28] Dreier, Mollenkopf, and Swanstrom, *Place Matters*, p. 118.

The Bay Area Council (BAC) in the San Francisco Bay Area provides a good example of the business leader type of corporate/city relationship. It not only participated in urban renewal during the 1960s, but continues to be active today. Founded in 1945 by business leaders, the Bay Area Council began developing plans and policies for the whole San Francisco Bay region, from San Jose to Santa Rosa. Its strategy has been one of funding research and providing proposals for local governments to implement. Chester Hartman, an activist and author, writes that the Bay Area Council shaped the current distribution of types of commerce in the Bay Area and then promoted a public transit system to connect them. In describing the BAC plan, he writes:

BAC also published industrial location surveys and directories that helped distribute the various economic functions "rationally" throughout the region. Thus, the East Bay is the locus for heavier industry, chemicals, and petroleum and also serves as the regional transportation hub. The Peninsula and South Bay areas for light manufacturing, electronic, and the aerospace industry. Alameda, Contra Costa, and San Mateo Counties support recent secondary office development. San Francisco is the center for administration, finance, consulting, and entertainment. An elaborate network of freeways and the Bay Area Rapid Transit (BART) system link all sectors of their regional economic unit to its administrative heart, the city.[29]

Some of the plans of the Bay Area Council were probably quite good. Some were never implemented, such as a freeway through Golden Gate Park, which is San Francisco's large city park. The business leadership model rests on the assumption that business leaders know what is best for the city, and city governments should follow their lead. The issue is more about who controls the city than who has the best plans. Still, even though this model may not be the ideal relationship between corporations and cities, it has probably produced better results than the next model, the competitive market model.

The competitive market model

This model construes the corporate/city relationship as similar to the competitive relationships among suppliers. Cities, in other words, are

---

[29] Chester Hartman, *City for Sale: The Transformation of San Francisco* (Berkeley: University of California Press, 2002), p. 6.

seen as belonging to the marketplace of exchanges. Corporations "trade" with public officials much as they trade with suppliers and customers. The basic formula is something like: "You do what I want, and I will do what you want." This type of relationship was especially prevalent in the booming 1990s when cities were competing against each other for corporate attention. City governments offered tax relief, advantageous loans, and other services for businesses to build in their cities. The authors of *Place Matters* see this type of "bidding war" among cities for business investments as a "race to the bottom" in which the tax burden shifts from businesses to residents.[30] As they point out, cities had become so accustomed to such tactics, they sometimes offered tax relief even when not necessary. In 1994, for example, the city of Los Angeles granted Dream Works, a new film company, a $75 million tax abatement to build its headquarters in the city, even though it was unlikely to locate anywhere else.[31]

Corporations are not the only players in these competitive games between cities and corporations. Cities have found they can play the game as well. They may demand what are called "exactions" from corporations, which are fees designed to offset any burdens caused by new developments. When Bayer Corporation moved to Berkeley, California, for example, they agreed to pay over $1 million for a biotechnology education program for local youth.[32] In essence, the competitive market type of corporate/city relationship assumes that each will work only in its own self-interest, so they cooperate only in getting the best deal they can. Although this competitive relationship continues today, one also finds examples of corporate/city relationships based on caring rather than competition.

The philanthropic model

In this model, corporations are seen as civic benefactors. Traditionally, this model referred to individuals, not to corporations, but more recently, corporations have set up foundations, contributed to various civic events, and promoted corporate philanthropy within the business community.

[30] Dreier, Mollenkopf, and Swanstrom, *Place Matters*, p. 100.
[31] Ibid., p. 189.
[32] See www.policylink.org/content/tools/50/73.1.asp.

Andrew Carnegie, whose name is chiseled into civic buildings throughout the United States, wrote extensively about the importance of philanthropy. He believed that those who had amassed great wealth should give most of it back to society, either through donations or taxes. In fact, he supported a strong inheritance tax. His reasoning was quite simple: "It should be remembered always that wealth is not chiefly the product of the individual under present conditions, but largely the joint product of the community."[33] His own philanthropic activity occurred primarily after he retired from Carnegie Steel Company. He did not urge the company to engage in philanthropy. Instead, he wrote about how labor was evolving to a position where they might have a greater share of the company profits. Carnegie proposed that some day, corporate wealth could be created by, and distributed to, both employees and employers.[34] He did not propose that some of this corporate wealth should be donated to cities. Individuals who did amass great wealth, on the other hand, should give most of it back to society.

In discussions today, there is not such a clear distinction between individual and corporate philanthropy. Many corporations today have extensive philanthropy programs. The food giant, General Mills, for example, reported in their "2002 Corporate Citizenship Report" that they contributed over $66 million to community programs. The monies were distributed through three different channels: food donations, $21.7 million; corporate contributions/strategic philanthropy/social investment, $26.8 million; and the General Mills Foundation, $18.2 million.[35] In 2000, corporate foundations donated almost $3 billion in the United States.[36] Corporate giving has become a significant aspect of corporate/city relationships.

A recent development in corporate philanthropy was the creation of the "Committee to Encourage Corporate Philanthropy." Chaired by Ken Derr from Chevron Texaco and the actor Paul Newman, the

---

[33] Andrew Carnegie, *Problems of To-Day: Wealth, Labor, and Socialism* (Garden City, NY: Doubleday, Doran and Company, 1933), p. 13.
[34] Ibid., p. 67.
[35] 2002 Corporate Citizenship Report, p. 7 at www.generalmills.com/ foundation.
[36] Foundation Yearbook (2002), The Foundation Center, www.dncenter. org/research/trends_analysis/pdf/yearbook.

committee's goal is to make corporate philanthropy "an integral part of a company's mission and business practices."[37] It seems that as government spending continues to decrease, corporations have taken on the role, or at least have been given the role, of providing funds for non-profit social work that earlier might have been provided by a government agency.

Closely related to corporate philanthropy is the practice of supporting employee voluntary contributions to community projects and non-profits. In the past decades, many corporations have given employees time off for civic participation. The time off may be for fund raising, but more often it is to participate in educational or nonprofit programs to help the disadvantaged. In 2000, for example, the online newsletter by the "Committee to Encourage Corporate Philanthropy" carried an article about Enron. Not only does the article state that Enron gave over $10 million a year to worthy causes, but also that it supported its employees volunteering to do work in schools and other civic organizations.[38] Enron's case may be exceptional, in terms of its inconsistent conduct, but it does make one wonder if a corporation's philanthropic programs serve as a reliable indicator of corporate integrity. After considering the partnership model, this issue can be addressed.

The partnership model

In many cities today, corporations have joined with community groups and government agencies to address common economic, social, and environmental problems. One finds quite a variety of such partnerships.

One of the most famous is the Shorebank Corporation, which celebrated its twentieth anniversary in 1993. Shorebank Corporation combined nonprofit and for-profit organizations to serve the housing and economic needs of the people in a section in Chicago called South Shore.[39] Its mission was to reverse the "disinvestment" of corporations

---

[37] See www.corphilanthropy.org.
[38] Charles Olson, "Enron Philanthropy: Smart, Bold, Ambitious, Innovative, United," at www.corphilanthropy.org.
[39] Richard P. Taub, *Community Capitalism: The South Shore Bank's Strategy for Neighborhood Revitalization* (Boston, MA: Harvard Business School Press, 1994).

from the South Shore area. It accomplished this by creating financial institutions that provided loans for housing and small business projects for the community and attracted investments from outside the community. These outside investments, from corporations and individuals, provided the capital for community development, and also provided a return for the investor. This was not called a "partnership," but in fact it functioned as one, with each side cooperating with the other to improve the lives of citizens.

Another example of a partnership is the current work of the Bay Area Council (BAC), which was mentioned earlier under the business leader model. The BAC appears to have evolved from the business leader model to a partnership model. This seems especially true when one reviews the following list of projects from a 2003 promotional brochure:

- Managing the regional Transportation Initiative in cooperation with 15 partner organizations . . .
- Managing the Bay Area Alliance for Sustainable Communities . . .
- Leading the Community Capital Investment initiative to attract investment into the poorest neighborhoods in partnership with community stakeholders.
- Sponsoring and staffing the Bay Area Education and Workforce Preparation Council.
- Mobilizing support for airport infrastructure improvement, international trade promotion, and workable privacy protections.

Alliances among corporations, government agencies, and citizens' action groups are common throughout the world today. One can find multiple examples of corporate/city partnerships in the World Business Council for Sustainable Development's book, *Walking the Talk*, as well as other books.[40] The growth of these partnerships reveals the growing awareness that the different agencies involved in improving urban life cannot succeed without mutual support and cooperation.

Reviewing the six different models of corporate and city relationships, how can we tell which ones promote corporate integrity and which ones do not? That decision depends on two different and yet

---

[40] Holliday, Schmidheiny, and Watts, *Walking the Talk*. There are also many websites that provide cases of corporate partnerships, such as the Business for Social Responsibility website at www.bsr.org.

related topics: the interdependence of corporations and cities, and what cities are good for – in other words, their mission.

The interdependence of corporations and cities

Of the many revelations that occurred on September 11, 2001, few were more visible than the interdependence of businesses and civic organizations. The World Trade Center towers stood as the pinnacle of global business in New York City. The airplanes that destroyed them attacked both the business and the civic community, and both responded. New York City firefighters and private security guards ran to save lives. Millionaires and minimum wage employees cared for each other as they tried to escape. No one distinguished between an "economic realm" and a "civic realm" on that day. When the towers fell into their civic context, what later became known as "ground zero" designated both a city's wound and a business disaster.

This interdependence between corporations and cities, however, is not equal, because corporations exist *in* cities but cities do not exist *in* corporations. Try to imagine corporations without cities. Take away the law enforcement agencies that enforce the laws. Take away the laws. Take away the moral communities that educate people to tell the truth, keep their promises, and expect others to do the same. Take away the order of stable societies. What will happen to corporations then? Either they will withdraw and wither away, or they will become fiefdoms, with their own security forces to protect them. Here, unfortunately, we do not need to use our imagination. The development of corporate fortresses in many cities has already happened. Still, until corporations are allowed to have their own judicial system and educational system, and can sustain many other public goods, they remain dependent on the city and the state in which they reside.

Corporations are dependent on cities and governments for the laws that protect them, for regulations that preserve their markets, for inspections that monitor their competition, and for the public goods that enable them to operate in good faith. Corporate development, in other words, depends on conditions that are not under corporate control. In spite of the ideology of "private" enterprise that assumes an independence from public resources, in fact, modern corporate existence depends on public resources.

Major cities today, of course, also depend on corporations. Corporations provide some of the economic base for a city's development. Today corporations are an essential part of the systemic creation of wealth and prosperity. They also provide jobs for a city's workforce. The importance of corporations for cities is what drives the competitive market model of corporate/city relations. Cities need the revenues and jobs that corporations provide. Cities may be civic communities, but they are also centers of trade and commerce. The question is whether economics or politics determines the character of civic life. For the sake of democratic institutions and self-rule, the balance must be weighted in favor of politics.

Imagine civil society as a drama, with many different actors, and the actors are writing and re-writing the script as events transpire. The title of the drama refers to the city, not corporations. Corporations have a part in the drama of city life. Corporations exist "in" this drama as actors, usually with important roles, but they should not control the play. The city directs the play. Other actors are also on stage and have their parts. The future acts of the play, of course, are not yet written. There is a lot of impromptu acting. And yet the city as a moral agent and a political entity has the responsibility to direct the play in the general direction of becoming the kind of community it envisions. The drama, in fact, is about the city's efforts to fulfill its mission.

Corporations and a city's mission

Although cities may have quite different missions, like corporations, they must have some good purpose, and must strive to be good cities. What is a good city? For John Friedmann, an urban scholar, the city has an obligation to create an environment where every person can flourish. He writes:

Every human being has the right, by nature, to the full development of their innate intellectual, physical, and spiritual capabilities in the context of wider communities. This is *the right to human flourishing*, and I regard it as the most fundamental of human rights.[41]

The source of Friedmann's comment is Aristotle's notion of human *eudaimonen* or the flourishing of the self. For humans to have the

---

[41] Friedmann, *The Prospect of Cities*, p. 110. Italics in original.

chance to flourish, Friedmann suggests that a good city must provide socially adequate housing, affordable healthcare, adequately remunerated work, and adequate social provisions.[42] Although others may have different ideas of what is socially necessary for human flourishing, it seems clear that these four requirements should at least be accepted as issues for deliberation; that is, they should become part of the conversation.[43]

One place to look for a city's view of human flourishing, as well as what a city is good for, is to look at its mission statement or charter. In the United States, cities were chartered by the states in which they are found with the right of home rule; that is, a city's right to govern its internal affairs. The preamble of the San Francisco City Charter expresses what home rule entails:

In order to obtain the full benefit of home rule granted by the Constitution of the State of California; to improve the quality of urban life; to encourage the participation of all persons and all sectors in the affairs of the City and County; to enable municipal government to meet the needs of the people effectively and efficiently; to provide for accountability and ethics in public service; to foster social harmony and cohesion, and to assure equality of opportunity for every resident: We, the people of the City and County of San Francisco, ordain and establish this charter as the fundamental law of the City and County. [44]

A modern city, of course, can be seen as a composite of different communities or neighborhoods, but this preamble shows, I think, a city that strives to be one community – one that ensures "equal opportunity for every resident" and fosters "social harmony and cohesion." Furthermore, it makes a claim for accountability and ethics in city government and public service. No one would claim that San Francisco has always been true to this mission, but it does serve as a guideline that can be used to justify, or to critique, city policies and proposals.

Given this mission, or some variation of it for other cities, how should corporations relate to it? For one thing, they should promote integrity on the cultural, interpersonal, and organizational dimensions.

---

[42] Ibid., p. 113.
[43] For an analysis of the social conditions for self-development, see Carol Gould, *Freedom and Social Cooperation in Politics, Economy, and Society* (Cambridge: Cambridge University Press, 1988).
[44] See www.sfgov.org/site/government_index.asp.

On these dimensions of corporate life, they should design communication patterns that are open to differences and disagreement, promote secure civic reciprocal interpersonal relationships, and pursue their worthwhile purpose in the social systems in which they exist. Practicing integrity on these three dimensions will aid in fulfilling a city's mission, because the communication patterns developed inside the corporation can be used to develop appropriate relationships among corporations and other civic organizations.

If corporations meet the challenges on the cultural, interpersonal, and organizational dimensions, they will have already learned how to develop appropriate boundaries. This is especially important since the modern world of competition and technology has set up conditions where boundaries are easily overlooked. There are also pressures to influence civic processes with money or threats of withdrawal, if city officials do not appear to be moving toward "business friendly" policies. Being a part of, rather than apart from, civic society is not always easy. It requires some release from the aggressiveness that competitors sometimes promote. If corporations discover their rightful place in civil society, they will have acquired what John Keene has suggested everyone in civic society has in common:

This global civil society is a haven of difference and identity – a space of many different, overlapping and conflicting moralities. Those who dwell within it have at least one basic thing in common: they have an ethical aversion to grandiose, pompous, power-hungry actions of those who suppose, falsely, that they are God, and try to act like God.[45]

For corporations to exist in civil society, in other words, they must participate in cosmopolitan conversations that facilitate openness to differences and disagreements, and from these conversations learn how to be a part of a larger context. Corporations also need to care about the integrity of civil society and even city government. The obligation can be expressed by the following principle of civic cooperation:

Business corporations have an obligation not to prevent and sometimes to promote the mission of a city.

The "not to prevent" refers to actions or policies that stifle the democratic participation of citizens in collective self-government, such as

---

[45] Keene, *Global Civil Society?* p. 208.

exerting undue pressure on city officials or employees to influence their decisions. Of the six models of corporate/city relationships, the ownership, unconscious, and competitive models appear to violate this principle. The business leader model could fall within a broad interpretation of the principle, if it were to move close to the partnership model. The partnership and the philanthropic models come closest to not preventing the city from achieving its mission. At the same time, there is currently a danger in the United States that corporate partnerships and philanthropic activities are disempowering democratic forms of collective self-government, in some cases in collaboration with nonprofits. So what is the appropriate set of relationships among governmental agencies, nonprofits, and corporations? Each case is probably different, but to explore some possibilities let us look at some recent developments in the funding of elementary education in the United States.

Civic cooperation and the funding of public education

In 2003 the *New York Times* reported that the Bill and Melinda Gates foundation has given $31 million to nonprofit groups to start small, alternative high schools for 36,000 students. These schools will provide education for what the foundation says are the children who are "failed and forgotten" by the nation's public schools.[46] Much of their money is going to nonprofits so that they can create schools for these students. On the one hand, when we consider the urgency to help these kids, one can only praise the Gates Foundation for taking up this cause. On the other hand, when we take a civic perspective and look for the integrity in collective self-government, there seems to be a failure here. Why are public schools doing so poorly with some students? Certainly, one reason is the lack of adequate funds for educational resources. So it seems that the Gates Foundation has exactly what public schools need: money. Still, does that mean that whoever has the money should determine which children will receive needed funds for an adequate education? Few would agree with that. Who should control the funds for public education depends on how we think education should be distributed in society.

Let us assume that resources, like the funding for public education, could be distributed either by the government (state and local elected

---

[46] See nytimes.com, February 26, 2003.

school boards), by the market (the privatization of public schools), or as gifts (individuals' and corporations' donations), or by some combination of the three. What sort of distribution would promote not only corporate and civic integrity, but also the integrity of public education? Following the work of Michael Walzer, who developed a notion of justice that is designed to answer just such questions, the just distribution of funds would depend on the social meaning of the goods that the funds support.[47] Walzer uses the term "social meaning" rather than just meaning, because the meaning of goods like education is socially constructed. If we consider different types of goods or things, we probably would agree that governments should distribute some things, such as citizenship, safe neighborhoods, and shelter for the homeless. We might also agree on some things that should be distributed by the market, such as beer, vacations, or cell phones. And finally some goods should be left as gifts, either because their meaning is tied to the act of giving or because some people see possibilities that others do not. Somewhat in the spirit of the entrepreneur, such funding creates new possibilities for others to consider. So how should public education be funded? Figure 5.3 shows the options.

	Market only	Mixed	Government only	Donations
Funding of education	○ ○	○ ○	○ ○	○ ○

Figure 5.3. The funding of public education

If we could check more than one circle, how much weight should be given to each one? It depends on what public education is for? It is for several things, but foremost its purpose is to teach our children to be citizens. If we rely on donations from philanthropists to fund our public schools, then what are we teaching our children about citizenship? Excluding our elected educational officials in running our schools would seem like the last thing to do. This does not mean that non-government schools, whether religious or secular, prevent civic integrity. It does mean that their mission should fit with the mission of public education and the mission of the cities in which they exist. Although donors to public education may be useful in the short term,

[47] Walzer, *Spheres of Justice*, p. 9.

to respond to emergency situations, to the extent that they do not support the development of inclusive democratic institutions and practices they should not control conversations about public education. The right balance here will probably differ in different situations, but the guideline can be fairly clear: corporations should not erode the civic and democratic practices of public education.

Does that mean that corporations should not be concerned with public education? Not at all. They do have a legitimate interest in whether public education is providing the skills necessary for the world of work, and their counsel can be very helpful in this matter. In fact, one could make a strong business case for corporate involvement in public education. This was Logsdon and Wood's argument – corporate citizenship is necessary for the survival of capitalism.[48] This argument, however, has the downside of justifying corporate involvement only as long as it is in the interest of corporations. Corporations need to be more reliable than that. A civic perspective adds something to the picture of civic cooperation: it looks at what corporations should do in terms of corporate integrity.

For the sake of corporate integrity, corporations sometimes do have an obligation to promote a city's mission because they are a part of civil society. That is the second half of the principle of civic cooperation. So what are some ways they might promote public education? First of all, we should examine how their policies and procedures already either prevent or promote public education. Consider the following questions: Does the corporate culture promote learning so that employees see education as important for themselves and therefore for their children? Are employees expected to work so many hours a week that they have little time to become involved in their children's education? Do employees have time to visit their children's schools and participate in parent activities? Do conversations at work promote secure civic reciprocal relationships that would increase workers' expectation and competency to become involved in civic and public forums? Does the profit that is generated by the community remain in the community in terms of wages and taxes? How a corporation answers these questions will probably have much more impact on the integrity of public education than its support of

---

[48] Logsdon and Wood, "Business Citizenship," p. 181.

employees volunteering a few hours a week in local schools or its donations of computers.

After examining corporate integrity on the cultural and interpersonal dimensions, which would require looking at corporate policies and procedures, corporations could then look at how they might engage in cooperative conversations with civic and governmental agencies. Remember the discussion of dialogue in chapter 1 where the beginning of dialogue was presented as a turning toward one another? On the social level, corporations and city agencies face a similar choice. They can either turn toward one another or turn their backs on one another. Participation in civil society requires that agencies turn toward one another and begin a conversation about how their city can achieve its mission. This conversation requires the conditions for public deliberation described in chapter 2, where the power of discourse determines policy and action rather than extraneous forces such as personality or money. In these conversations, where disagreement and differences become sources of mutual learning, corporations will learn how to engage in civic cooperation. They may learn that locating an office in a certain neighborhood will enhance its economic and social life. They may learn that retired citizens would like to spend time in company day-care centers. In more general terms, they will learn how to participate in the city's work of meeting human needs and respecting human rights.

In terms of Pearce's communicative cultures, the challenge for corporations is to move beyond modernistic solutions that assume that bigger and newer is better, and to move into cosmopolitan dialogues that enable the recognition of differences and mutual learning. The same is true for city agencies. What is at stake is not just the integrity of corporations, but the integrity of cities as well.

I have portrayed the city as the container for corporate activities, in the sense of providing the laws and frameworks necessary for corporate life. Sometimes it does seem like the container is leaking. Practices of government corruption, egoism, and cronyism may make any ethical perspective seem idealistic, and a product of wishful thinking. The development of trustworthy government is a struggle – a struggle that entails the development of a politics of inclusion. City government faces the same requirements for integrity as corporations – an openness to all who belong to its context. Until there is some trust that a city council is committed to a city's civic mission, the kind of conversations that could emerge from civil cooperation will probably not happen. In any concrete situation, however, the question is not whether a city has reached some ideal state, but whether it has the potential to elicit trust and participation.

Similar difficulties exist with many corporate leaders. In many cases, the problems arise from their positions of privilege, which in spite of their good intentions leave them unable to grasp the actual impact of corporate policies on others. Still, the conversations between corporations and government agencies can develop new possibilities for the enhancement of human flourishing in civic life. Corporations cannot facilitate the flourishing by themselves. They need public corporations and government agencies, just as public corporations and government agencies need them. For these conversations to have integrity, each participant needs to cooperate with the other, guided by the mission of the city and the dynamics of civic life.

One topic of these conversations, of course, will be the obligation of all participants to respect the natural environment. The natural environment is the context that holds civic society today, and how it prospers will finally determine the prosperity of cities and of corporations. Corporate integrity, as the next chapter demonstrates, requires not only that corporations engage in cooperative endeavors with cities, but that they also switch from developing human prosperity at the expense of the environment to developing natural prosperity that includes the flourishing of human and nonhuman nature.

From theory to practice

Questions for study and reflection

1. What are some of the major trends in the city or city-region in which you live that are determining the quality of life for its citizens? How are corporations responding to these trends?
2. How would you balance Boulding's triad of threat, exchange, and integrative strategies in corporations, in urban areas, in families?
3. What are the strengths and weaknesses of looking at the economy, civil society, and government from a contextual perspective?
4. How do corporations in your city support (or not support) democratic institutions?
5. What is your image of the corporate/city relationship?

6. What is your city's mission? How do your corporation's policies and procedures promote the city's mission?

Guidelines for the assessment worksheets in the appendix

Worksheet #10 allows an investigation of the relationships among corporations and cities in your region. You could examine different corporation/city relationships and evaluate how well they cooperate in fulfilling the city's mission.

Worksheet #11 offers an opportunity to think about how different goods should be distributed in terms of their social meaning. As you select either the market, government, or donations, or some combination of the three, you will also express your understanding of the social meaning of the goods.

6 | *Environmental integrity as natural prosperity*

The previous chapter concluded with the proposition that corporate integrity requires that corporations cooperate with other agencies in civil society in order to fulfill a city's mission. The chapter also showed how civil society serves as the context or container for such cooperative endeavors. This chapter addresses the final dimension of corporate integrity by exploring the container of both cities and corporations: the natural environment. How can corporations have integrity in their relationship with nature?

Understanding the relationship between corporations and nature may seem to rely completely on human imagination and knowledge. People may say that global warming is begging for attention, as though nature were speaking to us, but it is really the people who care about the future that are begging us to pay attention. There is a sense, however, in which we can hear nature by listening to our bodies. After all, we are creatures of nature. Our experiences of human vitality and fragility in different stages of life are nature's stories. So one way to understand an organization's view of nature is to review how it is designed to care for the health of its members.

Although any human community, by definition, is in part a natural community, some work communities have been designed so they are largely divorced from the rhythms of nature. The use of electric lighting, for example, creates a world of work separated from the earth's rhythm of light and darkness. The "24/7" world of global communications has largely erased the boundaries between times for work and times for family and community activities. As I argued in chapter 2, as long as the world of technology is embedded in modernistic culture, where whatever is new is better, it will be difficult to adequately recognize boundaries. This includes not only the boundaries of our human bodies, but all of nature. This is not to suggest that we should live only in nature. Nature can be brutal to human communities, through earthquakes, mudslides, and hurricanes. It can destroy our livelihoods. We do not need to throw away modern medicine, urban development, or information technology. Instead we need to create conversations that facilitate an understanding of the boundaries of technology. Instead of participating in modernistic conversations (as Pearce defines them) about how to adjust our communities to fit into a technological age, we need to begin talking about how to fit technology into a human age. For the sake of integrity, we need to design conversations that will open our eyes to the links between civil society and nature.

This chapter will review three different conversations that represent the complexity of current debates about the natural environment as the context for corporate integrity and corporate conduct. The three are the United Nations' sponsored conversations about sustainability, the Bretton Woods conversations about world trade and finance, and ecology conversations about the integrity of nature. Some corporations have been involved in each one of these conversations and their involvement can help us understand the conversations' possibilities and limitations.

All three conversations are global conversations, responding to global environmental issues. There are national and local conversations as well. In fact, between the 1960s and the 1990s corporations in the United States were involved in a series of conversations with environmental organizations and government agencies. A short summary of this story can serve as a prelude to the three global conversations, because the United States' story demonstrates some of the difficulties involved in balancing the involvement of corporations, nonprofits, and government agencies in conversations on sustainability. As this chapter will demonstrate, these three groups need to cooperate with each other not only for social integrity, as the last chapter demonstrated, but also for environmental integrity.

The United States' conversations on environmental protection

Andrew Hoffman, in his book *From Heresy to Dogma*, argues that the forty years between the 1950s and the 1990s witnessed a substantial change in corporate conversations about the environment.[1] As the title

---

[1] Andrew J. Hoffman, *From Heresy to Dogma: An Institutional History of Corporate Environmentalism* (San Francisco: New Lexington Press, 1997).

of his book indicates, he believes that the topic of the natural environment has moved from being an irritation to businesses to becoming a strategic part of their planning. He offers an example of this change by examining how people have changed their perceptions of smokestacks:

In the 1950s, prior to the advent of institutionalized environmental norms, [the smokestack] was viewed favorably, representing jobs, economic progress, and industrial strength. But in the industrial environmentalism period of the 1960s it came to symbolize something less desirable, an ugly and smelly nuisance. In the regulatory environmentalism of the 1970s, it represented the need for government controls. In the social responsibility period of the 1980s, it became the source of toxic pollution, hazardous to the health of the community. And finally, in the strategic environmentalism of the 1990s, it has come to symbolize wasted resources.[2]

These changes, from what Hoffman calls the "industrial environmentalism" of the 1950s to the "strategic environmentalism" of the 1990s represent different events both inside and outside of corporations. His story of these changes begins with the publication of Rachel Carson's *Silent Spring* (1962), which exposed the dangers of using DDT and, perhaps more importantly, questioned the prevailing optimism concerning technology. This technological optimism was also challenged by the Santa Barbara oil spill in 1969, and perhaps more dramatically by growing public awareness of environmental issues that culminated in the first Earth Day in 1970. Over twenty million people participated in rallies all across the nation, putting the environment on the national agenda.

In the following year, President Nixon signed into law the Environmental Protection Act, which changed the strategy for protecting the environment from corporate self-regulation to government regulation. Government took on the job of finding solutions to environmental problems. A key event during this period was the Love Canal incident in 1978. The Love Canal was a canal in Niagara Falls where Hooker Chemical Corporation had dumped over 21,800 tons of toxic chemicals. In 1953, Hooker covered over the landfill with a clay cap and sold it for one dollar to the city. After the city had built an elementary school and homes on top of the landfill, the toxic chemicals began to leak to the surface. As a result of

---

[2] Ibid., pp. 148–9.

this disaster, President Carter signed into law the Comprehensive Environmental Response, Compensation and Liability Act, which required businesses to clean up any toxic or hazardous sites they had created. Such regulation increased the tension between businesses and governmental environmental agencies.

When Ronald Reagan took office in 1981, he tried to resolve the tension by decreasing government regulations. As Hoffman points out, this had the opposite effect. Environmental groups turned directly to pressuring corporations and the focus changed from complying with government regulations to developing programs of corporate accountability.[3] The incident in Bhopal, India, in 1984, and others like it, such as the Exxon oil spill in 1989, turned environmental disasters into burdensome liabilities. As insurance carriers began to examine the environmental costs of such disasters, corporations began to integrate environmental issues into their strategic planning. In the 1990s, Hoffman witnessed a quite different conversation:

In effect, environmentalism is becoming less and less an environmental issue. As insurance companies apply environmental pressure on firms, environmental management ceases to be an environmental issue per se and becomes instead a risk-management issue. As competitors apply environmental pressure, it becomes an issue of competititive strategy. With investors, it becomes an issue of shareholder value. The firm's business channels are being altered to bring environmentalism to organizational attention through avenues related to marketing, accounting, finance, and so on.[4]

Hoffman's notion that environmental concerns have become part of everyday business practices makes one wonder whether corporations have taken over the environmental conversation so that they no longer need to participate in conversations that they do not control. Instead of being part of a larger whole, in other words, they have become a whole unto themselves. The question is, "Does strategic environmentalism represent the correct balance among nonprofits, corporations, and government agencies in conversations about preserving nature?" The story of the partnership between the fast-food giant McDonald's and the Environmental Defense Fund illustrates why the question needs an answer.

[3] Ibid., p. 88.
[4] Ibid., p. 183.

McDonald's and environmental action

In the 1980s, environmental groups such as the "Vermonters Organized for Cleanup" and the "Citizens Clearinghouse for Hazardous Wastes" built an international campaign against McDonald's extensive use of polystyrene foam packaging materials. The Environmental Protection Agency reported that the polystyrene production process generated the fifth-largest amount of toxic waste of any single chemical production process in 1986. The product also released cancer-causing chemicals when burned. In essence, it was dangerous to make, to use, and to dispose of. In 1987, McDonald's announced they would end the use of CFCs in their Styrofoam food packaging, which was praised by the Environmental Defense Fund (EDF), as well as the Natural Resources Defense Council and the Friends of the Earth.

After it was discovered that McDonald's had changed its terminology more than its practices, national and international grassroots groups resumed their protests. In 1990, McDonald's joined in a partnership with the Environmental Defense Fund, and promised to phase out their use of Styrofoam. This was seen as a new model of cooperation between corporations and environmental organizations. At the ten-year anniversary of the partnership, Fred Krupp, executive director of the EDF, and Jack Greenberg, McDonald's CEO and chairman, announced that McDonald's had:

- eliminated 150,000 tons of McDonald's packaging;
- purchased more than $3 billion worth of products made from recycled materials;
- recycled more than one million tons of corrugated cardboard, decreasing restaurant waste by 30 percent.[5]

These results show that partnerships can make changes. The McDonald's/EDF partnership appears to be a good example of the "civil economy" suggested in the previous chapter. The question is whether McDonald's has simply taken control of the conversation, with the help of the EDF, or whether they have become participants in a conversation about the preservation of nature as one agent among others. Have the three basic agencies of civil society, nonprofits, governments, and corporations, participated in this change in such a way that citizens can assume

---

[5] See www.environmentaldefense.org/pressrelease.efm?ContentID = 1299.

that the environment is protected? Or has the exclusion of the government agencies prevented the development of laws and regulations that would protect not only McDonald's integrity, but also the integrity of the fast-food industry? If McDonald's decreases its waste, but other fast-food companies stay the course, then the overall amount of waste will continue to increase. By partnering with McDonald's, nonprofits may have helped to mediate McDonald's organizational problem, but this help may have the unintended consequence of covering up the need for a system solution to a system problem, which would require not only the involvement of corporations and nonprofits, but also of government agencies.

The United States' story of corporate responsiveness to environmental issues has two messages. On the one hand, it confirms a basic assumption of this chapter: corporations can change their environmental practices if the conversations in which they participate change. On the other hand, it raises the question of whether environmental conversations in the United States, especially since the Reagan presidency, have tended to be private conversations between corporations and nonprofits, without enough involvement with government agencies. When we turn to the global conversations, the balance between these three agencies becomes even more crucial and at the same time more troublesome. Let us begin with the conversations about sustainability sponsored by the United Nations.

The United Nations' conversations on sustainability

The United Nations' conversations about sustainability had their beginnings, of all places, in worries about the weather. Shortly after the United Nations was founded, it began studying climate patterns and weather forecasting. For the first time, weather information from around the globe was assembled and standardized, which made it possible to notice changes in the global climate. In the years that followed, modern information technology enabled United Nations researchers to track the human impact on the natural environment.

In 1968, the UN General Assembly authorized the first Human Environment Conference to be held in 1972. At this conference, in Stockholm, Sweden, the participants encountered a major dilemma between the rich northern nations' interest in environmental protection and the poor southern nations' interest in economic growth. These different national agendas required that any global agreements needed to include both social and environmental concerns. The notion of sustainability became the key concept for working toward such agreements. Although the concept is used in different ways, its central meaning is that meeting current needs should not deny future generations the capacity to meet their needs. Since all nations had an interest in their future generations, it seemed like the future, if not the past or present, could serve as a unifying theme. At the end of the conference, the United Nations Environment Program (UNEP) was established to continue the conversation on sustainability.

The 1972 publication of *The Limits of Growth* by the Club of Rome added a more systemic analysis of the global context to the conversation on sustainability. Their publication was based on a four-year research project by a group of scientists and economists called together by Italian industrialist Aurelia Peccie and Scottish scientist Alexander King. They selected five factors – accelerating industrialization, rapid population growth, widespread malnutrition, depletion of nonrenewable resources, and a deteriorating environment – and examined how they reenforced each other through various feedback loops. Their conclusion was:

If the present growth trends in world population, industrialization, pollution, food production, and resource depletion continue unchanged, the limits of growth on this planet will be reached sometime within the next one hundred years. The most probable result will be a sudden and uncontrollable decline in both population and industrial capacity.[6]

Many saw their claim overly pessimistic, forgetting that they also made a second conclusion:

It is possible to alter these growth trends and to establish a condition of ecological and economic stability that is sustainable far into the future. The state of global equilibrium could be designed so that the basic material needs of each person on earth are satisfied and each person has an equal opportunity to realize his individual human potential.[7]

In fact, in 1992, the key researchers of *The Limits of Growth* reviewed and updated their analysis and concluded their statements were still justified, because "we realized that in spite of the world's improved technologies, the greater awareness, the stronger environment policies, many resource

[6] Donella H. Meadows, Dennis L. Meadows, Jorgen Randers, William W. Behrens III, *The Limits of Growth* (New York: Meridian Books, 1972), p. 29.
[7] Ibid.

and pollution flows had grown beyond their sustainable limits."[8] The global design they envisioned, where "the basic material needs of each person on earth are satisfied and each person has an equal opportunity to realize his individual human potential" has not yet occurred, even though many have tried to move the conversation in that direction.

One impetus was the formation of three groups: the World Conservation Strategy in 1980 by the International Union for the Conservation of Nature and Natural Resources (IUCN), the United Nations Environment Program (UNEP), and the World Wildlife Fund (WWF). They proposed a new ethic that combined respect for all natural communities:

Ultimately the behavior of entire societies towards the biosphere must be transformed if the achievement of conservation objections is to be assured. A new ethic, embracing plants and animals as well as people, is required for human societies to live in harmony with the natural world on which they depend for survival and well-being. The long-term task of environmental education is to foster or reinforce attitude and behavior compatible with this new ethic.[9]

Various other groups and conferences, including the 1987 publication of "Our Common Future," also called the Brundtland Report, named after the Norwegian Prime Minister, Gro Harlem Brundtland, continued the theme of the need for a new ethic based on global sustainability.[10] What was needed was more than just words. Nation states also needed to make new agreements about the design of the global community.

In 1992, at the Earth Summit in Rio de Janeiro, over 150 heads of state signed the Framework Convention on Climate Change (FCCC), the Rio Declaration, Agenda 21, the Convention on Biological Diversity, and the Forest Principles. These different statements covered both economic development and growing environmental threats, such as the destruction of biodiversity, and the continued increase in greenhouse gases.

The United Nations Framework Convention on Climate Change agreed that greenhouse gases had to be reduced, but they also knew

---

[8] Donella H. Meadows, Dennis L. Meadows, Jorgen Randers, *Beyond the Limits of Growth* (White River Junction, VT: Chelsea Green Publishing Company, 1992), p. xiv.

[9] Quoted in J. Ronald Engel and Joan Gibb Engel, "Introduction: The Ethics of Sustainable Development," in *Ethics of Environment and Development: Global Challenge, International Response* (Tucson and London: University of Arizona Press, 1993), p. 3.

[10] Ibid., p. 3.

the reductions could not come at the expense of economic development, especially in the poorer countries. So they agreed to a policy that asked all countries to decrease their greenhouse gases, but challenged developed countries to do more by voluntarily rolling back their greenhouse gas emissions to 1990 levels by the year 2000. This proposal was based on the observations that although the developed nations have only 20 percent of the global population, they use 80 percent of the world's natural resources, and contribute 70 percent of greenhouse gas emissions. In 1995, at a follow-up meeting, an assessment of the lack of reductions since Rio caused the 150 participating nations to increase their efforts at forging stronger agreements. Work began for the Kyoto conference on climate change, with the aim of attaining stronger commitments to reduce greenhouse emissions.

At the Kyoto conference in 1997 over 10,000 delegates, observers, and journalists participated in the third Conference of the Parties (COP), which had replaced the older International Negotiating Committee (INC) as the United Nations authority for the continued work on climatic change. At this meeting the conversations focused on the growing evidence of global warming. The conference was able to craft a legally binding agreement that industrialized countries would reduce their collective emissions of six greenhouse gases by 5.2 percent by 2008–12. To achieve this collective goal, industrialized nations could trade emission credits among themselves. If one nation surpassed its goal, for example, it could sell credits to another that had not met its goals. Industrialized nations could also get credit for developing sustainable projects. Even with this flexibility, time ran out before the protocols were signed. At the fourth Conference of the Parties, in 1998 in Buenos Aires, most of the 150 nations signed the protocols. Besides the signatures, of course, the agreements had to be ratified by the governments of the represented countries. Since the governments of some of these nations have not ratified the Kyoto protocols, most notably the United States, they have not yet gone into effect. Still, some nations set their own goals to meet the proposed reductions, and some multinational corporations have also taken on the challenge. To encourage corporate participation in these endeavors, the United Nations' secretary-general, Kofi Annan, initiated the Global Compact in the year 2000.[11] The compact

[11] See www.un.org/partners/business/gcevent/press/opening_remarks.htm.

The global compact asks companies to embrace, support and enact, within their sphere of influence, a set of core values in the areas of human rights, labor standards, the environment, and anti-corruption:

Human rights

- Principle 1: Businesses should support and respect the protection of internationally proclaimed human rights; and
- Principle 2: make sure that they are not complicit in human rights abuses.

Labor standards

- Principle 3: Businesses should uphold the freedom of association and the effective recognition of the right to collective bargaining;
- Principle 4: the elimination of all forms of forced and compulsory labor;
- Principle 5: the effective abolition of child labor; and
- Principle 6: the elimination of discrimination in respect of employment and occupation.

Environment

- Principle 7: Businesses should support a precautionary approach to environmental challenges;
- Principle 8: undertake initiatives to promote greater environmental responsibility; and
- Principle 9: encourage the development and diffusion of environmentally friendly technologies.

Anti-corruption

- Principle 10: Businesses should work against all forms of corruption, including extortion and bribery.

www.unglobalcompact.org/Portal/Default.asp

Figure 6.1. The Global Compact

invited multinational corporations to commit themselves to nine principles in the areas of human rights, labor, and the environment. In 2004 a tenth principle on anti-corruption was added (see figure 6.1). Nearly fifty corporations agreed to these principles in 2000, and others have joined the group since then. The compact represents an attempt by the United Nations to address the potential power of multinational corporations to create a sustainable economy. This was also the theme of the Johannesburg Earth Summit in 2002.

In Johannesburg the two themes of environmental protection and human development were more tightly woven together than ever before. Ensuring a clean water supply and restoring depleted fisheries, for example, were seen as meaningful ways of responding to poverty and to the environment. What had been interpreted as a conflict between the development of human communities and the preservation of nonhuman communities was now interpreted as a relationship of mutual dependence. What needed to be done seemed clearer than before, but how to get it done seemed more elusive.

For some, the best hope was projects like the Global Compact. Many of the corporations who were involved with the Global Compact had already been participants in the various UN conferences on sustainability we have just reviewed. In preparation for the Rio conference, for example, Maurice Strong, secretary-general of the conference, invited Stephan Schmidheiny, a Swiss industrialist, to be a business and industry adviser for the Earth Summit. Schmidheiny invited other leading business leaders to join him in representing the business community at the summit. This group formed the World Business Council for Sustainable Development (WBCSD), which has become one of the leading advocates for corporate environmental initiatives.

In the first major publication of the WBCSD, *Changing Course*, Schmidheiny argued: "The cornerstone of sustainable development is a system of open, competitive markets in which prices are made to reflect the costs of environmental as well as other resources."[12] Ten years later, in *Walking the Talk: The Business Case for Sustainable Development*, WBSCD continued their emphasis on the use of the market to promote sustainability. At the same time, they more fully recognized that corporations should work with other organizations to make the markets truly open to everyone. By working in partnership with other agencies, "Powerful synergies can emerge from partnerships that fuse the complementary capabilities of business, NGOs, and, in

---

[12] Steven Schmidheiny, *Changing Course: A Global Business Perspective on Development and the Environment* (Cambridge, MA: MIT Press, 1992), p. 14.

some cases, governments, parts of governments, and governmental institutions."[13] In this spirit of partnership, the WBCSD signed on to the Global Compact in 2002. For corporations that have joined the Global Compact, one of the key obligations is reporting on their environmental and social performance.

In the mid-1990s, some European corporations began reporting on their environmental and social performance as well as their financial performance. In 1997 a coalition of international groups, including UNEP, established the Global Reporting Initiative (GRI), an organization that provided corporate guidelines for triple line reporting.[14] The guidelines follow standard practices of accounting, including transparency, inclusiveness and accuracy. In 1999, twenty major companies, including Bristol-Myers Squibb, British Telecom, Proctor and Gamble, and Shell, implemented these guidelines. Although not all reporting companies follow the GRI guidelines, in the year 2000 almost half of the Fortune 500 companies issued annual reports that provided some information on how they were fulfilling their social and environmental responsibility.[15]

The practice of triple line reporting and the Global Compact has certainly changed the verbal conversation on sustainability in the past decade, but some wonder if the change is adequate. Simon Zadek believes that behind the skepticism are three questions: whether there exists a gap between what corporations say in public and do in private, whether this type of partnership with environmental groups and the UN forestalls more effective government regulations, and, finally, whether these partnerships serve to legitimize a global economic model that needs reform.[16] Perhaps these questions can be addressed by asking the following question. Is the image of relationships behind these conversations one of different isolated sectors or a contextual image like the image developed in chapter 5 that placed the economy

[13] Holliday, Schmidheiny, and Watts, *Walking the Talk*, p. 162.
[14] Ibid.
[15] Rosie Lombardi and Mel Wilson, "Globalization and its Discontents: The Arrival of Triple-Bottom-Line Reporting," *Ivey Business Journal* (September/October, 2001). Taken from website: www.pwcglobal.com/extweb/manissue.nsf/docid/F2C229B0D463808285256AEC005F1A37.
[16] Simon Zadek, *The Civil Corporation: The New Economy of Corporate Citizenship* (London and Sterling, VA: Earthscan Publications, 2001), p. 93.

in the context of civil society and the rule of law? To strive for sustainability without the rule of law to protect any progress should leave people skeptical.

Since the United Nations has not been elevated to a position where it can enforce the rule of law, and some nations have been unwilling to sign international treaties on environmental issues, the conversations about sustainability have lacked a global agent that would parallel the role of city governments as presented in the previous chapter on corporate city relationships. The result has been that the best argument for environmental stewardship has been the "business case," as evidenced by the latest publication of the World Business Council for Sustainable Development, which has the subtitle: "The Business Case for Sustainable Development."[17] If that were the only conversation determining our global future, one could argue that we should be patient for corporations to realize that a sustainable world is in their interests, but that is not the case. A second conversation not only rivals the conversation on sustainability, but also appears to be growing stronger. This conversation, on world trade and finance, was started by government agencies.

Conversations about world trade and finance

At the end of World War Two, in 1944, at Bretton Woods, New Hampshire, representatives from forty-five nations agreed to create institutions that would aid in the reconstruction of an economic order following the war, and to formulate a policy on international monetary exchanges. The resulting institutions were the International Bank for Reconstruction and Development, later named the World Bank, the International Monetary Fund (IMF), and the General Agreement on Tariffs and Trade (GATT), which would later, in 1987, become the World Trade Organization (WTO). These organizations came to be called the Bretton Woods organizations.

As a result of these agreements, the United States dollar, which was then linked to the gold standard, became the currency to which other national currencies were linked. The dominance of the United States in these financial and trade arrangements was to have significant

---

[17] Holliday, Schmidheiny, and Watts, *Walking the Talk*.

consequences for the conversations about trade and development in the coming decades. One consequence, which was already felt in the 1970s, was the United States' withdrawal of support from the United Nations' Conference on Trade and Development (UNCTAD).

UNCTAD was established in 1964 to promote the integration of developing countries into the world economy. Many leaders from the southern nations hoped that the United Nations would serve as a means for rectifying the inequalities between the northern and southern nations. In the 1960s they brought their proposals to UNCTAD, including the following:

- commodity price stabilization through the negotiation of price floors below which commodity prices would not be allowed to fall;
- preferential tariffs, which would have allowed Third World exports of manufactures, in the name of development, to enter First World markets at lower tariff rates than those applied to exports from other industrialized countries;
- an expansion and acceleration of foreign assistance.[18]

These proposals would have allowed southern developing nations to compete with the more mature economies of the north, but they also required some patience from the northern nations. Instead of joining this move toward more equality among nations, the United States withdrew its support for UNCTAD and transferred the international issues of trade and monetary policy to the Bretton Woods organizations.

Depositing the issues of world trade in organizations largely controlled by the United States had even more ominous consequences than one might have expected, because of unforeseen events. In the 1970s two events were particularly ominous – the decision to take the dollar off the gold standard in 1971 and the development of the Organization of Oil-Producing Countries (OPEC). The first opened the door to currency speculation, and the second filled Western banks with cash from OPEC countries. The banks, in turn, offered tempting loans to developing countries. With rising interest rates, many countries were unable to repay the loans. So the World Bank and the International Monetary Fund, which were designed to facilitate economic growth,

[18] Walden Bello, *The Future in the Balance: Essays on Globalization and Resistance* (Oakland, CA: Food First Books, 2001), p. 3.

became involved in saving Western bank loans. With precarious loans and floating currencies, the global financial system became unstable for many and disastrous for some. Furthermore, during the presidency of Ronald Reagan, the Bretton Wood policies took on a radical neo-liberal ideology of free trade and deregulation. These changes, according to Walden Bello, had the following consequences:

By the end of the 12-year long Reagan – Bush era in 1992, the South had been transformed: from Argentina to Ghana, state participation in the economy had been drastically curtailed: government enterprises were passing into private hands in the name of efficiency; protectionist barriers to northern imports were being radically reduced; and through export-first policies, the internal economy was more tightly integrated into the North-dominated capitalist world markets.[19]

In the 1990s, the World Trade Organization continued to push for open markets, in spite of the rising evidence that the free markets were mostly benefiting northern nations by giving them consumers for their products. This process came to a temporary halt in Seattle in 2001, when street demonstrators prevented delegates from attending meetings and the delegates finally went home without dismantling more trade barriers.

The conversations on world trade have not been limited to the Bretton Woods institutions and its critics, of course, but have also included international corporations and consumers. To the themes of free trade and open markets, corporations have added the theme of global consumption. Just as some corporations participated in conversations about sustainability, other corporations have participated in conversations about world trade. A major theme of these conversations has been how to promote consumption.

Conversations promoting consumption

One of the several revelations from the September 11th attack on the World Trade Center and the US Pentagon was how closely "the American way of life" has become connected with consumption. Within days, shopping bags adorned with US flags were seen across the country as a sign that those who hate us would not stop our

[19] Ibid., p. 12.

consumption. Shopping was patriotic. This valuing of consumption has a long history. Buchholz and Rosenthal wrote in 1998:

For the past forty years, with some exceptions, the overriding goal of people in advanced industrial societies has been one of buying more goods, acquiring more things, and increasing their stock of material wealth. Companies have profited from this consumer culture by catering to the consumer, making goods more convenient to buy, bombarding them with advertising – in general, promoting a consumer society by creating a certain materialistic conception of the good life. Because of this trend, the world's people have consumed as many goods and services since 1950 as all previous generations put together.[20]

The increase in global consumption through world trade has the added impact of increasing the environmental costs of transportation. These costs are not insignificant. On a round trip from New York to London, for example, a Boeing 747 spews out about 440 tons of carbon dioxide, "roughly the amount that 80 SUVs emit in a full year of driving."[21] In many cases, this environmental damage has been ignored. In *Walking the Talk*, the book by the World Business Council for Sustainable Development, for example, the authors celebrate the benefits of global travel.

Semiconductor chips might be designed in the US, where the basic wafers are also produced; these are then cut and assembled in Malaysia; and the final products are tested in and shipped from Singapore . . . The result is enhanced competitiveness, greater economies of scale, falling costs and a presence of new markets. [22]

These benefits may certainly be real, but so is the environmental damage caused by the transportation. It is not only computer chips. In major cities today we can find almost anything from everywhere. This is especially true of agriculture products. According to Vandana Shiva, the director of the Research Foundation for Science, Technology,

---

[20] Rogene Buchholz and Sandra Rosenthal, "Toward an Ethics of Consumption: Rethinking the Nature of Growth," in *The Business of Consumption: Environmental Ethics and the Global Economy*, ed. Laura Westra and Patricia Werhane (New York: Rowman and Littlefield, 1998), pp. 225–6.
[21] "Briefings," *The Green Business Letter* (March, 2003), p. 2.
[22] Holliday, Schmidheiny, and Watts, *Walking the Talk*, p. 44.

and Ecology in New Delhi: "The average chicken travels 2000 km before being eaten. Yoghurt and its ingredients make accumulated journeys totaling 3,500 km, and another 4,400 km could be added during distribution."[23] The average plate of food eaten in Western importing nations, according to the International Global Forum (IFG), is likely to have traveled fifteen hundred miles from its source.[24] Given the environmental cost of such extensive transportation, the IFG concludes: "It could be argued that the most important single act to improve the health of the planet and the quality of urban life would be to lessen the volume of international and long-distance transport."[25]

If the environmental costs of global transportation were reflected in the price of goods, consumers would at least know more about the impact of their purchases. Nevertheless, they still might buy such products, because of corporate advertising. The corporate investment in advertising is quite astounding. In 1986, advertising in the United States cost $100 billion. The amount had risen to $231 billion in the year 2000.[26] In 1998, global spending on advertising was around $437 billion.[27] Two of the three largest advertisers in the United States in 2001 were General Motors Corporation and Ford Motor Company.[28]

Ford's case is especially interesting because of their stance toward SUVs. In 2000, Ford issued its first "corporate citizenship report," in which it admitted that SUVs were three times as likely as cars to kill the other driver in a crash with a conventional car, were allowed to emit up to 5.5 times as much pollution as regular cars, and get only 10 to 13 miles per gallon of gasoline. In spite of these factors, Ford continues to produce SUVs because they are highly profitable. In the words of Ford's chairman, William C. Ford Jr.: "If we didn't provide that vehicle, someone else would, and they wouldn't provide it as

[23] Vandana Shiva, "The World on the Edge," in *Global Capitalism*, ed. Will Hutton and Anthony Giddens (New York: The New Press, 2000), p. 115.

[24] *Alternative to Economic Globalization: A Better World is Possible: A Report of the International Forum on Globalization* (San Francisco: Berrett-Koehler, 2002), p. 176.

[25] Ibid., p. 165.

[26] *New York Times 2003 Almanac*, p. 350.

[27] David Korten, *The Post-Corporate World: Life after Capitalism* (San Francisco, CA: Berrett-Koehler, 1999), p. 33.

[28] *New York Times 2003 Almanac*, p. 351.

responsibly as we do."[29] Ford's chairman, however, did not say that they were not only responding to customer demand, but also creating it. In 2001, Ford spent over $2 billion on advertising.[30]

The reliance of the global economy on unnecessary consumption presents a serious dilemma to those who believe that the market should serve sustainability. If the entire world were to consume as much as the average person in the United States, we would need two more earths to satisfy everyone.[31] Not all the world is consuming as much as we are. Although this may seem like a break for us, it also presents another dilemma. The inequality in consumption and in the production of wastes (US Americans waste nearly one million pounds of materials per person per year[32]) translates into an inequality in the destruction of the environment. As Mia MacDonald and Danielle Nierenberg point out:

> The ecological footprint of an average person in a high-income country is about six times bigger than that of someone in a low-income country – comparable to wearing either a size 7 shoe or an outsized 42. The one fifth of the world who live in the highest-income countries drive 87 percent of the world's vehicles and release 53 percent of the world's carbon emissions. [33]

This inequality in environmental impact is a serious challenge to the possibility of sustainability because it reinforces two trends that, instead of moving us toward sustainable communities, are moving us in opposite directions. The two trends are the growing gap between the rich and the poor and the increase in ethnic hatred.

The growing gap between the rich and the poor

In spite of the promise that increasing world trade would "raise all boats," the fact is that the gap between the rich and the poor has markedly increased, not decreased. As Noreena Hertz points out,

---

[29] Keith Bradsher, "Ford Admits SUVs are Irresponsible: Safety, Environmental Problems Noted, but so are Huge Profits," *San Francisco Chronicle,* May 12, 2000.

[30] *New York Times 2003 Almanac*, p. 351.

[31] Hawken, Lovins, and Lovins, *Natural Capitalism*, p. 51.

[32] Ibid., p. 53.

[33] Mia MacDonald and Danielle Nierenberg, "Linking Population, Women, and Biodiversity," in *State of the World, 2003* (New York: W.W. Norton 2003), p. 43.

even though inequality declined in many countries between 1945 and the 1970s, since the Reagan years and the dominance of neo-liberalism, there has been a reversal of this trend all over the world. She points out that, with the notable exception of East Asia, "the number of people living in extreme poverty – considered here as living on less than a dollar a day – has increased over this period in every developing country in the world."[34] There are several reasons for this. First of all, much of the wealth that globalization has created has not been the result of providing needed products and services, but of speculation in financial markets. "In 1998, on average, global currency markets exchanged every day the equivalent of US $1.5 trillion – that is, about 110 per cent of the UK's GDP in 1998."[35] David Korten, in his 1999 book, writes:

Nearly $2 trillion now changes hands in the world's currency exchange markets each day. Perhaps 2 percent of that money is related to trade in real goods and services. The rest, which is largely pursuing speculative profits, creates massive international financial instability while serving little if any public purpose.[36]

George Soros, whose success in exploiting global financial markets gives him some legitimacy to criticize them, gives the following reason for their excesses:

The global capitalist system is based on the belief that financial markets, left to their own devices, tend towards equilibrium. They are supposed to move like a pendulum: they may be dislocated by external forces, so-called exogenous shocks, but they will seek to return to the equilibrium position. This belief is false. Financial markets are given to excesses and if a boom/bust sequence progresses beyond a certain point it will never revert to where it came from. Instead of acting like a pendulum financial markets have recently acted more like a wrecking ball, knocking over one economy after another.[37]

---

[34] Noreena Hertz, *The Silent Takeover: Global Capitalism and the Death of Democracy* (New York: The Free Press, 2001), p. 41.
[35] Manuel Castells, "Information Technology and Global Capitalism," in *Global Capitalism*, pp. 52–74.
[36] Korten, *The Post-Corporate World*, p. 195.
[37] George Soros, *The Crisis of Global Capitalism: Open Society Endangered* (New York: Public Affairs, 1998), p. xvi.

One could disagree with Soros by pointing to Western domestic markets, which at least seem to run in business cycles. The global financial markets, however, do not have the controls that constrain domestic markets. Instead of being embedded in the legal institutions of civil society, global markets exist largely beyond national institutions. Large northern nations probably could exert more control than they seem willing to do, but small, poor nations, for the most part, exist at the mercy of global corporations. As David Korten points out:

In 1995, the combined sales of the world's top two hundred corporations – which employed only 18.8 million people, less than one-third of 1 percent of the world's population – equaled 28 percent of total world gross domestic product. The total sales of the Mitsubishi corporation were greater than the GDP of Indonesia, the world's fourth most populous country and a land of enormous natural wealth. The annual sales of Wal-Mart, the twelfth largest corporation, made its internal economy larger then the internal economies of 161 of the world's countries – including Israel, Poland, and Greece.[38]

If one believed that these gigantic corporations are governed only for the sake of their shareholders and owners, then one faces the startling conclusion: "The triumph of global capitalism means that more than half of the world's one hundred largest economies are centrally planned for the primary benefit of the wealthiest 1 percent of the world's people! It is a triumph of privatized central planning over markets and democracy."[39]

Viewing corporations as only responsible to their shareholders, however, is a violation of corporate integrity. It ignores the requirement for a worthwhile purpose that arises from a corporation's function in society, and it ignores that corporations exist in cities and in civil society. Still, the trend of the rich getting richer and the poor becoming poorer cannot be ignored. It not only makes sustainability more difficult, it also appears to increase ethnic hatred.

The increase in ethnic hatred

Amy Chua, a professor at Yale Law School, lost her aunt to ethnic violence in the Philippines in 1994. Her aunt belonged to the Filipino-

[38] Korten, *The Post-Corporate World*, p. 42.
[39] Ibid., p. 62.

Chinese minority that controls much of the country's wealth. The family chauffeur murdered her. As Chua tried to understand this family tragedy, she discovered that hatred between the ruling minority (the Chinese in this case) and the ethnic majority (the Filipinos) was fairly common. As she broadened her investigation, she came to the conclusion that the global expansion of capitalist markets and the promotion of democratic expectations have intensified the ethnic conflicts in developing countries.[40] Chua saw two main reasons for this development: the exported form of market capitalism was not the regulated market embedded in social structures as in the West, but rather a radical laissez-faire capitalism that had proven unworkable to the West, and the exported form of democracy was not embedded in the rule of law and deliberative practices as it had developed in the West, but was rather a simple entitlement of freedom. These two factors increased the existing tensions between the wealthy, market-dominant minority and the poor and resentful majority, because the majority perceived that the introduction of global markets worked to the advantage of the wealthy minority and to their disadvantage. She describes the formula that has been followed as follows:

Take the rawest form of capitalism, slap it together with the rawest form of democracy, and export the two as a package deal to the poorest, most frustrated, most unstable, and most desperate countries of the world. Add market-dominant minorities to the picture, and the instability inherent in this bareknuckle version of free market democracy is compounded a thousand-fold by the manipulable forces of ethnic hatred.[41]

Chua's research and analysis reminds us that integrity as wholeness should lead us to consider the consequences of actions as well as intentions. In fact, corporate responsibility means becoming accountable for one's actions, especially becoming accountable for those actions and policies that do harm. If someone knowingly lights a match in a room filled with gas, the person is responsible for the damage of the explosion, not for having offered someone a light to see in the dark. While the results of hatred are unpredictable, we do know

---

[40] Amy Chua, *World on Fire: How Exporting Free Market Democracy Breeds Ethnic Hatred and Global Instability* (New York: Doubleday, 2003).
[41] Ibid., p. 195.

that its escalation threatens all human and ecological communities. The continued escalation of these types of conflicts seems to have created communication patterns that are controlled only by force and the threat of force rather than by the power of public deliberation. Civil society and democratic practices are at risk for all parties involved.

In the long run, of course, things may work out. The fact is, however, that we are near the end of the long run. The development of the previous conversation on sustainability expresses an urgency to decrease consumption, increase conservation, and improve resource efficiency. This urgency, however, faces the resistance of a consumer economy that runs on oil, fear, and privilege. The dominant communication patterns here are ethnocentric that see things as "us and them" and that protect resources based on what was named in chapter 2 as the myth of scarcity. There are scarcities, of course, but in some cases the scarcity persists because of the unwillingness to change. There may be a scarcity of oil, for example, but not of energy, or there may be a scarcity of jobs, but not of work that needs to be done. In the near future, there will be a scarcity of healthy fish and of good drinking water if we do not change current trends. More importantly, there are also abundances, enough for every-one, if we turn to designing our communities and businesses to become integrated parts of nature.

For the earth, the conversation of world trade and consumption represents a growing threat to its vitality. Whether it can be contained or not is certainly questionable. If the only two conversations are the sustainability conversation based on voluntary compliance, and the business case and the work trade conversations based on continual growth and consumption, our chances for a sustainable future appear fairly slim. There is a third conversation, however, that could tip the balance so civic organizations could see more clearly how to meet the challenge of environmental integrity. That is the conversation about the integrity of nature.

Conversations about the integrity of nature

The conversations about the integrity of nature have many more creative voices than it is possible to review here. An enlightening trail, however, highlights the basic themes of the conversation. It begins with Aldo Leopold's land ethic, runs through E. F. Schumacher's notion that small is beautiful and Arnold Naess' deep ecology, and then ends with the understanding of nature as a living system.

A land ethic

In the previous story of environmental protectionism in the United States, Rachel Carson's *Silent Spring* was presented as a catalyst for new conversations about technology and nature. A less well-known book by Aldo Leopold, *A Sand Country Almanac*, written in 1949, was an earlier contribution to the field of ecology. A professional forester, Leopold grew to respect the complex interrelatedness of all of nature. This led him to call for a new ethic, which respected nature, as traditional ethics had called for respect of individuals and of society. The new "land ethic," as he said, "changes the role of *Homo sapiens* from conqueror of the land-community to plain member and citizen of it."[42] Although this ethic would require different behavior, he believed that first of all it required a different consciousness. He called it an "ecological consciousness." "It is inconceivable to me that an ethical relation to land can exist without love, respect, and admiration for land, and a high regard for its value. By value, I of course mean something far broader than mere economic value: I mean value in the philosophical sense."[43] The philosophical sense he had in mind required a sense of the land's integrity. He used the notion of integrity as a system concept. Sometimes he named this system the "biotic community" and sometimes "the land."

Land, then, is not merely soil; it is a fountain of energy flowing through a circuit of soils, plants, and animals. Food chains are the living channels, which conduct energy upward; death and decay return it to the soil. The circuit is not closed; some energy is dissipated in decay, some is added by absorption from the air, some is stored in soils, peats, and long-lived forests; but it is a sustained circuit, like a slowly augmented revolving fund of life.[44]

Given an awareness of the dynamics of the land, or biotic community, he offers the following ethical principle: "A thing is right when it tends

[42] Aldo Leopold, *A Sand County Almanac: And Sketches Here and There* (London: Oxford University Press, 1949), p. 204.
[43] Ibid., p. 223.
[44] Ibid., p. 216.

to preserve the integrity, stability, and beauty of the biotic community. It is wrong when it tends otherwise."[45] Leopold does not suggest that we discard other standards of conduct, such as economic or philosophical standards, but he wants us to add a third one: the ecological standard.

Leopold was not very hopeful that his country, the United States, would adopt this new ethic, because he believed that technological progress had captured its imagination. Land, as he says, was something that moderns felt they had "outgrown."[46] Why should we live according to nature's standards, when modern technology allows us to create our own? Still, since we are part of nature, perhaps we should figure out how to fit in. This is the message of E. F. Schumacher's slogan that "small is beautiful."

Small is beautiful

E. F. Schumacher, an economist, worried about the question of size and what he called "appropriate technology." He advocated that technological developments match the size of man. "Man is small, and, therefore, small is beautiful."[47] Furthermore, humans are part of a natural environment that has limits. So a yardstick for appropriate technology would be human development, not economic development. "An attitude to life which seeks fulfillment in the single-minded pursuit of wealth – in short, materialism – does not fit into this world, because it contains within itself no limiting principle, while the environment in which it is placed is strictly limited."[48]

The notion of limits, of course, violates one of the key principles of capitalist economics – unlimited human wants. That is what drives the economy of consumption. Schumacher is certainly aware of this ideology. He suggested a Buddhist economics as an alternative:

While the materialist is mainly interested in goods, the Buddhist is mainly interested in liberation ... The keynote of Buddhist economics, therefore is simplicity and non-violence ... For the modern economist this is very

[45] Ibid., pp. 224–5.
[46] Ibid., pp. 223–4.
[47] E. F. Schumacher, *Small is Beautiful: Economics as if People Mattered* (New York: Harper and Row, 1973), p. 159.
[48] Ibid., pp. 29–30.

difficult to understand. He is used to measuring the "standard of living" by the amount of annual consumption, assuming all the time that a man who consumes more is "better off" than a man who consumes less. A Buddhist economist would consider this approach excessively irrational: since consumption is merely a means of human well-being, the aim should be to obtain the maximum of well-being with the minimum of consumption.[49]

Is the Buddhist or the modern consumer irrational? Has the modern economy reversed the appropriate relationship between means and ends – between consumption and well-being? Do we eat to live, or live to eat? Is our well-being derived *from* nature or *with* nature? In other words, can human communities continue to prosper at the expense of nature, or is natural prosperity a condition for continued human prosperity? The answer depends on our assumptions about the relationship between human and non-human communities. The deep ecology movement has invited us to take this question seriously.

Deep ecology

The deep ecology movement proposes a transformation from an anthropocentric to a biocentric view of life. The anthropocentric view sees nature as a resource for humans. The biocentric sees humans as one aspect of nature. According to the founder of deep ecology, Arne Naess, "The flourishing of human and non-human living beings has value in itself. The value of non-human beings is independent of their usefulness to humans."[50] In deep ecology the environment is not merely a container for human flourishing, but rather a community of living beings, all with desires and equal rights to flourish. We are all part of a living system.

The biosphere as a living system

Implicit in the work of thinkers from Leopold to Naess is that the environment is a living system. J. E. Lovelock expressed this view with

---

[49] Ibid., p. 57.
[50] Arne Naess, "Sustainable Development and Deep Ecology," *Ethics of Environment and Development: Gobal challenge, International Response*, ed. John R. Engel and Joan Gibb Engel (Tucson and London: University of Arizona Press, 1993), p. 88.

his Gaia hypothesis that "the biosphere is a self-regulating entity with the capacity to keep our planet healthy by controlling the chemical and physical environment."[51] For Lovelock, Gaia was a name for what others have called the self-organizing capacity of the biosphere. When we consider the ecological systems of microclimates such as tide pools, or a regional biosphere such as a national forest, we can easily imagine the cyclical interconnected dynamics of these systems. The various parts of the system take care of each other's biological needs in such a way that the whole system remains healthy. It is this cyclical flow of food and waste and waste and food that has attached the interest of people interested in developing ecological organizations.

A popular scholar in this field, Fritjof Capra, argues:

The key to an operational definition of ecological sustainability is the realization that we do not need to invent sustainable human communities from scratch but can model them after nature's ecosystems, which are sustainable communities of plants, animals, and microorganisms.[52]

Capra's advice echoes that of other writers. David Orr, for example, has tried to design buildings that follow "the larger patterns and flows of the natural world."[53] Paul Hawken has also argued for "biomimicry," which means that organizational design would mimic biological design. A persuasive reason for considering such mimicking is that nature's systems are much more efficient than most human systems. As Hawken, Lovins and Lovins point out, compared to the efficiency of nature, which uses 100 percent of the materials that flow through its systems, the US economy uses only about 6 percent. The remaining 94 percent become waste.[54] If we could come closer to mimicking nature's patterns, we could become more efficient and cause less harm. This is the idea behind the principles of the Natural Step.

---

[51] J. E. Lovelock, *Gaia: A New Look at Life on Earth* (Oxford: Oxford University Press, 1979), p. xii.

[52] Fritjof Capra, *The Hidden Connections: Integrating the Biological, Cognitive and Social Dimensions of Life into a Science of Sustainability* (New York: Doubleday, 2002), p. 230.

[53] David Orr, *Nature of Design: Ecology, Culture and Human Intention* (Oxford: Oxford University Press, 2002), p. 20.

[54] Hawken, Lovins and Lovins, *Natural Capital*, p. 14.

The Natural Step

The Natural Step is an environmental program developed under the leadership of Dr. Karl-Henrick Robèrt in Sweden. He wrote in the foreword to *The Natural Step for Business*: "I am a cell scientist, and I see the cell as a metaphor for the whole Earth, as there must be a balance of all flows in both the cell and the Earth for each to survive."[55] The problem is that the earth's flow is seriously imbalanced. We are simply producing more than the earth can absorb. If we continually increase our use of the earth's resources, such as oil and water, and increase the production of things, as well as continue to destroy natural habitats, we will destroy the earth's furture. To reverse these trends and to meet human needs, the Natural Step proposes that corporations must change their treatment of nature. It sees the following four conditions for a sustainable society:

In a sustainable society, nature is not subject to systemically increasing . . .
1. . . . concentrations of substances extracted from the Earth's crust;
2. . . . concentrations of substances produced by society;
3. . . . degradation by physical means
   and in that society
4. . . . human needs are met worldwide.[56]

To meet these conditions, corporations must find new ways to design their resource use, production process, distribution process, and their products so that all "wastes" either become biological resources (biodegradable) or material resources (reuseable or recyclable). To use the title of a recent book by William McDonough and Michael Braungart, corporations need to think about their operations "from cradle to cradle" instead of from cradle to grave.[57] In nature, there are no graves, only cycles of growth – decay – growth. Several corporations have taken up this challenge to use nature's design as a model for designing their operations. One is the carpet company, Interface Inc.

---

[55] Karl-Henrik Robèrt, "Forword," in Brian Nattrass and Mary Altomare, *The Natural Step for Business* (Gabriola Island, British Columbia, Canada: New Society Publishers, 1999), p. xiii.
[56] Nattrass and Altomare, *The Natural Step*, p. 23.
[57] William McDonough and Michael Braungart, *Cradle to Cradle: Remaking the Way We Make Things* (New York: North Point Press, 2002).

The sustainability program of Interface Inc.

Interface Inc., a major carpet manufacturing company in the United States, is one of four corporations highlighted in Nattrass and Altomare's book on the Natural Step for business.[58] The other three are IKEA, Scandic Hotels, and Collins Pine Company. Each one is worthy of attention, but Interface Inc. will suffice. It has translated the Natural Step conditions into the following seven elements of sustainability.

1. Eliminating waste (anything that does not add values to our customers).
2. Eliminating harmful emissions to the biosphere.
3. Using renewable energy sources.
4. Creating self-sustaining, closed-loop products and processes.
5. Developing alternatives to the physical movement of people and material, using resource-efficient means of transportation.
6. Creating a culture that integrates the principles of sustainability into what we do everyday.
7. Creating a new model for business (redesigning it) by pioneering sustainable commerce.[59]

As Joseph DesJardins points out in his review of Interface's movement toward sustainability, the most impressive thing they have done is revise their view of their purpose.[60] Instead of a carpet company that produces and sells products, they see themselves as a carpet company that offers floor-covering services. This means that they continue to own the carpet itself, which creates an incentive to produce carpets that are durable, easily replaceable, and recyclable. Furthermore, these changes have resulted in improved efficiencies and reduced material and energy costs, which have benefited both customers and the company.

As Interface Inc. and other companies attempted to implement the principles of the Natural Step, their justification has primarily been the business case for doing well: it will improve the company's

---

[58] Nattrass and Altomare, *The Natural Step*.
[59] See www.interfaceinc.com.
[60] Joseph DesJardins, *An Introduction to Business Ethics* (New York: McGraw-Hill, 2003), p. 195.

performance. This case, as has been demonstrated in previous chapters, may be important from the economic perspective, but not sufficient for a civic perspective.

In terms of meeting the challenge of environmental integrity, emphasizing the business case may actually compromise the full persuasiveness of the ecological justification for preserving nature. Nature is the context of civil society, which is the context for corporations. As a member of civil society, and in cooperation with nonprofits and government agencies, corporations need to make environmental integrity a task of civil society. To make such a move, nature must be interpreted as a source of meaning and wisdom. Here is the dilemma. Nature has value only because it is valuable to us. At least that is the only value we can know. Its ultimate value to us, however, only becomes accessible when we see it as valuable in itself.

We need a healthy environment, but meeting that need depends on seeing nature as something more than a thing to meet our needs. It must also be seen holistically, as being integral and alive. This view is expressed in the declaration of the United Nations' 2002 Earth Charter:

The resilience of the community of life and the well-being of humanity depend upon preserving a healthy biosphere with all its ecological systems, a rich variety of plants and animals, fertile soils, pure waters, and clean air. The global environment with its finite resources is a common concern of all peoples. The protection of Earth's vitality, diversity, and beauty is a sacred trust. [61]

If corporations are to have environmental integrity, they will need to cooperate with nonprofits and government agencies to develop relationships among themselves that protect and restore nature.

The three conversations about sustainability, world trade, and the integrity of nature represent significant aspects of the relationships between members of civil society and nature. Some might wish the conversation on sustainability would dominate the other two, but that is not likely, nor is it sufficient, as long as it pays little attention to the need to cooperate with government agencies to develop international agreements and laws to protect the environment. Our best hope lies in the tension among all three conversations, working with the disagreements and differences, and striving to create a global civil society that

---

[61] See www.earthcharter.org.

has integrity in its relationship with nature. Within these three conversations are signs of hope and signs of despair. What has made them different from earlier conversations is that now the fate of nature and the fate of corporations are linked together. As Nattrass and Altomare have suggested, corporations have become part of evolution. For the first time, natural evolution is dependent on corporate conduct. Corporations and nature will either evolve or devolve together. To promote evolution, Nattrass and Altomare argue, corporations must develop an "evolutionary consciousness."

Evolutionary consciousness demands that every human system, whether it is a corporation, a family, a community, or a nation, take responsibility for designing or redesigning its system to safeguard the ecological balance that took billions of years to create and that human systems are changing in the course of decades. [62]

This evolutionary possibility will require corporate integrity on the cultural, interpersonal, organizational, and civic dimensions of corporate life as well as the natural. It requires communication patterns designed for cosmopolitan interactions among different members of civil society that can handle disagreement, respect each other's need for security and right to participate, pursue worthwhile goals, and develop guidelines for moving into the future. Although no one can tell exactly how these conversations will proceed, they will probably touch on these four basic themes: asking the right questions, practicing the principle of subsidiarity, selecting the appropriate boundaries, and promoting natural prosperity.

Four themes of natural integrity

Asking the right question

When my business students first become aware of the gravity of the environmental challenge, they think about what they can do personally, and often resign themselves to their powerlessness. Individuals, of course, can make appropriate responses, but the students are right in their underlying assumption: individuals cannot solve system problems. System problems need system solutions. Individuals, of course,

---

[62] Nattrass and Altomare, *The Natural Step*, p. 191.

need to call for such solutions, but the solutions themselves will come from imagining how to change the system, or, in the language of a communicative approach, how to change the conversations. So a more appropriate question is "What can we do?" and the "we" is the global community of citizens. First of all, we can give direction to the conversations in which we participate by asking the right questions.

Questions point to their answers, and the wrong question easily gets the wrong answer. If I look at a polluted river, for example, and ask how to protect people from the pollution, the answer might be to build a barrier along the river. If I ask how to make the water safe again, the answer might be to make a separate channel so the pollution does not get into the river. If I ask how to stop those polluting the river, the answer might be to support government regulation that forces all polluters to follow the same guidelines. If I ask how we can redesign the relationships between the market system and nature so that nature prospers as society prospers, then the answer might be to join with others in a cooperative effort not only to develop appropriate regulations, but also to develop educational programs to change the expectations of the social systems in which corporations operate. With this final question, I have moved from asking about how to protect individuals to how to change social systems. Intervention at this level could make a difference for both human and nonhuman communities.

Meeting the challenge of asking the right questions requires that we ask more than one. Sometimes, the right set of questions will include all five dimensions of corporate integrity. In other cases, the organizational and social system dimension will appear most urgent. Since the questions we ask arise out of the communication patterns in which we live, we also need to ask questions about the adequacy of these patterns. This requires reflection and dialogue with others. Engaging in organizational ethics today requires a multidimensional approach, so that we can become aware of what real change requires. Asking the right questions is the first step toward doing the right things. The second step is to imagine what types of actions are appropriate for different dimensions of an issue. The principle of subsidiarity can be helpful here.

The principle of subsidiarity

Subsidiarity refers to a political structure where "the authority of more distant levels of administration is *subsidiary*, or subordinate, to the authority of more local levels, which allow a greater opportunity for direct citizen engagement."[63] This principle, in other words, supports a bottom-up structure just as much as a top-down structure. In fact, it supports both. It suggests that issues should be addressed at the lowest level at which it is possible to make an adequate response. This is especially important for democratic practices. Direct involvement at the neighborhood and city level can prepare citizens for representative participation at higher levels. In the previous chapter, for example, the city was taken as the most appropriate level of analysis to explore the relationships among organizations in civil society, because cities provide most of the infrastructure, the people, and the culture that corporations require to exist. Global cities also participate in an emerging global civil society. At the same time, this global civil society depends on international laws and agreements in order to continue its development. It also depends on local initiatives at the neighborhood and district levels. The principle of subsidiarity allows us to affirm the necessity of working on all these different levels, and to make sure that communities at each level control as much of their lives as possible before one moves to the next level.

The principle of subsidiarity also applies to production and consumption. If you use wood products to make furniture, for example, it may be possible to find suitable local products or import somewhat higher-quality products. The principle of subsidiarity would encourage the use of local woods. Such choices decrease travel and greenhouse gas emissions. They also enable users to know about the growth, production, and distribution of the products they use. Furthermore, using local products can preserve the diversity of different communities.

The principle of subsidiarity matches the patterns of nature. The biosphere, after all, is both a global and a local system. "At all scales of nature, we find living systems nesting within other living systems – networks within networks. Their boundaries are not boundaries of separation but boundaries of identity. All living systems communicate with one another and share resources across their boundaries."[64]

These boundaries, of course, are just as important as the communication patterns that connect them. The awareness of boundaries, in

---

[63] *Alternatives to Economic Globalization*, p. 60.
[64] Capra, *The Hidden Connections*, p. 231.

fact, is just as important here in designing environmental integrity as it was in chapter 2 when we were designing cultural integrity.

Setting boundaries

In developed nations, corporations function in a civic context that sets formal and informal boundaries, from zoning laws to financial reporting. Although there are some "soft" agreements about appropriate international conduct, it would be misleading to speak of a global civil society as more than an emerging possibility. At the same time, in the long run, "No business, global business included, can properly function as business unless it draws upon and nurtures the non-market environment of civil society in which it is more or less embedded."[65] Civic boundaries are just as necessary in the global context as in the domestic. Still, even if we did have these civic boundaries, there is no guarantee that nature would be adequately represented in these civic conversations. How can corporations and cities become aware of how they are bounded by nature? It is not so much that nature has limits (nature by itself does just fine), but more that human communities must be limited if they are to live with nature. Instead of continually "pushing the envelope" so to speak, corporations, and even entrepreneurs, must acknowledge how nature envelops them.

One project that may play an important role in setting boundaries is the United Nations' 2002 Earth Charter. It contains four principles:

- respect and care for the community of life;
- ecological integrity;
- social and economic justice;
- democracy, nonviolence, and peace[66]

These four principles cover all of life. They unify human and non-human life. By themselves, corporations cannot create a world guided by such principles. They do have a place among the various agencies and peoples who must work together to create such a world. To effectively experience their proper place – their boundaries – corporations need to rely on their membership in the global civil society rather

[65] Helmut Anheier, Marlies Glasius, and Mary Kaldon (eds.), *Global Civil Society* (Oxford: Oxford University Press, 2001), p. 32.
[66] See www.earthcharter.org.

than on their possession of global resources. Just as corporations have an obligation to promote the mission of cities, they also have an obligation to promote the development of international laws and regulations that will create a context in which they can exist cooperatively with others. Only as one among others, who work together to develop prosperity, will they experience their appropriate boundaries. After all, corporate prosperity does not equal environmental integrity. Environmental integrity requires the prosperity of both human and nonhuman communities, or natural prosperity.

Natural prosperity

The emphasis on the local over the global also emphasizes the natural context. Our place is on the earth. Our awareness of our placement is easily overlooked because of technological illusions and ecological denial. The technological illusion imagines that, as a problem arises, so does a technological solution. Just before we run out of oil, we will develop a technology for hydrogen fuel. Just before global warming destroys our agricultural productivity, we will find new ways to produce food, or perhaps we will be able to produce food on the moon by then. And just before we run out of healthy sources for water, we will have technology to turn seawater into fresh water. Some of these developments may occur, and some probably will not. So how do we proceed?

First of all, we need to move from defending private interests to promoting the public good. The type of thinking required here is the "public thinking" of public deliberation. We seldom made decisions based on perfect knowledge, but we can decide either to be reckless with nature or to be cautious. The United Nations Rio Declaration suggests that we should apply what is called the precautionary principle in situations of contested knowledge. Principle 15 of the Declaration states:

In order to protect the environment, the precautionary approach shall be widely applied by States according to their capabilities. Where there are threats of serious or irreversible damage, lack of full scientific certainty shall not be used as a reason for postponing cost-effective measures to prevent environmental degradation.[67]

---

[67] See www.unep.org/Documents/Default.asp?DocumentID=78&ArticleID = 1163.

This principle, as Robyn Eckersley argues, should be incorporated into the values of democracy, and serve as one guide for making public decisions.[68] The principle does not provide answers, but it does decrease the risk of making mistakes. In the past few years, as the conversation on world trade and consumption has demonstrated, caution has not been a major theme of the political conversations in the United States. Instead, policies have been based more on what David Orr has labeled ecological denial.[69] The United States has refused to sign worldwide treaties to protect the environment, cut back on environmental protection, and tried to invade the Alaskan wilderness for oil. Who should get the benefit of the doubt here: the requirements of the consumer economy or the requirements of sustainability? The precautionary principle would side with the requirements for sustainability. When government agencies refuse to proceed with caution, it is certainly more difficult for corporations, since they require appropriate regulations not only to improve the systems in which they operate, but also to keep a level playing field among competitors in the same market. Still, corporations have a choice: they can take advantage of this denial or they can address it, and join with others in exploring together how to design conversations that focus on the flourishing of all of nature – human and nonhuman nature. The next chapter explores how civic leaders, both inside and outside corporations, can engage in this process of designing conversations that will promote integrity, not just in terms of nature, but also in the other four dimensions of corporate life: the cultural, interpersonal, organizational, and civic.

From theory to practice

Questions for dialogue and reflection

1. What is sustainability, and what must occur for it to be achieved?
2. How can the three conversations reviewed in this chapter be integrated?
3. What are some of the changes necessary for sustainability, on the individual, organizational, and systemic levels?

[68] Robyn Eckersley, *The Green State: Rethinking Democracy and Sovereignty* (Boston, MA: MIT Press, 2004), p. 135.
[69] Orr, *Nature of Design*, p. 86.

4. Is the Natural Step a good guide for reaching sustainability?
5. What are some current "best practices" that show the way to a sustainable future?
6. What are the strengths and weaknesses of the themes suggested for future conversations about natural prosperity?

Guidelines for the assessment worksheets in the appendix

For the sake of integrity, the three conversations presented in the chapter must become parts of an inclusive, civic conversation. Use Worksheet #12 to begin an integration of these conversations by exploring the various questions listed.

New conversations could well include the themes offered in the final section of this chapter. Worksheet #13 offers a chance to assess what would need to change in current conversations for these themes to be included.

7 | *Corporate integrity and organizational leadership*

I n the course of the previous five chapters, the quest for understanding corporate integrity began with the challenges of culture and ended with the challenges of nature, the two basic foundations of human communities. In a sense both nature and culture are always given; we are born into them and live in their context. Today, however, we no longer experience them as simply there. Their quality largely depends on current interpersonal, organizational, and civic relationships and these relationships depend on the design of the conversational patterns in which they exist. When these communication patterns do not promote corporate integrity, organizational leaders need to change them. This process of leading by changing communication patterns is the theme of this final chapter.

Organizational leaders who intend to promote corporate integrity will discover the possibilities and limitations for doing so embedded in the quality of the conversational patterns that constitute a corporation's cultural, interpersonal, organizational, civic, and natural dimensions. Because these five dimensions of corporate integrity are interconnected, the possibilities for developing corporate integrity are actually greater than one might first imagine. Reviewing some of these connections can set the stage for exploring how leaders can improve corporate integrity.

The connections among the five dimensions of integrity

When the last chapter concluded with the suggestion that corporations must become aware of their boundaries and limits, it was actually reiterating a suggestion already presented in chapter 2. In that chapter on Pearce's four types of communication patterns, awareness of boundaries was suggested as an antidote to the excesses of modernistic communication patterns. Valuing differences requires an awareness of the other. When I acknowledge someone as a

particular person, I also experience my own particularity, my boundaries. I share a whole that belongs to others just as much as it belongs
to me. For us to live well together, we need to become aware of
boundaries in the cultural, interpersonal, civic, and natural dimensions
of organizational life.

There is also an implicit connection between the recognition of the
need for secure relationships at work, which chapter 3 highlighted,
and relationships with nature, which we explored in chapter 6. If
conversations at work are guided by the need for safety and the right
to participate, it will be much easier to participate in conversations
with environmental agencies about caring for nature. Striving to meet
human needs, in other words, will make it easier to recognize the needs
of nature. But if employees are treated as expendable and easily
replaceable, it will be more difficult to recognize the co-dependence
between human and nonhuman nature.

The clearest conclusion that can be drawn from the implicit connections of the five dimensions is that they all should reinforce each other.
Progress in creating integrity in one dimension should aid the process
of creating integrity in the others. Perhaps nothing prevents this type
of synergy as much as the lack of a clear and worthwhile corporate
purpose. The omission of a *telos* for organizations, or the substitution
of individual or social purposes, such as profit or social prosperity, for
an organization's purpose, compromises the human desire for working
toward something good. Profit is not bad. It is a useful result of good
work. Social prosperity is also valuable, when linked with natural
prosperity. A strong notion of organizational purpose does not negate
the significance of the individual or social interests in wealth. But it just
makes sure that these interests do not become a substitute for an
organization's purpose. Only a clear idea of what businesses are good
for will enable the five dimensions of corporations to become fully
integrated.

A great example of the power of a strong purpose to increase the
integrity of all dimensions of a corporation's life is the experience of
Fetzer Vineyards, one of the largest suppliers of wine in the United
States. The following mission statement guides their workforce:

We are an environmentally and socially conscious grower, producer and
marketer of wines of the highest quality and value. Working in harmony
and with respect for the human spirit, we are committed to sharing

information about the enjoyment of food and wine in a lifestyle of modera-
tion and responsibility. We are dedicated to the continuous growth and
development of our people and our business.[1]

Paul Dolan, the president of Fetzer Vineyards, sees this mission statement as a set of talking points for creating the business's context and
culture. It provides an identity that can run throughout the company,
from interpersonal relationships to relationships with nature. Although
Dolan does not use the terminology developed here, I believe he would
agree that the key to corporate integrity is an inclusion of all five
challenges to corporate integrity in a business's everyday communications.[2] In many cases, however, some of the five dimensions are
included, but others are not.

   When I was involved in an ethics and compliance program at a mid-
size company in San Francisco we talked about culture, interpersonal
relationships, and the corporation's mission, but not about the corporation's relationship with the city in which it existed, or about its
relationship with nature. We did use the notion of integrity, but it was
only the integrity of the corporation. Such a program would have been
improved if it had included the civic and natural dimensions of corporate integrity. In fact, including these two dimensions might have made
the other three much more challenging.

   Some ethics and corporate responsibility programs seem to go in the
opposite direction. They focus on the relationship between corporations and nature, or perhaps corporations and society, but not on
the interpersonal relationships at work or on developing a culture that
honors differences and diversity. A worst-case scenario would be a
corporation partnering with non-profits to help the homeless while
needlessly downsizing and laying off workers. There are many examples where the left hand does not know what the right hand is doing.
In some cases, different activities are so separated that knowledge of a
whole system would require more than imagination. It would require a
change in organizational structure.

   In most office buildings today, for example, office workers come in
the morning and leave at night, and office cleaners come in the night

---

[1] Paul Dolan, *True to our Roots: Fermenting a Business Revolution*
(Princeton, NJ: Bloomberg Press, 2003), p. 61.
[2] Ibid., p. 64.

and leave in the morning. They never see each other, and yet they are dependent on each other. Not only do they not see each other at work, they seldom see each other outside of work. They live in different neighborhoods and belong to different clubs and associations. Worse still, their images of each other are largely determined by either the local news or television shows. This separation of citizens from each other not only prevents corporate integrity, but civic integrity as well.

As long as our work and living environments are designed so that the people who work in the same building never see each other, how will it be possible to integrate corporations or cities? If our work life is designed so it prevents encounters of differences and therefore disagreements, how can a culture that promotes openness develop? If cultures are not open to differences and disagreements, how can corporations develop cooperative relationships with other agencies in the civic realm, or learn from groups that have different views of corporate responsibility? If things were static, it might appear as though corporate integrity was impossible. Things are not static. Change is the order of the day. That does not mean that all change is good. As we have seen in the previous chapters, some changes, such as an increase in ethnic hatred, are terrible. Still, at least we know we are not stuck with what we have. The five dimensions of corporate integrity also suggest that work on one dimension can influence the other dimensions, especially if people include all five dimensions in their ongoing communications. In fact, adequate responses to many current issues in corporate ethics would benefit from exploring the challenges they present and the questions they raise on all five dimensions of corporate integrity. Figure 7.1 illustrates this point by examining the issues of diversity in the workplace.

Just as diversity can be explored in all five dimensions, so can other issues, such as health and safety or employee privacy. Most decisions will focus only on one dimension, but an awareness of the other dimensions will increase the possibility of making better decisions, especially if the decision makers ensure that they are asking the right questions and practicing the principle of subsidiarity.

Not one of these decisions, of course, can happen by itself. People need to lead the way. Who leads and how they know the way, however, depends on the communication patterns in which they exist. Remember the discussion on the nature of the self in chapter 1? There the self was presented in two guises: as a relational self (the who-am-I? question) and

Corporate Dimension	Challenges	Questions
Cultural	Openness to cultural differences Capacity to handle disagreements	How can we develop a diverse workforce and honor its diversity?
Interpersonal	Need for security Employee participation in setting standards Reciprocity	Do our communication patterns provide security and participation for all social groups?
Organizational	Quality of products and services Character of work community	Do our products and advertising respect the diversity of our communities?
Civic	Corporation as member of civil society Corporate members as citizens	Do our practices and policies, such as our choice of locations or work schedules, support a city's mission of creating equal opportunity?
Natural	Sustainability Overconsumption and violence Natural prosperity	Are we supporting diversity globally? What are we doing to reverse trends of growing ethnic tension?

Figure 7.1. Issues of diversity and the five dimensions of corporate integrity

an acting self (the what-should-I-do? question). Leaders have a similar duality. Leaders are relational. No one to lead, no leaders. But leaders are also actors or agents. They lead. They lead, however, in a relational context that gives them their legitimacy as leaders. At least that is how it appears from the contextual model of communication. True, there are models of leadership that conform more to the post office model, but these models are not very helpful in figuring out how to actually improve corporate integrity.

From the contextual model of communication, leading always occurs in the ongoing verbal and nonverbal communication patterns that constitute organizations. The communication patterns include decision making processes, hierarchies, roles, and assigned responsibilities. It also includes the distribution of rewards and punishments, structures of control, influence, accountability, and recognition. These communication patterns create the context in which some people lead others.

From a civic perspective, the ongoing communication patterns that create the context for leadership should enable persons to be seen as citizens and corporations to be seen as participating in civil society. Does this mean that corporate leaders should be seen as civic leaders? If so, are there any relevant differences between business and political leaders? Exploring this question can clarify the meaning of organizational leadership.

Comparing business and political leaders

Until the twentieth century, as Barbara Kellerman points out, the differences between business and political leaders far outweighed the similarities. In fact, business people were not called leaders, but managers, because work relationships were seen as based on coercion, not influence.

As the United States made the nineteenth-century transition from becoming a society that was largely agrarian to one largely industrial, the exigencies of work resulted in rigid organizational structures . . . The notion of the manager rather than the leader grew out of this circumstance. The word *leadership* implies a contract of some kind between the leader and the led. Ideally at least, leaders are supposed to do their work on behalf of the led, and they are supposed to influence rather than coerce.

But for most of this century the notion of influence was quite irrelevant to the workplace . . . By most measures the relationship between those in charge and those under them was autocratic rather than democratic.[3]

This view of the business manager corresponds with the master-and-servant image of relationships highlighted in chapter 3. As I argued there, even though this image still remains in force in some business practices today, such as employment at will, it has for the most part been replaced

---

[3] Barbara Kellerman, *Reinventing Leadership: Making the Connection Between Politics and Business* (New York: State University of New York Press, 1999), p. 3. Italics in original.

by market and team relational images. Kellerman traces a similar change in leadership theory. The command and control style of the manager has at least been modified by a greater reliance on persuasion. To illustrate her point, she quotes William May, the chairman and president of the American Can Company, who in 1968 said:

A chief executive has to persuade as much as command. He has to evoke consent as well as assent among his subordinates, to say nothing of his board of directors. People talk about "decision making" as if it were some kind of instant action. In actuality, it's a fearfully time-consuming process, because you've got to mobilize people behind those decisions.[4]

As she points out, a city mayor, a governor, or even the President of the United States could have said the same thing.

Not only have business leaders become more like political leaders, in terms of relying more on influence and less on coercion, but political leaders, Kellerman argues, have become more like business leaders. The similarity is not that they use more coercion than before, but rather that they have become more focused on business issues, ranging from the need for efficiency in government to managing the national economy. In the United States, for example, presidents are now judged by how well the economy is doing more than by how well public institutions are doing. Furthermore, people expect government to be more efficient and to be held accountable for their expenses, much like a financial manager would be in a business. Mayors of cities and governors of states are praised for their economic development successes more than for their successes in improving the possibilities for participatory democracy.

While political leaders have become more business-like, business leaders have in certain respects become more democratic. Even more so, the leadership literature has become more concerned with democratic practices. Kellerman offers the following list of ideas that she has found in books on corporate leadership:

- Create a vision
- Level with everyone
- Communicate everything – and then some
- Rethink motivation
- Foster diversity

[4] Ibid., p. 36.

- Empower everyone
- Create networks
- Form teams
- Go horizontal
- Hang loose
- Always learn.[5]

This list applies not only to corporate and political leaders, from Kellerman's perspective, but also to nonprofit leaders. "The key tasks are the same [for for-profits and nonprofits]: creating a vision, communicating the vision, enlisting and empowering others, planning strategically and tactically, and implementing."[6] So at least in the literature on leadership Kellerman sees little difference between corporate, government, and non-profit leaders. This is not to say that all leaders are following the leadership literature. After her review of business practices in the 1990s Kellerman concluded:

Because the mantra of the decade has been "lean and mean," and because downsizing continues to play so large a part in the life of corporate America, the niceties touted by leadership theorists have remained largely unrealized. In fact, if truth be told, as the century draws to a close, America is still focusing its attention not on employees, supposedly the key followers, but on figures of authority, on the men (almost always) who hold the title of chief executive officer.[7]

This observation, however, does not deter Kellerman from proposing to close the gap between business and political leaders. The similarities, for her, overpower the differences. The similarities she cites are the following: both share an ideology of collaboration between leaders and followers, both are expected to provide meaning and purpose, both are embedded in international and national environments, both must be familiar with global markets, both are subject to public scrutiny, both are expected to be efficient managers, both face similar challenges in the fast-paced world of technology and globalization, both suffer from a gap between what is said and what is done, and finally, both fall short of the "moral model typically espoused."[8]

---

[5] Ibid., p. 125.
[6] Ibid., p. 180.
[7] Ibid., p. 157.
[8] Ibid., p. 160.

So business and political leaders seem very similar, except that they have different followers. How important is that? While Kellerman does recognize this difference, she does not give it much attention, apparently for two reasons. First of all, she believes that when push comes to shove, the "iron law of oligarchy" will prevail. This is the view developed by Robert Michels in 1911 that in large organizations the few at the top will eventually control the organization.[9] If the leader-and-follower relationship is not strong enough to prevent leaders from breaking it, then the relationship is also probably not strong enough to make much difference in a leader's identity.

A second assumption that seems to guide Kellerman's discounting of the role of followers in a leader's identity is a bit more complicated. It is based on her view of the business of business. She writes: "The business of politics is making public policy; and the business of business is making money."[10] Chapter 4 has already demonstrated that, in terms of organizational integrity, making money is a consequence of pursuing a worthwhile purpose, not a worthwhile purpose itself. If business leaders are organizational leaders, then their followers must be identified by their membership in the organization, not their private motive for joining the organization. From the perspective of organizational leadership, employees do not need a leader to make money; they need leaders to clarify the company's worthwhile purpose within continually changing social systems and to help them achieve it. This view assumes that the business of business is the pursuit of a worthwhile purpose in larger social systems. If the business of business is making money, business leaders probably do not need followers; they just need money. But are they then really leaders?

Political leaders serve as leaders because their followers, or at least a majority, have elected them. In some sense, they have an obligation to represent their followers' public concerns, and in some ways they receive their identity from them. Although modern media campaigns have made political leaders sometimes equivalent to entertainment stars, they still, at the end of the day, have to represent somebody. Is the same true for business leaders? Do they represent any followers? If leadership is a relational term, then where do business leaders receive their relational identity? The answer to these questions contains an

---

[9] Ibid., p. 204.
[10] Ibid., p. 218.

important principle for organizational leaders who want to promote corporate integrity. It all depends on how one sees the leader-and-follower relationship.

The leader-and-follower relationship

Some scholars in leadership studies appear to ignore the relational question while others see it as central. Joseph Badaracco and Richard Ellsworth, for example, in their *Leadership and the Quest for Integrity*, give the following definition of the leader with integrity:

Integrity is a consistency and coherence among three elements. One is a leader's aspiration for his or her organization. Another is a leader's own personal values... Left alone, however, organizational aims and personal aspirations run the risk of being irrelevant. They must be translated into action [the third element] through behavior that will move a company toward the ideal organization, one that is consistent with the leader's personal values in a dilemma-dominated world.[11]

Remember the four meanings of integrity presented in chapter 1? They included integrity as consistency, relational, inclusive, and pursuing a worthwhile purpose. Badaracco and Ellsworth's definition only touches on two of them: consistency and worthwhile purpose, or what they call a "sense of moral soundness."[12] The relational meaning of integrity is missing. Their definition of integrity appears to be so focused on the individual leader that it misses the relationships that create leaders in the first place. Ignoring the relationship between leaders and followers certainly makes it easier to imagine the similarities between different types of leaders, because they are seen only as individuals instead of as individuals-in-relationships. Without the relational connection, however, people no longer function as leaders.

In contrast to Badaracco and Ellsworth's view of leadership, Joseph Rost emphasizes the importance of the leadership relationship. In his *Leadership for the Twenty-First Century*, he first reviews various views

[11] Joseph L. Badaracco, Jr. and Richard R. Ellsworth, *Leadership and the Quest for Integrity* (Boston, MA: Harvard Business School Press, 1989), p. 109.
[12] Ibid., p. 98.

of leadership (many of which include the leader-and-follower relation-ship). He then offers his definition, where relationship is central: "Leadership is an influence relationship among leaders and followers who intend real changes that reflect their mutual purposes."[13] Rost further defines the relationship as follows:

Leadership as an influence relationship has two characteristics: (1) it is multidirectional, in that influence flows in all directions and not just from the top down; and (2) it is noncoercive, meaning that it is not based on authority, power, or dictatorial actions but is based on persuasive behaviors, thus allowing anyone in the relationship to freely agree or disagree and ultimately to drop into or out of the relationship.[14]

Rost's two characteristics of the leader-and-follower relationship do seem to fit with the image of secure civic reciprocal work relationships. They also fit with our understanding of the conditions for dialogue and deliberation. At the same time, they do not match the experience of many of us who work in organizations. In fact, our supervisors or leaders do tell us what to do, and many of us are not really free to disagree, at least not without severe consequences. So how can we square Rost's view of the leader-and-follower relationship with our everyday experience of supervisors and managers?

Rost's answer is that leaders and managers do not belong to the same category. For him, managers have positions of authority, from which they may use coercion. Leaders do not use coercion; they use influence instead. Also managers coordinate the activities of subordinates to produce goods and services, while leaders intend real change. Finally, leaders participate in a mutual purpose with followers. This mutual purpose is absent in the management/subordinate relationship.[15] These differences, for Rost, do not necessarily reside in different persons, so managers could lead, or leaders could manage.[16] Whether a manager really does lead depends on whether the relationship with workers is

---

[13] Joseph C. Rost, *Leadership for the Twenty-First Century* (Westport, CT: Praeger Publishers, 1991), p. 102. Other writers have also emphasized the importance of the relational dimension of leadership. See Georges Enderle, "Some Perspectives of Managerial Ethical Leadership," *Journal of Business Ethics*, vol. 6 (1987), pp. 657–63.

[14] Ibid., p. 107.

[15] Ibid., pp. 149–51.

[16] Ibid., p. 151.

one of influence, rather than coercion, and whether workers and managers share a mutual purpose.

Separating the process of leading from managing, as Rost does, raises a couple of problems. As Kellerman suggested earlier, business people now want to be seen as leaders, using persuasion rather than command and control. If the language of persuasion, however, hides the practice of command and control, then the result is what Joanne Ciulla has named "bogus empowerment." Bogus empowerment is when the verbal communication of collaboration and teamwork does not match the nonverbal patterns of command and control.[17] For Ciulla, leadership relations do involve the exercise of power, and can involve power transfers or empowerment of followers, but these transfers between leaders and followers must be based on a moral relationship that entails honesty, sincerity, and authenticity.[18] In other words, it is the moral character of the leader-and-follower relationship that makes all the difference.

Although it is certainly true that honest, sincere, and authentic relationships may be necessary for appropriate leader-and-follower relationships, are they sufficient? Is it possible, for example, that the type of master/servant relationships described in chapter 3 could be honest, sincere, and authentic? It probably is. Coercive relationships could also be honest, sincere, and authentic, and yet violate corporate integrity. As I argued in chapter 3, interpersonal relationships at work should recognize workers as citizens. Citizens, of course, should not be coerced. By separating leading from managing, Rost may have freed leaders from coercive relationships, but he has not freed the worker. His perspective, in other words, does not seem to adequately recognize the civic dimension of work relationships. The moral character of relationships among citizens (and both workers and managers are citizens) should not only be honest, sincere, and authentic, but should also respect each other's civic rights.

Does this mean that only corporations owned by workers can have integrity? Although such arrangements certainly would make citizenship more visible, I do not think they are necessary. Even in organizations that

---

[17] Joanne B. Ciulla, "Leadership and the Problem of Bogus Empowerment," in *Ethics: The Heart of Leadership*, ed. Joanne B. Ciulla (Westport, CT: Praeger, 1998).
[18] Ibid., p. 84.

are worker-owned, some people will still probably give directives for others to obey. The issue is not about who owns and controls corporate property, but who has the right to control corporate employees. The question is about the control of people, not property. Or even more to the point: why should some citizens at work submit to the directives of other citizens? To answer that question, and to advance our exploration of the notion of the leader-and-follower relationship, we need to develop a civic view of authority in the workplace.

A civic view of authority in the workplace

Corporate integrity requires that workers be treated as citizens, not just when leaders are leading them, but also when managers are managing them, which means that workers have a right to participate in the arrangement of their work life. This is not a new argument. Chapter 3 argued that the right to participate could be supported by a strong notion of interpersonal integrity that recognized that the core of civic relationships must be recognized in work relationships. This argument depended on a relational view of the self. A similar conclusion can be supported from a more individual notion of the self that emphasizes human freedom. George Brenkert argues from this perspective for worker participation in a recent article on the issue of corporate democracy: "Accordingly, a necessary condition for one's freedom to be respected is that one enjoy a right to participate in the decisions of organizations of which one is a member."[19] So both relational and individual notions of the self support the requirement for the recognition of the right to participate. This right has another side, of course, which is the freedom from coercion. Citizenship is not compatible with subjugation. Given this belief, why should employees obey the directives of managers? Christopher McMahon provides us with an answer: domination or coercion, he says, is not the same as subordination.[20]

---

[19] George G Brenkert, "Freedom, Participation and Corporations: The Issue of Corporate (Economic) Democracy," *Business Ethics Quarterly*, vol. 2, no. 3 (July, 1992), pp. 251–69.

[20] Christopher McMahon, *Authority and Democracy: A General Theory of Government and Management* (Princeton, NJ: Princeton University Press, 1994).

A relation of subordination may involve domination if it serves only the
interests of the person in the superior position . . . If it serves the interests of
the person in the subordinate position, however, in the sense of enabling him
to better comply with the reasons that apply to him – it is not a relation of
domination.[21]

So employees could obey their employer when it is in their interest to
do so. As McMahon points out, this is similar to a widely held justification for obeying laws in general. Obeying laws provides stability
and order, which most people believe is to their advantage.[22] For
McMahon, workers obey the directives of the manager because the
directives are good for the employees as a group.

To understand McMahon's argument here, we need to understand
his three different types of authority: E-authority, or the authority
of experts, P-authority, which is the authority based on promises,
and C-authority or a "cooperation-facilitating kind of authority."[23]
E-authority is fairly straightforward. If another person knows how to
do something and I do not, and if I want it done, I need to grant her
authority to do the work. A problem arises, of course, when authority
in one area is transferred to another area in which the person's expertise does not apply, such as when someone who is an expert in running
a computer company is then assumed to be an expert in public education or healthcare, as some business executives seem to assume.

P-authority is based on promises, such as the promise that if you do
the work, you will receive wages in return. As McMahon points out,
when one has reasons to question whether or not to obey one's supervisor, such promises would only be one of several moral reasons for
continuing to be obedient.[24] There could be occasions, for example,
where one's moral obligations to one's family would override the
moral obligation to keep one's promises at work. Even more significant
for citizens at work, however, is that obedience based only on promises
may ignore the quality of the relationship between employees and
employers. P-authority encounters the same problem as relying only
on contracts to establish relationships, rather than also emphasizing
the idea of membership. Relationships at work are certainly reciprocal,

---

[21] Ibid., p. 45.
[22] Ibid., p. 4.
[23] Ibid., p. 44.
[24] Ibid., p. 220.

but they should also include the need for security and the right of participation. Only the third possibility, C-authority, sets forth the conditions for such a complex relationship.

C-authority, or "cooperation-facilitation authority" can legitimately require obedience because employees can see it as facilitating the attainment of goods they desire. To understand McMahon's point here, it is necessary to take a collective or organizational view rather than that of the individual. As a collective, following the directives of managers allows employees to cooperatively achieve ends they could not achieve without such facilitation. In the workplace, these ends should be the worthwhile purposes of the corporation – the development and distribution of excellent products and services that meet the needs of customers in the context of various social systems. Wages, from this perspective, are not merely part of an exchange contract, but also a form of social justice. Much like the notion of reciprocity from chapter 3, those who contribute to attaining corporate objectives should be rewarded for their contribution.[25]

Leading by facilitating cooperation may not appear to match the official obligations of most business leaders. Do they not also have a responsibility to manage corporate property? Of course they do. Why else would business schools give degrees in business administration? But sometimes business administrators are also business leaders. These people appear to be caught in a dilemma between their obligations to manage corporate property and their obligations to respect workers as citizens. Although completely resolving this dilemma is probably impossible, the notion of corporate integrity would suggest that the dilemma's mediation could occur through remaining connected to the corporation's purpose, which provides both the reason for its existence and a common cause for both employers and employees. In any case, as McMahon points out, the right to control corporate property does not entail the right to control labor. He uses the analogy of someone using his car.

My ownership of my car, for example, gives me the right to tell someone who is driving it to refrain from certain courses of action – to exclude them – but it does not give me the right to direct her to do anything with it ... Similarly,

[25] Ibid., p. 246.

property rights in productive resources cannot provide a moral basis for managerial authority, understood as the authority to tell employees what to do, as opposed to what to refrain from doing.[26]

If the analogy holds, and I think it does, then corporate administrators have the right to keep people from using their machinery or knowledge technology, but they cannot force anyone to use them. To enlist workers to do the work, they need to show that following their directives will facilitate getting the work done. This assumes of course, that the work is worthwhile doing. Workers need to be connected to the larger purpose of the work, to see their part in the larger whole, and to accept this purpose as worthwhile. Their work, in other words, has to have integrity – it needs to be part of a meaningful whole.

If organizations have a worthwhile purpose, the manager-and-worker or leader-and-follower relationship receives its legitimacy from belonging to a common endeavor to do something well. The leadership principle implicit here is that the exercise of authority at work should facilitate the workers' accomplishment of corporate purposes. In some cases, this authority will belong in a particular position and in other cases it may emerge out of a process of deliberation. We could interpret the exercise of authority from one's position as the work of management and the exercise of authority in the deliberative process as the work of leaders. Such labels, however, may prove more misleading than helpful. In both cases, the exercise of authority must be civil and *for* the employees. If there is a need to make a difference between managing and leading, it probably should not be a very large one. Leading is a process that is *for* the followers, who in turn are working *for* the corporation's worthwhile purpose. Wherever directing occurs, its legitimacy will depend on the quality of the relationship in which it exists. A civic view of authority in the workplace highlights that the human relationships of participants in the ongoing communications that constitute organizations should be relationships of consent, not coercion. Leaders can facilitate the development of integrity in these communicative relationships in two ways: by designing the context for integrity and by showing signs of integrity.

[26] Ibid., pp. 16–17.

Designing the context for corporate integrity

Of the five dimensions of corporate integrity, the dimension that most clearly expresses the intricacies of the leader-and-follower relationship is the interpersonal. So this section will focus on leading teams, which was the image of work relationships that most closely matched the need for secure civic reciprocal relationships. Of course, not all teams are alike. Some have much more autonomy than others.

J. Richard Hackman outlines four different levels of team self-management: (1) manager-led teams, which are teams that only have authority to execute the task assigned by management; (2) self-managing teams, which are teams that have responsibilities in monitoring their process of meeting management directives; (3) self-designing teams, where managers still give directives, but the team has authority to decide how to meet objectives; and (4) self-governing teams, where team members have responsibility for deciding what is to be done and how to do it.[27] One way to interpret the difference among Hackman's types is in terms of the balance of position and deliberative authority. The first type relies mostly on the authority of the managers to give them directions, while the fourth type would rely mostly on the process of deliberation as the source of directions. At the same time, if the management directives of these teams are sufficient for the team's task and the task is connected to a worthwhile purpose, then designing the appropriate context for each type of team can promote the integrity of the whole corporation.

In Hackman's book on leading teams, he focuses mostly on the characteristics of effective teams, and then from this perspective looks at what leaders should do.[28] Contrast this approach with leadership programs that begin with characteristics of leadership and then think of groups to lead.[29] A strong relational view of leadership favors Hackman's approach. His description of the characteristics of an effective team, in fact, appears to parallel most of the integrity

---

[27] J. Richard Hackman, *Leading Teams: Setting the Stage for Great Performances* (Boston, MA: Harvard Business School Press, 2002), p. 53.
[28] Ibid.
[29] See, for example, Charles J. Palus and David M. Horth, *The Leader's Edge: Six Creative Competencies for Navigating Complex Challenges* (San Francisco, CA: Jossey-Bass, 2002).

challenges covered in the previous chapters. Look at the following diagnostic questions that he believes teams should be able to answer:

Is the team a real team, bounded and stable over time, that requires members to work interdependently to achieve some common purpose? Is the team's direction clear, consequential, and challenging? Does the team's structure – its task, composition, and norms – facilitate good performance processes? Does the organizational context – the rewards, information, and educational systems – provide the team with the supports that the work requires? And is there expert coaching available to the team to help members minimize the inefficiencies in their performance processes and instead harvest the potential synergies of teamwork?[30]

The first two questions about a "real team" and a "common purpose" would be supported by the integrity requirements for secure relationships and a worthwhile purpose. The questions about the team's structure would be supported by the integrity requirements for the citizens consenting to follow directives. The question of the organizational context would fit with the integrity requirement of reciprocal relationships. The suggestion about expert coaching is not part of the integrity requirement, but also would not exclude it. So, it seems that leading teams for effectiveness is very much like leading teams for integrity: it is largely a matter of design. As Hackman says:

A leader cannot make a team great, but a leader can create the conditions that increase the chances that moments of greatness will occur – and moreover, can provide a little boost or nudge now and then to help members take the fullest possible advantage of these favorable conditions.[31]

Designing and redesigning teams is largely a process of changing the verbal and nonverbal communication patterns in which teams perform. Much of the work has to do with making the available resources that teams need to be effective. Instead of teams existing in their own worlds, they need to be connected with other aspects of the organization so communication easily occurs when necessary. This is especially true of teams that have a tendency to move toward ethnocentric patterns of communication and engage in us-and-them thinking. Leaders can enable them to discard any myth of scarcity by showing that resources match

---

[30] Hackman, *Leading Teams*, p. 212.
[31] Ibid., p. 253.

responsibilities and that every team is a part of a larger whole that provides them with resources and gives them direction so they can be effective and have integrity. Paul Dolan has made a similar point in arguing that leaders must give workers knowledge about the bigger picture so they see where their work fits into the whole enterprise.

As leaders, our job is to cultivate our people, bringing out their best and create a rich, human whole greater than the sum of the parts. That's culture: something bigger than the individuals within a group, which they nevertheless are an integral part of. Teamwork becomes more natural, because everyone knows why the work the next person is doing is valuable. If they're talking about that context all the time, if they are constantly looking at their workplace, their products, and their processes from the standpoint of fulfilling themselves and their purpose, you can hardly keep up with the ideas they bring forth.[32]

The importance of paying attention to the context has also been emphasized in Krogh, Ichijo, and Nonaka's book on creating knowledge.

The enabling context must be energized so that individuals or the organization can create and amplify knowledge. For that purpose, managers need to provide the following conditions: the right amount of autonomy for participants; a certain level of creative chaos, redundancy, and variety to make the environment stimulating; and again, a high-care organization – one that fosters mutual support and commitment.[33]

This enabling context is not only relevant for the human need for security but also for the civic right of participation. As Michael Walzer has said:

The citizen must be ready and able, when his time comes, to deliberate with his fellows, listen and be listened to, take responsibility for what he says and does. Ready and able: not only in states, cities, and towns, but wherever power is exercised, in companies and factories, too, and in unions, faculties, and professions.[34]

---

[32] Dolan, *True To Our Roots*, pp. 64–5.
[33] Georg Von Krogh, Kazuo Ichijo, and Ikujiro Nonaka, *Enabling Knowledge Creation: How to Unlock the Mystery of Tacit Knowledge and Release the Power of Innovation* (New York: Oxford University Press, 2000).
[34] Walzer, *Spheres of Justice*, p. 310.

The readiness of citizens, of course, depends largely on the expectations that the ongoing conversations communicate. Perhaps more than anything else, leading teams and groups involves giving signs of appropriate expectations. These expectations are not only about coming forth and speaking one's mind, but also about the appropriate boundaries between persons and among different teams, as well as between corporations and other civic organizations.

Just as the setting of boundaries is important for moving beyond the excesses of modernistic communication (chapter 2), for participating in conversations with other agencies in civic society (chapter 5), and for living within natural limits (chapter 6), it is also important for designing teams. Instead of striving to rise above all others, we need to learn how to live with others. The aggression of modernistic communication, which tends to drive everything from child rearing to technological development, becomes more and more of a liability as the population becomes larger and the earth becomes smaller. Teams should be excellent; they do not need to be the best. Corporations do not have to be great. They can just be really good. Being the "best" almost always requires the sacrifice of some part of a whole for the advancement of another part. It almost always signals, in other words, a lack of integrity. Designing communication patterns that ensure high-quality work, and that carry the interconnections among different groups and projects throughout the organization, can help each team to know its place in a larger whole, and how other groups depend on its quality work.

Designing the communication patterns that provide the context for teams does not exhaust the leadership role of organizational leaders. They can also be participants in team deliberations, and through their participation display that corporate integrity is not only a possibility, but also a reality. Corporate integrity becomes apparent when people practice openness, provide safety, voice their concerns, refer to worthwhile purposes, cooperate with others, and include nature in their strategic plans. Just as the integrity of political leaders is connected to how they represent the public concerns of their constituency, the integrity of business leaders depends on how they represent or signify the integrity of the corporations to which they belong, whether in conversations with representatives from other civic agencies or with co-workers. The organizational leader displays by words and deeds the direction to take in order to increase the integrity of the corporation to which she belongs. This aspect of leadership, as Hackman says, is very much a "shared activity."[35] It is the work of displaying or showing signs of corporate integrity.

Showing signs of corporate integrity

Corporations come in all sizes, and large corporations certainly have more leadership positions than smaller ones. These leadership positions are not only created and maintained by various ongoing communication patterns, but people in these positions can change the patterns by how they lead. The leaders with the greatest capacity for promoting or preventing appropriate conversations in all five dimensions of corporate life are the members of a senior leadership team and especially the CEO. Most CEOs have more duties than leading followers, such as their duties to the corporate board, but in terms of corporate integrity, their relationship with followers is essential. Even though they cannot have a concrete relationship with the thousands of employees who obey corporate directives, they can actively lead employees through promoting the *design* of appropriate communication patterns throughout the corporation and acting as a visible *sign* of how employees should participate in these conversations.

In a recent study of ethical leadership by senior management, Trevino, Hartman, and Brown examined the importance of corporate executives actively demonstrating their ethical leadership. According to their research, executives need to make their ethical actions visible to their employees in order for the employees to see what the corporation expects of them.[36]

Our study identified a number of ways moral managers can increase the salience of an ethics and values agenda and develop a reputation for ethical leadership. They serve as a role model for ethical conduct in a way that is visible to employees. They communicate regularly and persuasively with employees about ethical standards, principles, and values. Finally, they use

---

[35] Ibid., p. 211.
[36] Linda Klebe Trevino, Laura Pincus Hartman, and Michael Brown, "Moral Person and Moral Manager: How Executives Develop a Reputation for Ethical Leadership," *California Management Review*, vol. 42, no. 4 (Summer, 2000), pp. 128–42.

the reward system consistently to hold all employees accountable to ethical standards.[37]

These recommended actions are essential for creating an expectation for high ethical performance throughout an organization. Signaling expectations is perhaps the most important aspect of leadership in large organizations. This process of showing signs of corporate integrity can actually occur at all levels of the organization, especially in the process of corporate deliberations.

Sometimes the leader is seen as the one who has the last word, the speaker who ends the conversation. Particular conversations do have an ending, of course, but in terms of dialogue and deliberation, the leader is more often the one who deepens, redirects, and continues conversations. One of the key virtues for deepening and directing the conversation is curiosity. Curiosity is not only a remedy for monocultural communication patterns; as suggested in chapter 2, it can also facilitate team dialogue.

Remember the exploration of dialogue in chapter 2? It is in dialogue that the shared activity of leadership occurs most readily. Dialogical leaders enter into conversations with others and work together to articulate their best potential through discovering the possibilities that become available through the dialogical process. In other words, leaders emerge from the dialogical process itself as those who become responsible for realities that the process defines. Especially in a cosmopolitan organization (one that practices cosmopolitan communication) different resources from different participants are acknowledged as valuable. It is not necessary for all to rely on the same resources, or to believe in the same stories. Instead, each person's resources provide a base for designing coordination patterns that enable people working together to accomplish common projects.

Who becomes the leader in this process will not always be determined by designated leadership positions. In fact, a responsibility of those in leadership positions is to facilitate the conditions for cooperative dialogue that enable any follower to step forward and say what needs to be said, and thereby lead others where the group needs to go. Someone must begin the conversation, or at least take up the continuing conversation again, but if this person's initial contributions

---

[37] Ibid., p. 134.

dominate the conversation, then the group will be stuck in monological soliloquies rather than being open to dialogue. Leadership in dialogical conversations emerges from the process itself, as participants are called forth into responsible activities.

In many cases, the initiation of a resourceful dialogue begins with asking the right questions. This issue surfaced in the last chapter in the analysis of how corporations could participate in current conversations about nature. Asking the right questions is also relevant here, not only in terms of setting the right boundaries for an inquiry, but also in terms of different types of knowledge, and the relationships among them. Since managers and leaders often share information and knowledge in teams, and teams themselves are carriers of information and knowledge, it is important to understand the process of sharing knowledge.

Suppose you have seen your company's new product, and from your perspective it seems designed for a more upscale buyer than previous models. You ask if that is true and learn you are right. It will be more expensive. So your observation was right. Do you now know what is going on? Hardly. In fact, with this small amount of information you may be more puzzled than enlightened. To understand what is going on, you will need more than just the facts, because facts always exist in and receive their meaning from a particular context that is constituted not only by facts, but also by values and assumptions. How many times have we failed to understand something because we interpreted the "facts" from our perspective rather than the perspective from which the facts originated? Giving people "just the facts" sometimes does more harm than good, especially when the listener does not understand the speaker's context that gives the facts their meaning.

The contextual aspect of facts can be clarified by making a distinction between technical information and tacit knowledge. Most practices, from riding a bike to reading a business ledger, involve both technical information and tacit knowledge. We "know" how to ride a bike or read a ledger because we have a kind of somatic knowledge in the sense that it is embedded in our bodies; sometimes in our whole body, such as riding a bike, and sometimes in our minds, such as when reading business ledgers. Without this tacit knowledge, employees may be baffled by information that is disconnected from actual practices.

In some cases, the facts cannot be adequately understood because one does not know the value and assumptions that make them relevant. The facts we talk about are always selections from the myriad of things we could talk about. The selection process depends on our values and assumptions.[38] Values give significance to "facts" when they support something that we think should be done. Assumptions, on the other hand, provide the worldview in which a particular set of values and observations make sense.

Remember the four communicative cultures presented in chapter 2? The differences in how people treat resources and others, as well as their temporal orientation, were all based on different assumptions about how things work and the way things are. To understand activities within communities, people need to understand their history, traditions, and stories, their awareness of things, and their expectations for the future. Every community is embedded in a culture that provides the participants of that community with a foundation for interpreting the world in a particular manner. To listen to information without knowing the values that made the information significant or the assumptions that lead people to understand the information in a certain manner is to create opportunities for misunderstanding and mistakes. To share information, on the other hand, by knowing or communicating the values and assumptions that provide their context, enables effective and collaborative leadership.

If you want to share information, you need to consider how to share the values and assumptions that give the information meaning.

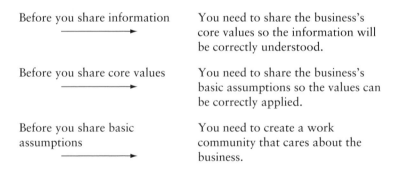

Figure 7.2. Conditions for sharing information

---

[38] For a detailed analysis of the differences and relationships among observations, values, and assumptions, see my *Working Ethics; Strategies for Decision Making and Organizational Responsibility* (San Francisco, CA: Jossey-Bass, 1990, and Oakland, CA: Regent Press, 2000).

Figure 7.2 shows some of the needed conditions for the successful sharing of information.

You not only share information, values, and assumptions, you also receive the same from others, if they are open to you. The process of receiving knowledge from others somewhat repeats the flow chart we just developed, but there is another dimension that needs attention – the likelihood that another's information, values, and assumptions will be different from one's own. So we need to explore the conditions for listening to and valuing differences. Figure 7.3 attempts to illustrate this dynamic.

Before you receive information ⟶	You need to prepare yourself to hear something you might not have said.
To prepare yourself to hear something you might not have said ⟶	You need to acknowledge that others know things that you do not know.
To acknowledge others as knowing what you do not know ⟶	You need to accept that different experiences have different meanings for different people.
To acknowledge that people are different ⟶	You will need to learn how others see you as different from how you see yourself.
To learn how others see you differently than you see yourself ⟶	You will have to create a context where everyone feels safe to say what needs to be said.
To create such a context ⟶	You can show others that you feel comfortable listening to them.

Figure 7.3. Conditions for receiving information

Showing others that you feel comfortable can display the safety that will allow dialogue to occur and for leadership to become a shared activity. Participants will then have the opportunity not only to say what needs to be said, but also speak in such a way that other members respond to and join in a common endeavor of understanding the task at hand as a collaborative project.

If there is a difference between a manager and a leader in this process, it will reveal itself in terms of who provides a sign of the deeper meanings of human integrity. I think this is what Hackman may have in mind when he writes of the need for "emotional maturity."[39] He writes of emotional maturity mostly in terms of being able to handle anxiety, but I think it goes further than this. Daniel Goleman's extensive work on "emotional intelligence" might be of some help here. In his book on "primal leadership," he sees the leader as "the group's emotional guide."[40] According to Goleman and the other authors of *Primal Leadership*, the choices for leaders are either to lead with "resonance," which would be to share similar emotions with followers, or "dissonance," which would mean a disconnection between the leaders' and followers' emotions. This distinction seems very important, as does another distinction these authors make between alignment and attunement. Groups can be in alignment with the organization's purpose and with their leaders, but not in attunement. The emotional element would be missing in alignment, but present in attunement. Displaying the relational attunement of people and projects could be one hallmark of the leader.

In spite of these important categories, a closer reading of *Primal Leadership* reveals that the book not only displays a modernistic lack of awareness of boundaries (as defined in chapter 2), but also reveals that it is based on a post office model of communication. The book's model of emotional leadership is for an individual to first get his or her emotional life together, and then to connect with others. The contextual model of communication would proceed quite differently. It would lead one to examine how the context evokes individual emotions, instead of interpreting the emotional response as primarily located in the individual. Emotional responses, in other words, indicate something about the situation and especially about human relationships. People certainly bring their own emotional history with them, and they may have different degrees of maturity, but to assume that emotions are independent of group interactions is to make the talk about emotions so abstract that people will overlook how emotional awareness can provide important knowledge about issues and situations. Giving signs of integrity does require emotional maturity, but it also requires an

[39] Hackman, *Leading Teams*, p. 226.
[40] Daniel Goleman, Richard Boyatzis, and Annie McKee, *Primal Leadership: Realizing the Power of Emotional Intelligence* (Boston, MA: Harvard Business School Press, 2002), p. 5.

empathy with the emotional climate of a group process. Perhaps this type of attunement with a group's emotional life is what gives a leader the capacity to facilitate group learning and transformation that the manager prepares for. In its most complete form, this attunement not only grasps a group's emotional life, but also acknowledges the group's potential for transforming their expectations of themselves. This emergent possibility is close to what Pearce called the mystery of cosmopolitan communication.

Another way of thinking about the difference between the manager and the leader is in terms of providing signs of mystery. The emergence of mystery in cosmopolitan communication enables an acknowledgment that there is always more than has been said. This "more" humanizes our communities. It is what provides space for entering into generative dialogue to revitalize the center that holds everything together. It is this "more" that gives virtues and actions meaning, so that instead of just wanting to be satisfied, people strive for excellence. If work teams can come to experience this "more," it will not only affect their work together, but also their production and service. The writer Michael Ignatieff refers to this "more" in the following quote about meeting the needs of others.

Giving the aged poor their pension and providing them with medical care might be a necessary condition for their self-respect and their dignity, but it is not a sufficient condition. It is the manner of the giving that counts and the moral basis on which it is given; whether strangers at my door get their stories listened to by the social workers, whether the ambulance man takes care not to jostle them when they are taken down the steep stairs of their apartment building, whether a nurse sits with them in the hospital when they are frightened and alone. Respect and dignity are conferred by gestures such as these. They are gestures too much a matter of human art to be made a consistent matter of administrative routine.[41]

There is a meaning, a mystery, and an emotional dimension to the work of leading teams, and more generally to the work of organizational leadership. It is, however, as Hackman has said, a shared activity. We all need to become involved in designing and redesigning

---

[41] Michael Ignatieff, *The Needs of Strangers: An Essay on Privacy, Solidarity, and the Politics of Being Human* (New York: Penguin Books, 1984), p. 17.

conversations, sometimes in terms of creating more appropriate conditions so people can share their knowledge, and sometimes by saying what we believe and saying it in such a way that the dialogue grows. This may allow us to see the outlines for designing corporate integrity in such a way that we can trust corporations as partners in creating our common future.

The notion of integrity is a calling: a calling to relate, to include. It means that the stranger is recognized not as apart from us, but rather as a part of us. When strangers are like us, they are easy to include. When the stranger is different from us or disagrees with us, it is more difficult. At its more profound dimension, integrity calls for an inclusion where everyone is equally a stranger and equally at home. No one owns the home we want to enter, it belongs to all of us. We will only feel safe when we all belong. We can only enter into an integrated community when we leave behind a world of us versus them, move away from structures of privilege, and become strangers together. Once we all become strangers, then we can work in designing conversational patterns at different dimensions of personal and organizational life, in which we can talk together about our need for security and our right to participate, our desire to live for something worthwhile, and our common aspiration to live at home on the earth.

From theory to practice

Questions for dialogue and reflection

1. What changes need to occur in your organization before all five dimensions of corporate integrity could be addressed?
2. What dimensions of corporate integrity can you most directly influence and what can you do?
3. What do you see as the similarities and differences between business and political leaders?
4. What should be the relationship between leaders and followers?
5. Which of McMahon's three types of authority is used in your workplace?
6. What do you see as the differences between managers and leaders?
7. What conditions are necessary for you to be a leader in your organizations?

Guidelines for the assessment worksheets in the appendix

The five dimensions of corporate integrity provide a comprehensive framework for addressing business issues. Worksheet #14 provides an example of developing questions on the issue of advertising ethics, and then provides a worksheet for interpreting other issues from all five dimensions of corporate integrity.

Many corporations today provide a yearly report of their economic, social, and environmental performance. Worksheet #15 provides an opportunity for examining what values and assumptions should be communicated for others to understand such "information."

Appendix: Assessment Worksheets

Worksheet #1

Chapter 1: The context for corporate integrity

Five dimensions of corporate integrity

Select recent conversations, or communication patterns and analyze the explicit or implicit theme or message about the five challenges to corporate integrity:

cultural openness

relational awareness

worthwhile purpose

civic cooperation

natural prosperity.

Worksheet #2

Chapter 1: The context for corporate integrity

Looking at your organization as an ongoing conversation

How has the ongoing conversation changed?

How has the ongoing conversation remained the same?

How does the ongoing conversation need to change to increase corporate integrity?

Worksheet #3

Chapter 1: The context for cultural integrity

Models of corporate responsibility

On many corporate websites, corporations have their mission statements and corporate responsibility programs. Analyze these statements in terms of how they include or balance the five theories of corporate responsibility.

Classic

Contractual

Stakeholder

Corporate agent

Corporate citizen

Worksheet #4

Chapter 2: Cultural integrity as openness

Analyzing communicative practices

Logic	Pre-figurative	Contextual	Implicative	Practical	(Reflexive)
Expressions	Because of what has happened	To affirm my "situation"	To change my "situation"	In order to	Think about it
Types of culture	Monocultural	Monocultural Ethnocentric	Modernistic Cosmopolitan	Modernistic Cosmopolitan	Modernistic Cosmopolitan
Time-frame	Past	Present	Present	Future	Present

List eight persons you interact with in the first column, and then evaluate the interaction in terms of the different kinds of force (What's driving the interaction?). Distribute 10 points among the five different types of forces for each personal interaction.

Persons	Pre-figurative	Contextual	Implicative	Practical	Reflective

Worksheet #5

Chapter 2: Cultural integrity as openness

Dialogue worksheet

List eight different persons or groups you communicate with in the first column in the chart below. Include settings at work, at home, at play, and in your public and private life. Then evaluate the communication patterns with them on each of the following aspects of dialogue, using the scale from 5 to 1.

A. See others as different	Strong	5 4 3 2 1	Weak
B. Ask questions of inquiry	Many	5 4 3 2 1	Few
C. Acknowledge resources	Often	5 4 3 2 1	Seldom
D. Explore the unknown	Often	5 4 3 2 1	Seldom
E. Develop thought	Often	5 4 3 2 1	Seldom
F. Gain self-understanding	Often	5 4 3 2 1	Seldom

Dialogue partners	A	B	C	D	E	F

Worksheet #6

Chapter 3: Interpersonal integrity as relational wholeness

Images of relationships

Draw your images of family, civic, and work relationships in the squares below.

	Family relationships	Civic relationships	Work relationships
Your realistic image of			
The "official" image of			
Your ideal image of			

After completing the worksheet, explore what are possible expectations for developing secure civic reciprocal relationships at work.

Worksheet #7

Chapter 3: Interpersonal integrity as relational wholeness

Evaluating the conditions for public deliberation

Select a conversation at work, assess it by using the questions below, and then talk with others about what conditions could be improved and how to improve them.

1. What is the degree of safety?
   High 5 4 3 2 1 Low

2. What is the degree to which everyone feels free to participate?
   High 5 4 3 2 1 Low

3. What is the degree to which decisions are based on good reasons?
   High 5 4 3 2 1 Low

4. What is the degree of cooperation?
   High 5 4 3 2 1 Low

5. What is the degree of publicity (reasons are available to everyone)?
   High 5 4 3 2 1 Low

Worksheet #8

Chapter 4: Organizational integrity as pursuing a worthwhile purpose

Organizational talk

How would the meaning of the following terms change when they are applied to individuals, to for-profits or to nonprofits?

Motives

Agency

Decision making

Intentions

Purposes

Character

Desires

Self-government

Integrity

Worksheet #9

Chapter 4: Organizational integrity as pursuing a worthwhile purpose

Corporate purpose as a worthwhile function in a larger social system

Place a corporation in the middle circle, include other agencies that belong to the circle, and identify the larger social systems in the outer rings. (Some possible larger systems are healthcare, education, sports, entertainment, food, welfare, transportation, finance, and information.)

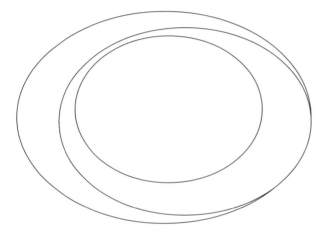

How do you see the relationships among the different parts of the whole? What is the purpose of the whole system? How do the different parts contribute to the whole?

Worksheet #10

Chapter 5: Social integrity as civic cooperation

Corporate and city relationships

Which of the six models of corporate/city relationships matches your business's interactions with the city in which it exists?

Ownership model
Unconscious model
Business leader model
Competitive model
Paternalistic model
Partnership model

How would you describe the integrity (wholeness) of that relationship?

How would changes in the conversations between corporations and cities increase integrity?

Worksheet #11

Chapter 5: Social integrity as civic cooperation

Select how you think the goods in the first column should be distributed in society, and justify your choices in terms of what you think about their social meaning.

The Distribution of Goods

	Market only	Mixed	Government only	Private donations
Housing	○	○	○	○
Education	○	○	○	○
Life insurance	○	○	○	○
Police protection	○	○	○	○
Healthcare	○	○	○	○
Automobile	○	○	○	○
Care	○	○	○	○
Jobs	○	○	○	○
Childcare	○	○	○	○
Safe environment	○	○	○	○

Worksheet #12

Chapter 6: Environmental integrity as natural prosperity

Designing new conversations

Select two other conversation partners. As a group of three, let each person represent one of the three conversations on sustainability, world trade, or the integrity of nature. From these different positions, develop a new conversation by answering the following questions about the future.

What do we know is true?

What do we not know?

What are the most general shared values?

What are the basic assumptions we share?

What does integrity require?

How should we proceed?

Worksheet #13

Chapter 6: Environmental integrity as natural prosperity

Talking about natural prosperity

How could organizations, in which you are involved or have knowledge of, include the following four themes in their conversations?

Asking the right questions

Practicing the principle of subsidiarity

Setting boundaries

Promoting natural prosperity.

Worksheet #14

Chapter 7: Corporate integrity and organizational leadership

Using the five dimensions of corporate integrity to ask the right questions

Use the example below on the issue of advertising as a model for developing questions on the five dimensions of corporate integrity. Use the worksheet on the next page to address issues you have selected.

The Five Dimensions of Corporate Integrity and Ethics of Advertising

Corporate dimension	Challenges	Sample questions
Cultural	Openness to cultural differences Capacity to handle disagreements	How can our advertising respect different cultures and customs?
Interpersonal	Need for security Employee participation in setting standards	Does our advertising play on people's fears and anxieties? Does it reflect our standards for interpersonal relationships?
Organizational	Quality of products and services Character of work community	Is there a clear match between our products and social needs and our advertisements?
Civic	Rights of citizens at work Corporation as member of civil society	Does our advertising exploit the vulnerabilities of particular communities? How do they fit with our city's mission?
Natural	Environmental threats Sustainability	How could commercial advertising promote sustainability?

Asking the Right Questions

Issue:		
Corporate dimension	*Challenges*	*Questions*
Cultural	Openness to cultural differences, capacity to handle disagreements	
Interpersonal	Need for security, employee participation in setting standards	
Organizational	Quality of products and services, character of work community	
Civic	Rights of citizens at work, corporation as member of civil society	
Natural	Environmental threats, sustainability	

Worksheet #15

Chapter 7: Corporate integrity as organizational leadership

Designing conditions for understanding

Select a corporation and research the relevant facts, values, and assumptions that members would need to know to become engaged leaders in achieving the company's goals.

Type of Knowledge	Information (the facts)	Values	Assumptions
Company purpose			
Social performance			
Environmental performance			
Economic performance			

Bibliography

Alternative to Economic Globalization: A Better World is Possible: A Report of the International Forum on Globalization, San Francisco: Berrett-Koehler, 2002.

The American Heritage Dictionary of the English Language, third edition, Boston: Houghton Mifflin, 1992.

Amin, Ash and Thrift, Nigel, *Cities: Reimagining The Urban*, Malden, MA: Blackwell Publishers, 2002.

Anheier, Helmut, Glasius, Marlies, and Kaldon, Mary (eds.), *Global Civil Society*, Oxford: Oxford University Press, 2001.

Arendt, Hannah, *The Human Condition*, Garden City, NY: Doubleday, 1959.

Aristotle, *Nicomachean Ethics*, The Library of Liberal Arts, trans. M. Ostwald, Englewood Cliffs, NJ: Prentice Hall, 1962.

Austin, James E., *The Collaboration Challenge: How Nonprofits and Businesses Succeed Through Strategic Alliances*, San Francisco: Jossey-Bass, 2000.

Badaracco, Joseph L. Jr. and Ellsworth, Richard R., *Leadership and the Quest for Integrity*, Boston, MA: Harvard Business School Press, 1989.

Barber, Benjamin, *Strong Democracy: Participatory Politics for a New Age*, Berkeley, Los Angeles, and London: University of California Press, 1984.

Becker, Lawrence C., *Reciprocity*, Chicago and London: University of Chicago Press, 1986.

Bello, Walden, *The Future in the Balance: Essays on Globalization and Resistance*, Oakland, CA: Food First Books, 2001.

Boatright, John, *Ethics and the Conduct of Business*, fourth edition, Upper Saddle River, NJ: Prentice Hall, 2003.

Bohman, James, *Public Deliberation: Pluralism, Complexity, and Democracy*, Cambridge, MA: MIT Press, 1996.

Boulding, Kenneth, *Three Faces of Power*, New York: Sage, 1990.

Bowlby, John, *A Secure Base: Parent–Child Attachment and Healthy Human Development*, New York: Basic Books, 1988.

Bradsher, Keith, "Ford Admits SUVs are Irresponsible: Safety, Environmental Problems Noted, but so are Huge Profits," *San Francisco Chronicle*, May 12, 2000.

Brenkert, George G., "Freedom, Participation and Corporations: The Issue of Corporate (Economic) Democracy," *Business Ethics Quarterly*, vol. 2, no. 3 (July, 1992), pp. 251–69.

Brown, Marvin T., *Working Ethics: Strategies for Decision Making and Organizational Responsibility*, San Francisco, CA: Jossey-Bass, 1990, and Oakland, CA: Regent Press, 2000.

   The Ethical Process: An Approach to Disagreement and Controversial Issues, third edition, Upper Saddle Lake, NJ: Prentice Hall, 2003.

Bruyn, Severyn T., *A Civil Economy: Transforming the Market in the Twenty-First Century*, Ann Arbor: University of Michigan Press, 2000.

Buber, Martin, *I and Thou*, trans. R. Gregor-Smith, New York: Charles Scribner's Sons, 1958.

   On Intersubjectivity and Cultural Creativity, ed. S. N. Eisenstadt, Chicago and London: University of Chicago Press, 1992.

   Between Man and Man, trans. R. Gregor-Smith, London and New York: Routledge, 2002.

Buchholz, Rogene A. and Rosenthal, Sandra B., "Toward an Ethics of Consumption," in *The Business of Consumption: Environmental Ethics and the Global Economy*, ed. Laura Westra and Patricia Werhane, New York: Rowman and Littlefield, 1998.

Burke, Kenneth, *A Grammar of Motives*, Berkeley and Los Angeles: University of California Press, 1969.

Capra, Fritjof, *The Hidden Connections: Integrating the Biological, Cognitive and Social Dimensions of Life into a Science of Sustainability*, New York: Doubleday, 2002.

Carnegie, Andrew, *Problems of To-Day: Wealth, Labor, and Socialism*, Garden City, NY: Doubleday, Doran and Company, 1933.

Castells, Manuel, *The Informational City*, Oxford: Blackwell Publishers, 1991.

   "Information Technology and Global Capitalism," in *Global Capitalism*, ed. Will Hutton and Anthony Giddens, New York: The New Press, 2000.

Chua, Amy, *World on Fire: How Exporting Free Market Democracy Breeds Ethnic Hatred and Global Instability*, New York: Doubleday, 2003.

Churchman, C. W., *The Systems Approach*, New York: Dell Publishing Co., 1968.

Ciulla, Joanne B., "Leadership and the Problem of Bogus Empowerment," in *Ethics: The Heart of Leadership*, ed. Joanne B. Ciulla, Westport, CT: Praeger, 1998.

Coase, R. H., "The Nature of the Firm: Origin (1937)," in *The Nature of the Firm: Origins, Evolution, and Development*, ed. Oliver E. Williamson and Sidney G. Winter, New York and Oxford: Oxford University Press, 1993, pp. 18–33.

Cohen, Allan and Bradford, David, *Influence Without Authority*, New York: John Wiley, 1991.

Cohen, Jean L. and Arato, Andrew, *Civil Society and Political Theory*, Cambridge, MA: MIT Press, 1992.

Collins, James C. and Porras, Jerry I., *Built to Last: Successful Habits of Visionary Companies*, New York: HarperBusiness, 1997.

Collins, Jim, *From Good to Great: Why Some Companies Make the Leap ... and Others Don't*, New York: HarperBusiness, 2001.

DeGeorge, Richard T., *Competing with Integrity in International Business*, New York and Oxford: Oxford University Press, 1993.

    Business Ethics, fifth edition, Upper Saddle River, NJ: Prentice Hall, 1999.

Delucchi, Mark A., *The Annualized Social Cost of Motor-Vehicle Use in the U.S., 1990–1991: Summary of Theory, Data, Methods, and Results*, UCTC No. 311, University of California, Berkeley: University of California Transportation Center, June, 1997.

DePree, Max, *Leadership is an Art*, New York: Dell Publishing, 1989.

DeSimone, Livio D. and Popoff, Frank, *Eco-Efficiency: The Business Link to Sustainable Development*, Cambridge, MA: MIT Press, 2000.

DesJardins, Joseph, *An Introduction to Business Ethics*, New York: McGraw-Hill, 2003.

Devall, Bill and Sessions, George, "Interview with Arne Naess," in *Deep Ecology*, Salt Lake City: Peregrine Smith Books, 1985.

Dolan, Paul, *True to our Roots: Fermenting a Business Revolution*, Princeton, NJ: Bloomberg Press, 2003.

Donaldson, Thomas and Dunfee, Thomas W., *Ties That Bind: A Social Contracts Approach to Business Ethics*, Boston, MA: Harvard Business School Press, 1999.

Dreier, Peter, Mollenkoph, John, and Swanstrom, Todd, *Place Matters: Metropolitics for the Twenty-First Century*, Lawrence, KS: University Press of Kansas, 2001.

Eckersley, Robyn, *The Green State: Rethinking Democracy and Sovereignty*, Boston, MA: MIT Press, 2004.

Ellsworth, Richard R., *Leading with Purpose: The New Corporate Realities*, Stanford, CA: Stanford University Press, 2002.

Enderle, Georges, "Business Ethics and Wealth Creation: Is There a Catholic Deficit?" Occasional Papers of the Erasmus Institute, 2004 Series, no. 1, University of Notre Dame.

    "Some Perspectives of Managerial Ethical Leadership," *Journal of Business Ethics*, vol. 6 (1987), pp. 657–63.

    "Towards Business Ethics as an Academic Discipline," *Business Ethics Quarterly*, vol. 6, no. 1 (January, 1996), pp. 43–65.

Engel, Ronald J. and Engel, Joan Gibb, "Introduction: The Ethics of Sustainable Development," in *Ethics of Environment and Development: Global Challenge, International Response*, ed. J. Ronald Engel and Joan Gibb Engel, Tucson and London: University of Arizona Press, 1993.

Feenberg, Andrew, *Questioning Technology*, London and New York: Routledge, 1999.

Fort, Timothy L., *Ethics and Governance: Business as Mediating Institution*, New York: Oxford University Press, 2001.

Frederick, William C., *Values, Nature, and Culture in the American Corporation*, New York: Oxford University Press, 1995.

Freeman, R. Edward, "A Stakeholder Theory of the Modern Corporation," in *Ethical Theory and Business*, sixth edition, ed. Tom Beauchamp and Norm Bowie, Upper Saddle River, NJ: Prentice Hall, 1997.

Freeman R. Edward, and Gilbert, Daniel R. Jr., *Corporate Strategy and the Search for Ethics*, Englewood Cliffs, NJ: Prentice Hall, 1988.

French, Peter A, *Collective and Corporate Responsibility*, New York: Columbia University Press, 1984.

Friedman, Milton, *Capitalism and Freedom*, Chicago: University of Chicago Press, 1962.

  "The Social Responsibility of Business Is to Increase its Profits," in *Ethical Theory and Business*, sixth edition, ed. Tom Beauchamp and Norm Bowie, Upper Saddle River, NJ: Prentice Hall, 2000, pp. 51–5.

Friedmann, John, *The Prospect of Cities*, Minneapolis and London: University of Minnesota Press, 2002.

Gadamer, Hans-Georg, *Truth and Method*, rev. trans. J. Weinsheimer and D. Marshall, New York: Crossroad, 1989.

Galbraith, John, *The Anatomy of Power*, Boston: Houghton Mifflin, 1983.

Gewirth, Alan, "Can Any Final Ends Be Rational?" *Ethics*, vol. 102, no. 1 (October, 1991), pp. 66–95.

Gilligan, Carol, *In a Different Voice: Psychological Theory and Women's Development*, Cambridge, MA: Harvard University Press, 1993.

Goleman, Daniel, Boyatzis, Richard, and McKee, Annie, *Primal Leadership: Realizing the Power of Emotional Intelligence*, Boston, MA: Harvard Business School Press, 2002.

Gould, Carol, *Freedom and Social Cooperation in Politics, Economy, and Society*, Cambridge: Cambridge University Press, 1988.

Hackman, J. Richard, *Leading Teams: Setting the Stage for Great Performances*, Boston, MA: Harvard Business School Press, 2002.

Hartman, Chester, *City for Sale: The Transformation of San Francisco*, Berkeley: University of California Press, 2002.

Hartman, Edwin M., *Organizational Ethics and the Good Life*, New York: Oxford University Press, 1996.

Hawken, Paul, Lovins, Amory and Lovins, L. Hunter, *Natural Capitalism: Creating the Next Industrial Revolution*, Boston: Little Brown and Company, 1999.

Hawley, James P. and Williams, Andrew T., *The Rise of Fiduciary Capitalism: How Institutional Investors Can Make Corporate America More Democratic*, Philadelphia: University of Pennsylvania Press, 2003.

Heidegger, Martin, *Discourse on Thinking*, trans. John M. Anderson and E. Hans Freund, New York: Harper and Row, 1966.

Held, Virginia, *Feminist Morality: Transforming Culture, Society, and Politics*, Chicago and London: University of Chicago Press, 1993.

Hertz, Noreena, *The Silent Takeover: Global Capitalism and the Death of Democracy*, New York: The Free Press, 2001.

Hoffman, Andrew J., *From Heresy to Dogma: An Institutional History of Corporate Environmentalism*, San Francisco, CA: New Lexington Press, 1997.

Holliday, Charles O. Jr., Schmidheiny, Stephan, and Watts, Philip, *Walking the Talk: The Business Case for Sustainable Development*, San Francisco, CA: Berrett-Koehler, 2002.

Holston, James (ed.), *Cities and Citizenship*, Durham, NC, and London: Duke University Press, 1999.

Ignatieff, Michael, *The Needs of Strangers: An Essay on Privacy, Solidarity, and the Politics of being Human*, New York: Penguin Books, 1984.

Isaacs, William, *Dialogue and the Art of Thinking Together*, New York: Currency, 1999.

Johnson, Susan, *Creating Connection: The Practice of Emotionally Focused Marital Therapy*, New York: Brunner/Mazel, 1996.

Kaptein, Muel and Wempe, Johan, *The Balanced Company: A Theory of Corporate Integrity*, Oxford: Oxford University Press, 2002.

Keene, John, *Global Civil Society?* Cambridge: Cambridge University Press, 2003.

Kegan, Robert, *The Evolving Self: Problem and Process in Human Development*, Cambridge, MA: Harvard University Press, 1982.

Kellerman, Barbara, *Reinventing Leadership: Making the Connection Between Politics and Business*, New York: State University of New York Press, 1999.

Koehn, Daryl, *Rethinking Feminist Ethics: Care, Trust, and Empathy*, London and New York: Routledge, 1998.

Korten, David, *When Corporations Rule the World*, San Francisco, CA: Berrett-Koehler, 1995.

   The Post-Corporate World: Life after Capitalism, San Francisco, CA: Berrett-Koehler, 1999.

LeClair, Debbie Thorne, Ferrell, O.C., and Fraedrich, John, *Integrity Management: A Guide to Managing Legal and Ethical Issues in the Workplace*, Tampa, FL: University of Tampa Press, 1998.

Leopold, Aldo, *A Sand County Almanac: And Sketches Here and There*, London: Oxford University Press, 1949.

Logsdon, Jeanne M. and Wood, Donna J., "Business Citizenship: From Domestic to Global Level of Analysis," *Business Ethics Quarterly*, vol. 12, no. 2 (April, 2002), pp. 155–87.

Lombardi, Rosie and Wilson, Mel, "Globalization and its Discontents: The Arrival of Triple-Bottom-Line Reporting," *Ivey Business Journal* (September/October, 2001), www. pwcglobal.com/servlet.

Lovelock, J. E., *Gaia: A New Look at Life on Earth*, Oxford: Oxford University Press, 1979.

MacDonald, Mia and Nierenberg, Danielle, "Linking Population, Women, and Biodiversity," in *State of the World, 2003*, New York: W.W. Norton, 2003.

McDonough, William and Braungart, Michael, *Cradle to Cradle: Remaking the Way We Make Things*, New York: North Point Press, 2002.

McIntosh, Malcolm, Leipziger, Deborah, Jones Keith, and Coleman, Gill, *Corporate Citizenship: Successful Strategies for Responsible Companies*, London: Financial Times Management, 1998.

McMahon, Christopher, *Authority and Democracy: A General Theory of Government and Management*, Princeton, NJ: Princeton University Press, 1994.

Meadows, Donella H., Meadows, Dennis L., and Randers, Jorgen, *Beyond the Limits of Growth*, White River Junction, VT: Chelsea Green Publishing Company, 1992.

Meadows, Donella H., Meadows, Dennis L., Randers, Jorgen, and Behrens, William W. III, *The Limits of Growth*, New York: Meridian Books, 1972.

Meikle, Scott, *Aristotle's Economic Thought*, Oxford: Clarendon Press, 1995.

Mitchell, William J., *City of Bits: Space, Place, and the Infobahn*, Cambridge, MA: MIT Press, 1999.

Nace, Ted, *Gangs of America: The Rise of Corporate Power and the Disabling of Democracy*, San Francisco: Berrett-Koehler, 2003.

Naess, Arne, "Sustainable Development and Deep Ecology," in *Ethics of Environment and Development: Global Challenge, International Response*, ed. John R. Engel and Joan Gibb Engel, Tucson and London: University of Arizona Press, 1993.

Nattrass, Brian and Altomare, Mary, *The Natural Step for Business: Wealth, Ecology and the Evolutionary Corporation*, Gabriola Island, British Columbia, Canada: New Society Publishers, 2003.

Newton, Lisa H., "The Chainsaws of Greed: The Case of Pacific Lumber," in *Case Studies in Business Ethics*, fourth edition, ed. Thomas Donaldson and Al Gini, Upper Saddle River, NJ: Prentice Hall, 1996.

Ethics and Sustainability: Sustainable Development and the Moral Life, Upper Saddle River, NJ: Prentice Hall, 2003.

The New York Times 2003 Almanac, ed. John W. Wright, New York: Penguin Reference Books, 2003.

Niebuhr, Reinhold, *Reinhold Niebuhr on Politics*, ed. Harry R. Davis and Robert R. Good, New York: Charles Scribner's Sons, 1960.

North, Douglass C., *Institutions, Institutional Change and Economic Performance*, Cambridge: Cambridge University Press, 1990.

O'Meara Sheehan, Molly, "Uniting Divided Cities," *State of the World, 2003: The Worldwatch Institute*, ed. Linda Starke, New York: W.W. Norton, 2003.

Orr, David, *Nature of Design: Ecology, Culture and Human Intention*, Oxford: Oxford University Press, 2002.

Orren, Karen, *Belated Feudalism: Labor, the Law, and Liberal Development in the United States*, Cambridge and New York: Cambridge University Press, 1991.

Ostwald, Martin, "Translator's Introduction," in Aristotle, *Nicomachean Ethics* trans. Martin Ostwald, Englewood Cliffs, NJ: Prentice Hall, 1962.

O'Toole, James, *Vanguard Management: Redesigning the Corporate Future*, Garden City, NY: Doubleday, 1985.

Paine, Lynn Sharp, "Managing for Organizational Integrity," *Harvard Business Review* (March/April, 1994), pp. 106–17.

Value Shift: Why Companies Must Merge Social and Financial Imperatives to Achieve Superior Performance, New York: McGraw-Hill, 2003.

Palmer, Tom, "Classical Liberalism and Civic Society: Definitions, History, and Relations," in *Civil Society and Government*, ed. Robert C. Post and Nancy L. Rosenblum, Princeton and Oxford: Princeton University Press, 2002.

Palus, Charles J. and Horth, David M., *The Leader's Edge: Six Creative Competencies for Navigating Complex Challenges*, San Francisco, CA: Jossey-Bass, 2002.

Pateman, Carole, *Participation and Democratic Theory*, Cambridge: Cambridge University Press, 1970.

Pearce, W. Barnett, *Communication and the Human Condition*, Carbondale and Edwardville: Southern Illinois University Press, 1989.

Petrick, Joseph A. and Quinn, John F., *Management Ethics: Integrity at Work*, Thousand Oaks, CA: Sage, 1997.

Post, Robert C. and Rosenblum, Nancy L., "Introduction," in *Civil Society and Government*, ed. R. Post and N. Rosenblum, Princeton, NJ, and Oxford: Princeton University Press, 2002.

Redner, Harry, *Ethical Life: The Past and Present of Ethical Cultures*, Lanham: Rowman and Littlefield, 2001.

Rion, Michael, *The Responsible Manager: Practical Strategies for Ethical Decision Making*, Amherst, MA: Human Resource Development Press, 1996.

Robèrt, Karl-Henrik, "Forword," in Nattrass B. and Altomare, M., *The Natural Step for Business*, Gabriola Island, British Columbia, Canada: New Society Publishers, 1999.

Rost, Joseph C., *Leadership for the Twenty-First Century*, Westport, CT: Praeger Publishers, 1991.

Roy, William G., *Socializing Capital: The Rise of the Large Industrial Corporation in America*, Princeton, NJ: Princeton University Press, 1997.

Sagoff, Mark, *The Economy of the Earth: Philosophy, Law, and the Environment*, Cambridge: Cambridge University Press, 1988.

Salamon, Lester M., *America's Nonprofit Sector: A Primer*, second edition, New York: The Foundation Center, 1999.

Sandel, Michael J., *Democracy's Discontent: America in Search of a Public Philosophy*, Cambridge, MA: The Belknap Press of Harvard University, 1996.

Sashkin, Marshall and Kiser, Kenneth, *Putting Total Quality Management to Work*, San Francisco: Berrett-Koehler, 1993.

Sassen, Saskia, *The Global City: New York, London, Tokyo*, Princeton, NJ: Princeton University Press, 1991.

   "Whose City is It? Globalization and the Formation of New Claims," in *Cities and Citizenship*, ed. James Holston, Durham, NC, and London, Duke University Press, 1999.

Scalet, Steven and Schmidtz, David, "State, Civil Society, and Classical Liberalism," in *Civil Society and Government*, ed. R. Post and N. Rosenblum, Princeton and Oxford: Princeton University Press, 2002.

Schmidheiny, Stephen, *Changing Course: A Global Business Perspective on Development and the Environment*, Cambridge, MA: MIT Press, 1992.

Schmookler, Andrew B., *Out of Weakness: Healing the Wounds That Drive Us to War*, New York: Bantam Books, 1988.

Schumacher, E. F., *Small is Beautiful: Economics as if People Mattered*, New York: Harper and Row, 1973.

Sclove, Richard, *Democracy and Technology*, New York and London: The Guilford Press, 1995.

Scott, Allen, Agnew, John, Soja, Edward W., and Storper, Michael, "Global City-Regions," in *Global City-Regions*, ed. Allen Scott, Oxford: Oxford University Press, 2001.

Sen, Amartya, "Does Business Ethics Make Economic Sense?" *Business Ethics Quarterly*, vol. 3, no. 1 (January, 1993), pp. 45–54.

Senge, Peter. M., *The Fifth Discipline: the Art and Practice of the Learning Organization*, New York: Doubleday Currency, 1990.

Shiva, Vandana, "The World on the Edge," in *Global Capitalism*, ed. Will Hutton and Anthony Giddens, New York: The New Press, 2000.

Siegel, Daniel, *The Developing Mind: Towards a Neurobiology of Interpersonal Experience*, New York: The Guilford Press, 1999.

Simpson, Lorenzo C., *Technology Time and the Conversations of Modernity*, New York: Routledge, 1995.

Smith, Adam, *The Wealth of Nations*, ed. E. Cannan, New York: The Modern Library, 1937.

Solomon, Robert C., "Corporate Roles, Personal Virtues: An Aristotelian Approach to Business Ethics," *Business Ethics Quarterly*, vol. 23 (1992), pp. 317–39.

  Ethics and Excellence: Cooperation and Integrity in Business, New York and Oxford: Oxford University Press, 1993.

  A Better Way to Think About Business: How Personal Integrity Leads to Corporate Success, New York: Oxford University Press, 1999.

Soros, George, *The Crisis of Global Capitalism: Open Society Endangered*, New York: Public Affairs, 1998.

Spinosa, Charles, Flores, Fernando, and Dreyfus, Hubert L., *Disclosing New Worlds: Entrepreneurship, Democratic Action, and the Cultivation of Solidarity.* Cambridge, MA and London: MIT Press, 1997.

Srivastva, Suresh and Associates, *Executive Integrity: The Search for High Human Values in Organizational Life*, San Francisco and London: Jossey-Bass, 1989.

Srivastva, Suresh and Barrett, Frank J., "Foundations for Executive Integrity: Dialogue, Diversity, Development" in *Executive Integrity: The Search for High Human Values in Organizational Life*, ed. Suresh Srivastva and Associates, San Francisco, CA: Jossey-Bass, 1989.

Taub, Richard P., *Community Capitalism: The South Shore Bank's Strategy for Neighborhood Revitalization*, Boston, MA: Harvard Business School Press, 1994.

Tichy, Noel M., McGill, Andrew R., St. Clair, Lynda St. (eds.), *Corporate Global Citizenship: Doing Business in the Public Eye*, San Francisco: New Lexington Press, 1997.

Til, Jon Van, *Growing Civil Society: From Nonprofit Sector to Third Space*, Bloomington and Indianapolis: Indiana University Press, 2000.

Trevino, Linda Klebe, Hartman, Laura Pincus, Brown, Michael, "Moral Person and Moral Manager: How Executives Develop a Reputation for Ethical Leadership," *California Management Review*, vol. 42, no. 4 (Summer, 2000), pp. 128–42.

Ulrich, Peter, "Ethics and Economics," in *Ethics in the Economy: Handbook of Business Ethics*, ed. Laszlo Zsolnai, Oxford: Peter Lang, 2004, pp. 9–37.

Velasquez, Manuel, "Debunking Corporate Moral Responsibility," *Business Ethics Quarterly*, vol. 13, no. 4 (2003), pp. 531–62.

Von Krogh, Georg, Ichijo, Kazuo, and Nonaka, Ikujiro, *Enabling Knowledge Creation: How to Unlock the Mystery of Tacit Knowledge and Release the Power of Innovation*, New York: Oxford University Press, 2000.

Waddock, Sandra, "Parallel Universes: Companies, Academics, and the Progress of Corporate Citizenship," *Business and Society Review*, vol. 109, no. 1 (Spring, 2004), pp. 2–42.

Walzer, Michael, *Spheres of Justice: A Defense of Pluralism and Equality*, New York: Basic Books, 1983.

Watson, Charles E., *Managing with Integrity: Insights from American CEOs*, New York: Praeger, 1991.

Weinberg, Alvin M., "Can Technology Replace Social Engineering?" *Technology and The Future*, ninth edition, ed. Albert H. Teich, Belmont, CA: Wadsworth/Thomson Learning, 2003.

Weisbord, Marvin R., *Productive Workplaces: Organizing and Managing for Dignity, Meaning, and Community*, San Francisco, CA: Jossey-Bass, 1987.

Werhane, Patricia H. and Radin, Tara J., "Employment at Will and Due Process," in *Ethical Theory and Business*, sixth edition, ed. Tom Beauchamp and Norman Bowie, Upper Saddle River, NJ: Prentice-Hall, 2001.

Williamson, Oliver E. and Winter, Sidney G. (eds.), *The Nature of the Firm: Origins, Evolution, and Development*, New York and Oxford: Oxford University Press, 1993.

Wood, Donna J. and Logsdon, Jeanne M., "Business, Citizenship: From Individuals to Organizations," in *Ethics and Entrepreneurship: The Ruffin Series No. 3*, special issue of *Business Ethics Quarterly* (2002), pp. 59–94.

Zadek, Simon, *The Civil Corporation: The New Economy of Corporate Citizenship*, London and Sterling, VA: Earthscan Publications, 2001.

Index

3M, 119
advertising, and corporate investment,
    185
Agnew, J., 140
Altomare, M., 195, 196, 198
American Express 119
Amin, A. 139
Anheier, H. 201
Arato, A. 142, 144
Arendt, H. 93–4
Aristotle 7, 13
    ethics subservient to politics 28, 30
    human flourishing 159
    notion of purpose 120, 128
    see also civic ethic
Arthur Anderson 2
Association for Professional and
    Practical Ethics 23
attachment theory 85–6
authority
    based on promises 219–20
    cooperation-facilitating 220–21
    of experts 219

Badaracco, J. L. Jr. 215
Barber, B. 26, 89–92
Barrett, F. 6
Bay Area Council, corporate/city
    relationship 153, 157
Bayer Corporation, exactions to
    Berkeley 154
Becker, L. C. 79
Behrens, W. W. III 175
Bello, W. 182, 183
biomimicry 194
Boatright, J. R. 14, 17
Boeing 119
bogus empowerment 217
Bohman, J. 92, 94
Boulding, K. 146

Bowlby, J. 85–6, 88
Boyatzis, R. 231
Bradford, D. 78
Bradsher, K. 186
Braungart, M. 195
Brenkert, G. G. 218
Bretton Woods agreements 181
    free trade and deregulation 183
Brown, M. T. 226, 229
Brundtland Report 176
Bruyn, S. T. 149
Buber, M. 36, 58–60
Buchholz, R. 184
Buddhist economics 192
Burke, K. 40
business ethics 9, 12, 30

calculative thinking 63
Capra, F. 194, 200
Carnegie, Andrew, corporate
    philanthropy 155
Carson, R. 171, 191
Castells, M. 187
Chua, A. 188–89
Citicorp 119
cities
    connection with networks 139
    missions of 159–160
        and corporations 160–62,
        165
    regional places 140–42
    size of 139
    trustworthy government 165
Ciulla, J. B. 217
civic cooperation 4, 13, 218–21
civic ethic
    Aristotle 28, 119
    business values 29–30
    development of private ethic 29
    economy and politics 30, 31

263